450

JE 812 M6142e
Easy plays for boys and girls; a collection of short,
royalty-free plays for special days, and every ...
Gotwalt, Helen Louise Miller.

EASY PLAYS FOR BOYS AND GIRLS

Easy Plays for Boys and Girls

A collection of short, royalty-free plays for special days—and every day

by
HELEN LOUISE MILLER

Publishers   **PLAYS, INC.**   *Boston*

Copright © 1963 by
HELEN LOUISE MILLER
All Rights Reserved

CAUTION

All material in this volume is fully protected by copyright law. All rights, including motion picture, recitation, television, public reading, radio broadcasting, and rights of translation into foreign languages, are strictly reserved.

NOTICE FOR AMATEUR PRODUCTION

These plays may be produced by schools, clubs, and similar amateur groups without payment of a royalty fee.

NOTICE FOR PROFESSIONAL PRODUCTION

For any form of non-amateur presentation (professional stage, radio or television), permission must be obtained in writing from the publisher. Inquiries should be addressed to PLAYS, INC., 8 Arlington Street, Boston 16, Massachusetts.

Library of Congress Catalog Card Number: 63-15351

MANUFACTURED IN THE UNITED STATES OF AMERICA

CONTENTS

For Every Day

The Little Nut Tree (*Legend*)	3
Bandit Ben Rides Again (*Western*)	16
Sourdough Sally (*Alaska*)	31
Aloha, Mother (*Hawaii*)	46
So Long at the Fair (*Spring*)	55
The Glass Slippers (*Fairy Tale*)	68
The Mouse that Soared (*Space*)	82
Smokey Wins His Star (*Safety*)	95
Meet Mr. Muffin (*Health*)	109

For Special Days

The Admiral's Nightmare (*Columbus Day*)	118
Which Way to Halloween? (*Halloween*)	132
The Runaway Unicorn (*Book Week*)	147
The Parrot and the Pirates (*Book Week*)	160
The ABC's Thanksgiving (*Thanksgiving*)	172
Bartholomew's Joyful Noise (*Thanksgiving*)	181
The Runaway Toys (*Christmas*)	195
Squeaknibble's Christmas (*Christmas*)	206
Gifts for the New Year (*New Year's Day*)	215
Lincoln's Library Fine (*Lincoln's Birthday*)	227
Princess Lonely Heart (*Valentine's Day*)	239
Washington's Lucky Star (*Washington's Birthday*)	251

The White House Rabbit (*Easter*) 262
Baskets or Bonnets (*Easter*) 275
Merry-Go-Round for Mother (*Mother's Day*) 289
The Magic Pencils (*Promotion Day*) 306
Production Notes 319

EASY PLAYS FOR BOYS AND GIRLS

THE LITTLE NUT TREE

Characters

HENRY POOLE
MRS. POOLE, *Henry's mother*
MR. POOLE, *Henry's father*
MARY
ANN
ELIZABETH
GEORGE
JOHN
EDWARD
GUIDE
SIGHT-SEERS
LORD MAYOR
DON CARLOS, *King of Spain's Minister*
PRINCESS JOANNA, *King of Spain's daughter*
HERALDS
LADIES-IN-WAITING

TIME: *Many years ago in England.*
SETTING: *The garden of Henry Poole, where a little nut tree occupies a prominent place slightly right of center stage.*
AT RISE: HENRY *is standing on a stool or stepladder polishing the large silver nutmeg which hangs down from the tree. His bottles of polish and extra cloths are on a small bench near the base of the tree. Six children,* MARY, ANN, ELIZABETH, GEORGE, JOHN *and* EDWARD, *are helping. Three are weeding at the base of the tree and three are watering it from sprinkling cans. All are singing "The Little Nut Tree."* *

---

* The music for this song may be found in *Together We Sing* (Lower Grades), by Wolfe and Fullerton, Follett Publishing Co., and also in many other elementary school music books.

CHILDREN:
> I had a little nut tree;
> Nothing would it bear,
> But a silver nutmeg
> And a golden pear.
> The children in the village
> Came to work with me
> To water it and care for
> My little nut tree.

HENRY: There! I've finished! How does it look?

CHILDREN (*Stopping work to look up and admire*): Beautiful! Beautiful!

MARY: I never saw it so bright and shining.

HENRY: I mixed up a new silver polish yesterday.

JOHN: What about the golden pear? It looks mighty dull to me.

HENRY (*Coming down from ladder*): I'll do that next.

ANN (*Shaking bottle of polish*): I'll shake up the polish so it will be rich and foamy.

HENRY: Thank you, Ann. I could never take care of my little nut tree without the help all of you give me.

EDWARD: We love to come.

GEORGE (*Rising from weeding*): There's not a single weed left under that tree.

ELIZABETH: I think we've given it enough water for today.

HENRY (*Stooping to feel the ground*): That's just right. Not too wet and not too dry.

EDWARD: We'll move your ladder to the other side so

you can reach the golden pear. (BOYS *move ladder and* HENRY *mounts it.*)

MARY: I'll put the polish on your rag and hand it up to you. (*Does so*)

HENRY: That's fine. Thanks.

JOHN: Can you reach it?

ANN: Be careful! Don't fall.

HENRY (*As he polishes the golden pear*): I won't.

MRS. POOLE (*Enters with basket on arm. She is unnoticed by* CHILDREN *who are all gazing up at* HENRY. *Angrily*): Henry Henderson Halliburton Poole! What are you doing up there? (CHILDREN *jump in surprise.*)

HENRY: Sakes alive, Mother, you scared the life out of me!

CHILDREN: He's polishing the golden pear.

MRS. POOLE: Polishing the golden pear indeed! Come down out of that tree this minute!

HENRY: Just three more rubs and I'll be finished.

MRS. POOLE: This minute! Do you hear me?

HENRY: Yes, Mother. I'm coming. (*Comes down ladder*)

MRS. POOLE: What do you mean by spending your time on that worthless tree, when there's work to be done?

HENRY: But, Mother, the silver nutmeg had to be polished.

JOHN: And the golden pear was quite dull.

MRS. POOLE: All of you children are wasting too much

time on this silly tree. There's plenty of work for you to do at home.

MARY: We were just leaving, Mistress Poole.

MRS. POOLE: Then be on your way. Your mothers will be looking for you.

GEORGE: We'll come back tomorrow, Henry, if you need us.

MRS. POOLE: I can tell you right now he won't need you. His father is going to cut that tree down this very night.

CHILDREN: Oh, no! No! He mustn't! He mustn't!

HENRY: Please, please, Mother, don't let him do such a thing.

MRS. POOLE: And why not? Just tell me why not!

HENRY: There's not another tree like this in the whole kingdom . . . maybe not even in the whole world!

MRS. POOLE: And what good is it? We can't eat a silver nutmeg and a golden pear! We can't even sell them because no one can pick them.

HENRY: But that's a good thing. They would have been stolen long ago if anyone could have pulled them loose from the tree.

MRS. POOLE: I can't argue about it now. I have too much work to do. And as for you, there is wood to be chopped, water to be carried, and floors to be scrubbed. Now send those children home and come into the house at once. (*Exits right*)

HENRY: Yes, Mother.

EDWARD: I guess we'd better go.

MARY: Don't worry, Henry. I am sure your father won't cut down the tree.

HENRY: I'm afraid he will, Mary. He says it's not good for anything.

ANN: But it is so beautiful.

ELIZABETH: Every day more and more people come to see it.

HENRY: Yes, I know. But that's another thing that angers Father.

JOHN: Doesn't he want people to enjoy the tree?

HENRY: He says they trample all over the garden. They step on the vegetables he is trying to raise.

GEORGE: My father wouldn't like that either.

MRS. POOLE (*Calling from offstage*): Henry! I want you this minute.

HENRY: I'm coming, Mother.

CHILDREN: Goodbye, Henry. We'll come back tomorrow. (CHILDREN *exit left.*)

HENRY (*As he turns to right exit*): Poor little nut tree! Nobody loves you as much as I do. (*As he exits right,* GUIDE *enters left with a group of* SIGHT-SEERS. *A sign on his hat and a badge on his chest say "Guide."*)

GUIDE: Right this way, folks. Right this way for the only tree of its kind in the world.

WOMAN (*Pointing*): Is this the tree?

GUIDE: This is it, madam. And there you can see the silver nutmeg and the golden pear.

1ST CHILD: Are they *real* silver and *real* gold?

GUIDE: Oh, yes, yes indeed.

MAN: They must be worth a great deal of money.

WOMAN: It's a wonder someone doesn't steal them.

GUIDE: That is impossible, madam. No one has been able to pick them. Some of the strongest men in the village have tried.

BOY: I bet I could pick them. May I try?

GUIDE: You may try, little boy. But I'm warning you, it's no use.

BOY (*Mounting ladder*): I want the silver nutmeg.

GIRL: Try to get the golden pear for me. I want the golden pear!

WOMAN: Be careful! Don't fall.

BOY (*Tugging at nutmeg*): It won't come off.

MAN: Maybe if I shake the tree, it will help. (*Shakes trunk of tree*)

MR. POOLE (*Entering*): Here! Here! What's going on? What are you folks doing in my garden?

GUIDE: They wanted to see the little nut tree.

MR. POOLE: You must all leave at once. This is private property.

GUIDE: We are doing no harm.

MR. POOLE: I will not have strangers trampling around in my garden.

WOMAN: Very well. We will go.

MAN: I think the whole thing is a fake.

BOY: I don't even believe that nutmeg is real silver. It's just tin.

GIRL: And that golden pear is only made of brass.

MAN: If I had that thing in my yard, I'd chop it down.

MR. POOLE: That's just what I am going to do as soon as you people leave.

WOMAN: Come on, Sylvester. We can take a hint! (GUIDE *and* SIGHT-SEERS *exit left.*)

MR. POOLE: Henry! Henry! Come here at once and bring me my axe.

HENRY (*Entering right*): Father! Father! What are you going to do?

MR. POOLE: I'm going to chop down this tree. It's more bother than it's worth.

HENRY: Oh, please, Father, please! Don't cut down my little tree.

MR. POOLE: Henry, listen to me. We are very poor. We need every bit of land to raise food. And besides, I have some very bad news.

HENRY: What is it, Father?

MRS. POOLE (*Entering right with axe*): Here is your axe. I heard you asking for it.

HENRY: Father says he has some bad news.

MRS. POOLE: What is it, Charles?

MR. POOLE: We will soon be at war with Spain. I must leave tomorrow for the army.

HENRY: Will you be a soldier, Father, and carry a gun?

MR. POOLE: I am afraid so.

MRS. POOLE: Oh, this is terrible, terrible! What shall we do without you?

MR. POOLE: Henry is a big boy now. He will have to take my place. That is why I want to cut down this tree today. He must not waste his time with it.

HENRY: Father, I promise to take good care of Mother and do all the work. Only, please, please, let me keep my little nut tree.

MR. POOLE: It's no use, Henry. My mind's made up.

MRS. POOLE: Maybe we could let him keep it one more day.

MR. POOLE (*Taking axe*): No use waiting. I'll do it now. Stand back. Out of my way! (*As* MR. POOLE *swings back on the axe, the* 6 CHILDREN *run in.*)

CHILDREN (*Calling*): Wait! Wait! Wait!

JOHN (*Grabbing* MR. POOLE'S *arm*): Don't do it, Mr. Poole. Don't do it!

GEORGE: Have you heard the news?

ANN: The most wonderful thing has happened.

HENRY, MRS. POOLE *and* MR. POOLE: What is it?

ELIZABETH: The King of Spain's daughter is coming.

MR. POOLE: Coming where?

MARY: Coming here to your house.

MRS. POOLE: I don't believe it. Why would she be coming here?

EDWARD: She has heard about Henry's little nut tree and she is coming to see it.

MR. POOLE: Impossible! We are about to go to war with Spain. The King's daughter would never be coming here.

CHILDREN: But she is! She is!

JOHN: We saw her in her golden coach.

ELIZABETH: We ran as fast as we could to tell you.

MARY: She'll be here any minute.

ANN: The Lord Mayor himself is riding by her side. (*Offstage sound of trumpets.*)
HERALDS (*Offstage*): Make way! Make way for the Princess Joanna!
MRS. POOLE: She really is coming! (2 HERALDS *enter with trumpets and stand at attention as the* LORD MAYOR *enters with* PRINCESS JOANNA, *followed by* 2 LADIES-IN-WAITING *and* DON CARLOS.)
HERALDS: Make way! Make way for the Princess Joanna!
LORD MAYOR (*To* MR. POOLE): Are you Charles Poole?
MR. POOLE: I am, Your Honor.
LORD MAYOR: I have the honor to present the Royal Princess, Joanna, Daughter of His Majesty, the King of Spain.
ALL (*Bowing*): We are honored.
DON CARLOS: I am Don Carlos, the King's Minister.
ALL: We are at your service. (*Bow*)
DON CARLOS: The Royal Princess desires to see with her own eyes the remarkable nut tree which bears nothing but a silver nutmeg and a golden pear.
PRINCESS: I cannot believe there is such a tree in all the world.
HENRY: There it is, Your Royal Highness. See—there is the silver nutmeg and there is the golden pear!
PRINCESS: It is really true! Look how the silver nutmeg shines in the sun! And see how the golden pear glows like a ball of fire!
LADIES-IN-WAITING: It is truly beautiful, Your Highness.

PRINCESS: And well worth coming hundreds of miles to see! Ever since I heard about the tree from one of my father's prisoners, I have thought of nothing else. (*Pointing to* MR. POOLE) Is this gentleman the owner?

MR. POOLE: The tree belongs to my son, Henry, Your Highness.

PRINCESS: You must love the tree very much, Henry.

HENRY: Oh, I do love it, Your Highness.

PRINCESS: Do you love it too much to part with the silver nutmeg and the golden pear? I would pay you a great sum of money.

HENRY: Alas, I would gladly give them to Your Highness, but . . .

PRINCESS: But what, Henry?

HENRY: But no one can pick them.

DON CARLOS: Nonsense! If Your Highness so orders, I will climb up there and pull them down myself.

MR. POOLE: It's no use, sir. My son speaks the truth. The strongest men in the country have tried and failed.

PRINCESS: The prisoner who told me about your little nut tree also told me something else.

HENRY: What did he tell you?

PRINCESS: He told me this rhyme. Listen carefully:
There is a little nut tree;
Nothing will it bear,
But a silver nutmeg
And a golden pear.
And no amount of money
This fruit will ever buy,
Until a lady claims them

With a teardrop in her eye!
HENRY: Do you have a teardrop in your eye, Princess?
PRINCESS (*Dabbing at her eyes with a handkerchief*): I think so, Henry! Would you care to look?
HENRY (*Tilts back her head to look in her eye*): Yes, yes! You do have a teardrop. It's as bright as silver . . . as bright as my silver nutmeg!
PRINCESS: Then you will try to get them for me?
HENRY: I'll try at once. (*Climbs ladder*)
DON CARLOS: No tricks, young man.
HENRY: Here is the silver nutmeg, Princess. It almost dropped into my hand. (*Gives it to* PRINCESS) Now for the golden pear. (*Picks pear and gives it to* PRINCESS)
PRINCESS: Thank you! Thank you! I know I am the luckiest Princess in the world. Don Carlos, bring in the treasure chest.
HENRY: Oh, no, Princess. I will not take your money. I give them to you freely.
PRINCESS: But you must have a reward.
HENRY (*Kneeling*): Then tell the King, your father, not to make war on our people. Let us live in peace.
PRINCESS: It shall be done. I will tell my father that you and your people are the kindest folk in the world.
MRS. POOLE: Oh, thank you, thank you, Princess.
MR. POOLE: A thousand thank you's, Princess. Now I can stay at home with my family.
LORD MAYOR: This is a great day for our people, Princess. I will proclaim the news at once.

HENRY: And I can keep my little nut tree forever and ever.

CHILDREN: But there's nothing on it.

PRINCESS: I will send the finest gardeners from Spain to help you care for the tree. Perhaps it will bear other fruit in years to come.

LORD MAYOR: And even if it doesn't, it is the most famous tree in the world. I will give orders that this garden be made into a public park where people can come and gaze at the tree which saved them from war.

MR. POOLE: But what about us, Your Honor?

LORD MAYOR: You and your family will move into the city palace at once.

MR. *and* MRS. POOLE: Oh, thank you, thank you.

LORD MAYOR: And I further decree that the history of this little nut tree shall be celebrated in song and story throughout our land.

HENRY: Perhaps we could make up the story right now. I'll begin it.

I had a little nut tree, and nothing would it bear,

MRS. POOLE: But a silver nutmeg and a golden pear.

HENRY: The King of Spain's daughter came to visit me,

MR. POOLE: And all for the sake of the little nut tree.

DON CARLOS: Her dress was all of crimson,

LORD MAYOR: Coal black was her hair.

PRINCESS: I asked you for the nutmeg and the golden pear.

HENRY: I said: "So fair a Princess, never did I see,
I'll give to you the fruit of my little nut tree!"

LORD MAYOR: Excellent! Excellent! I hereby command that all children everywhere learn the words of this little song and sing it.

PRINCESS: Musicians, give us the tune!

ALL (*Note: Autoharp accompaniment is especially effective*):
I had a little nut tree, nothing would it bear,
But a silver nutmeg and a golden pear.
The King of Spain's daughter came to visit me,
And all for the sake of my little nut tree.

Her dress was all of crimson, coal black was her hair.
She asked me for the nutmeg and the golden pear.
I said: "So fair a princess never did I see,
I'll give to you the fruit of my little nut tree."
(*Curtain*)

THE END

BANDIT BEN RIDES AGAIN

Characters

WILD BILL
PEANUT BUTTER PETE } *cowboys*
JESSE JONES
SAD SAM
SHERIFF BUNCOMBE, of *Hokum County*
MIRANDA, *his daughter*
RED CHIEF
RED SQUAW
WHITE CHIEF
WHITE SQUAW
BLUE CHIEF
BLUE SQUAW
YELLOW CHIEF
YELLOW SQUAW
GREEN CHIEF
GREEN SQUAW
TILLY
MILLY } *city slickers*
WILLY
BANDIT BEN

TIME: *Just after the days of the wild and woolly West.*
SETTING: *A sign proclaims the place as the Bar-B.Q. Ranch. Another crudely lettered sign at left reads "Sheriff's Office."*
AT RISE: *Four cowboys,* WILD BILL, PEANUT BUTTER PETE, JESSE JONES *and* SAD SAM *are perched on a rail fence left stage, idly twirling their lassos.* SHERIFF BUNCOMBE *is slouched in a swivel chair, his hat on the back of his head, his feet on the desk; he is polishing his badge with his bandanna. There is a large hand bell on the desk.*

COWBOYS (*Singing to the tune of* "*Git Along, Little Dogie.*"):
We're four little cowboys
From Bar-B.Q. Ranch,
We're four little cowboys
Just waiting our chance
To do something useful,
To do something bold,
Like real western heroes
In brave days of old.
WILD BILL: We've counted our cattle,
We've herded our sheep.
PEANUT BUTTER PETE: There's nothing to do
But to eat and to sleep.
JESSE JONES: We're quick on the trigger,
We're fast on the draw,
SAD SAM: We'd risk any danger
Upholding the law.
ALL: But we've run out of robbers
And Bad Men, you see,
'Cause all of them lately
Have jobs on TV!
SHERIFF (*Singing to the tune of* "*Reuben, Reuben.*"):
I'm the Sheriff of Hokum County
And I'm shining up my star,
'Cause it's getting kind of rusty
With affairs the way they are.

Oh, it's been a month of Sundays
Since I've had a man in jail,

And my horse is out of practice
On a rough and rocky trail.

And there hasn't been a hold-up
Since I couldn't tell you when,
And the rustlers do not rustle
Since they're honest cattlemen.

So my star is getting rusty,
And my pistols are the same,
And my saddle's getting dusty,
Now the West is strictly tame!

WILD BILL: Well, boys, what shall we do this afternoon?

PEANUT BUTTER PETE: I'm going to make some fresh peanut butter sandwiches.

JESSE JONES: I'm going to write a letter.

SAD SAM: I'm going to read a sad, sad story, so I can have a good cry.

WILD BILL: In that case, I might as well take a nap. (*Yawning and stretching*) Heigh-ho! I'm getting sleepy already.

PEANUT BUTTER PETE: When you get up from your nap, I'll give you one of my sandwiches and a glass of milk.

JESSE JONES: I'll let you read my letter.

SAD SAM: And I'll tell you my story, so you can cry, too.

WILD BILL (*As they prepare to exit*):
It's back to the bunkhouse
For me and for you,
Because there's just nothing,
Just nothing to do! (COWBOYS *exit*.)

SHERIFF:
I might as well go fishing.
There's no one to arrest.
I can't believe it's happened
To our wild and woolly West!

Oh, Miranda, will you please bring me my fishing rod and that can of worms in the shanty?

MIRANDA (*Entering with fishing rod and bait can. She also carries a workbasket containing a long strip of varicolored knitting*): Oh, Father, don't tell me you're going fishing again!

SHERIFF: Why not? There's nothing else to do, daughter. A man has to busy himself somehow.

MIRANDA: But we've eaten so many fish lately, I've started to sprout fins. I do hope you don't catch any.

SHERIFF: But I'm the Sheriff. I have to catch something! If I can't catch any outlaws, I might as well catch fish. (*Exits with fishing pole and bait can*)

MIRANDA (*Sitting in* SHERIFF's *chair*): Poor Father. He still misses the old days when these rocks and hills were full of Bad Men, and there was a highwayman behind every bush. Now as for me, I like it this way. It gives me a chance to catch up with my knitting. (*She pulls out long strip of knitting. Ten* INDIANS, *five* CHIEFS *and five* SQUAWS, *enter in single file. They are costumed in colors according to their names. The* CHIEFS *are empty-handed. The* SQUAWS *carry the equipment mentioned in their lines.*)

INDIANS (*Singing*): One little, two little, three little Indians,

Four little, five little, six little Indians,
Seven little, eight little, nine little Indians,
Ten little Indians all!

RED CHIEF: This good place for camp.
RED SQUAW: Me settum up wigwams in shade, Red Chief.
WHITE CHIEF: Not in shade, Red Squaw. Me want more sun tan.
WHITE SQUAW: Me, too. Without sun tan, folks take us for palefaces.
BLUE CHIEF: Make sure tepees face north. Me likum North Star.
BLUE SQUAW: Will do, Blue Chief.
YELLOW CHIEF: Put bows and arrows in dry place. Don't want 'em damp.
YELLOW SQUAW: Why bother, Yellow Chief? No more hunting parties. Buy food at supermarkets now.
GREEN CHIEF: Take good care of war paint, Green Squaw. Maybe soon go on warpath.
GREEN SQUAW: What warpath? All palefaces heap big friends now. (SQUAWS *place equipment center stage.*)
MIRANDA: Howdy, strangers.
INDIANS: Howdy.
MIRANDA: You aim to pitch camp here?
RED CHIEF: Yep.
MIRANDA: That's fine. Welcome to Hokum County.
RED SQUAW: What you knitting? Heap small blanket?
MIRANDA: Oh, no. That's not a blanket. It's a muffler for my father. And I'm doing it with a fancy stitch I made up myself. (SQUAWS *gather around her to admire.*)

BANDIT BEN RIDES AGAIN

SQUAWS: Ummm! Heap pretty colors!
WHITE SQUAW: Someday I show white squaw blanket I weave.
BLUE SQUAW: I show you new basket I make.
YELLOW SQUAW: I show you bead necklace.
GREEN SQUAW: I show you pictures on pottery.
MIRANDA: That will be nice. It's good to have some new neighbors.
RED CHIEF: You all alone here? No men folks on place?
MIRANDA: Only my father. He's the Sheriff of Hokum County. But he's out fishing right now.
WHITE CHIEF (*Pointing in direction of Bar-B.Q. Ranch*): Who live there? More palefaces?
MIRANDA: Yes, that's the Bar-B.Q. Ranch. The cowboys will also be glad for new neighbors.
BLUE CHIEF: This good place for camp?
MIRANDA: Oh, yes. But it's terribly dull. Nothing ever happens here.
TILLY, MILLY *and* WILLY (*Enter, screaming in terror*): Help! Help! Police! Murder! Help! Help! Police! Murder!
MIRANDA *and* INDIANS: What's the matter?
TILLY, MILLY *and* WILLY: Help! Help! Police! Murder! Help! Help! Police! Murder!
MIRANDA: Stop that screaming and tell us what's wrong.
TILLY, MILLY *and* WILLY: We've been robbed! We've been robbed!
MIRANDA: Impossible! I don't believe it. Who are you?
TILLY, MILLY *and* WILLY:
We're three City Slickers

As green as can be.
We don't know a cactus
From a Joshua Tree!
TILLY: I'm Tilly!
MILLY: I'm Milly!
WILLY: I'm Willy!
MIRANDA: How did you get here? Where are your horses?
TILLY, MILLY *and* WILLY:
We never ride horses,
We're fresh from New York.
Our stagecoach was held up
At Red River Fork!
MIRANDA: How exciting!
RED CHIEF: Palefaces make joke.
BLUE CHIEF: Heap big storytellers.
TILLY, MILLY *and* WILLY (*Screaming with renewed terror*): Indians! Indians! Help! Help!
MIRANDA: Oh, for goodness' sake, be quiet! These Indians won't hurt you.
TILLY: I know we'll be murdered!
MILLY: And burned at the stake!
WILLY (*Falling on his knees and clasping his hands*):
Spare us, oh, spare us,
For dear heaven's sake!
WHITE CHIEF: Too long on desert. Too much sun make Palefaces funny in head.
YELLOW CHIEF: This calls for council. Sit down. Let palefaces tell story. (INDIANS *squat in semicircle, with*

TILLY, MILLY *and* WILLY *in center.* MIRANDA *stands near the desk.*)

MIRANDA: Now let's have your story. What really happened to you?

TILLY: It was just the way we told you.

MILLY: Our stage was held up at Red River Fork.

WILLY: By a big bandit wearing a black mask.

MIRANDA: Are you sure he was a real bandit?

TILLY: He took all of my rings.

MILLY: And all of my bracelets.

WILLY: And all of our money.

TILLY, MILLY *and* WILLY: He was a real bandit, all right.

GREEN CHIEF: What happen to stagecoach driver?

TILLY: The horses ran away with the coach and the driver.

WILLY: The bandit is a dangerous man. You must catch him at once!

MIRANDA: I'll call my father. He'll know what to do. This is our alarm bell. (*Rings bell*) We always ring it in time of trouble. (*Ringing bell louder and louder*) This will also rouse the boys at the Bar-B.Q. Ranch. We haven't had so much excitement in years. (COWBOYS *enter from left.* PEANUT BUTTER PETE *is munching on a sandwich.*)

COWBOYS: What's up?

MIRANDA: Plenty. A bandit just held up the stage at Red River Fork. These people were robbed.

WILD BILL: Come along, Sam. We'll see if the cattle are all right.

JESSE JONES: Finish that sandwich, Pete, and we'll saddle the horses. (COWBOYS *exit*.)
RED CHIEF (*To* RED SQUAW): Bring bows and arrows.
GREEN CHIEF (*To* GREEN SQUAW): Bring 'em war paint.
MIRANDA: Where do you think you're going? You won't need war paint to catch a bandit.
GREEN CHIEF: War paint good medicine. Make 'em bandit heap much scared.
SHERIFF (*Entering with rod and pail*): What in tarnation is going on here? You scared the daylights out of me with that bell, and besides, my biggest fish got away.
WILLY: Oh, Sheriff, we're so glad you're here.
TILLY: Our stage was held up at Red River Fork.
MILLY: And the bandit took all our money and jewelry.
WILLY: You must catch him at once.
SHERIFF: That's just what we'll do, young man. Sheriff Buncombe always gets his man. I'll get up a posse at once.
WHITE CHIEF: Red brothers ready to ride with paleface.
SHERIFF: Where did these Indians come from?
MIRANDA: They're our new neighbors, Father, and they're very friendly.
SHERIFF (*To* INDIANS): Then get your horses at once. (INDIAN CHIEFS *exit*.) Did you see which way the bandit went?
TILLY, MILLY *and* WILLY (*Pointing*): He went that-a-way!
SHERIFF: Did you call the boys from Bar-B.Q. Ranch?

MIRANDA: They've gone to see to their cattle and saddle their horses.
SHERIFF: Good. I'll saddle Old Paint and be ready to ride. (*Exits.* COWBOYS *enter on broomstick horses.*)
WILD BILL: That dad-busted bandit has stolen some of our best cattle.
JESSE JONES: We'll hang that varmint on a sour apple tree. (INDIANS *enter on broomstick horses.*)
MIRANDA: Our new Indian neighbors are joining the posse.
COWBOYS: Good.
SHERIFF (*Entering on broomstick horse*): No doubt he's hiding in Cabbage Canyon, but we'll cut him off at Snake Tooth Gap.
WILLY: Maybe I'd better go with you.
SHERIFF: You stay here with the ladies. Come on, boys, let's go. (COWBOYS *and* INDIANS *circle stage once, yelling and shouting, then exit left.*)
MIRANDA: How I wish I could go along.
TILLY *and* MILLY: Not me!
YELLOW SQUAW: No good for women. We stay home and get camp ready for braves.
MIRANDA (*To* TILLY, MILLY *and* WILLY): Make yourselves at home. I guess I'd better go back to my knitting. (SQUAWS *busy themselves with camp equipment, their backs to audience.* MIRANDA *knits.* MILLY, TILLY *and* WILLY *sit on floor beside her.* BANDIT BEN *enters, wearing a black handkerchief as a half-mask. He carries a bag of loot in one hand and brandishes toy pistol in the other.*)

BANDIT: Stick 'em up! (SQUAWS *wheel around in surprise*. MIRANDA, TILLY, MILLY *and* WILLY *jump to their feet.*)
ALL: The bandit! The bandit!
BANDIT: Stick 'em up, I said, and reach for the sky! (ALL *raise their hands.*) That's better. Aha! Nobody home but the ladies. Where are all the men?
WILLY: Right here. And if you think I'm afraid of that gun, you . . . you're *right*.
MIRANDA: What's your name? And what do you think you're doing here?
BANDIT (*Removing mask*):
  I'm a big, bad bandit, by the name of Ben.
  I'm a rootin', tootin' rascal from El Gaucho Glen!
  All the cowboys tremble and their horses shy,
  And the Injuns quake and quiver when I just ride by!
  I'm a big, bold, bad man from the wild, wild West,
  And of all the old-time outlaws, I'm the last and the best!
  I'm a big, bad bandit, as bad as I can be,
  And it does no good to chase me, 'cause you can't catch me!
MIRANDA: Well, my father will catch you. He's out looking for you right now.
BANDIT: A lot of good it will do him. I knew he'd go that-a-way, (*Pointing*) so I came this-a-way.
MILLY *and* TILLY: Help! Help!
BANDIT: Stop that screeching. I never did like a screaming woman. Do as I say, and you won't be hurt.
MIRANDA: What do you want?

BANDIT: First of all, I want something to eat. Have any pie?
MIRANDA: I—I don't know. I think so.
BANDIT: Then bring me a nice big piece. And while you're at it, you can fry some potatoes and cook a steak. I like it rare and juicy.
MIRANDA: I'm not the cook here.
BANDIT: Don't put on airs. (*Brandishing gun*) Get into the house and do as I say.
MIRANDA: But I'm really not the cook. Ching Lee is the cook at our house. He's a good cook, too.
BANDIT: Then tell Ching Lee to bring me some grub. I'm starved.
MIRANDA (*Reaching for bell*): He—he's not here right now. He's out at the barn. But I can call him.
BANDIT: No tricks, little lady. You stay right here where I can see what you're doing.
MIRANDA: Oh, I don't need to go to the barn. I can call him with this bell. He'll come running the minute he hears it.
BANDIT: Then go ahead and ring it, and make it plenty loud.
MIRANDA (*Rings violently and pauses*): I guess he's inside the barn. Maybe he can't hear me. I'll ring again. (*Rings louder and louder. As she rings, the* SHERIFF, COWBOYS *and* INDIANS *gallop back onstage.*)
COWBOYS *and* INDIANS: The bandit! The bandit!
SHERIFF: At him, men! (COWBOYS *and* INDIANS *disarm* BANDIT, *and* COWBOYS *tie him up.*) I told you Sher-

iff Buncombe always gets his man. Now what shall we do with him?

INDIAN CHIEFS: Scalp him.

SQUAWS: Burn him at the stake.

MIRANDA: Put him in jail.

SAD SAM: Shoot him.

PEANUT BUTTER PETE: Ride him on a rail.

JESSE JONES: Hang him.

WILD BILL: Hanging's too good for him.

SHERIFF: Easy, boys, easy. We must give him a trial.

RED CHIEF: Make him run the gantlet.

SHERIFF: Now that's not a bad idea.

MIRANDA: Oh, Father, you can't do that. You must stand for law and order.

SHERIFF: But this man is a dangerous character.

WILLY: Please, Sheriff, I have an idea.

SHERIFF: We don't want any of your big city ideas. We have our own laws here in the West.

WILLY: But this is a great idea, sir.

SHERIFF: O.K. Let's hear it.

WILLY: I want you to give him to me.

ALL: Give him to you?

SHERIFF: What for? Why should we give him to you? What would you do with him?

WILLY (*Producing card and handing it to* SHERIFF): You don't know who I am, sir. Here is my card.

SHERIFF (*Reading*): Willy Winkum, President of Terror Television, Incorporated!

WILLY: If you give him to me, Sheriff, I can put him

on television, and keep him there for the rest of his life.
BANDIT: Oh, please, Sheriff. Anything but that. Please don't put me on television.
TILLY: The last of the Bad Men!
MILLY: He'll be a big star!
BANDIT: I don't want to be a Bad Man on television. The Bad Men never win. The bandits are always caught.
SHERIFF: Well, you're caught now, and it's up to us to decide. All those in favor of putting this wretch on television, say "aye!"
ALL: AYE!
SHERIFF: So be it! Mr. Winkum, he is your prisoner.
WILLY: Fine! Splendid! I promise you he will never escape. He will always be caught and punished as he deserves.
ALL: Hurray! Hurray!
WILD BILL: And now, little friends,
When you're watching TV,
JESSE JONES: Just think how unhappy
This bandit will be!
PEANUT BUTTER PETE: No matter how quick,
The hero is quicker!
SAD SAM: No matter how slick,
The good guys are slicker!
SHERIFF: And not once, but always,
Again and again,
They'll capture the bandit,

And that will be Ben!
MIRANDA: 'Twill be a lot safer
For you and for me,
To keep this bold bandit
For life on TV!
INDIANS: For no one will help him,
He'll not have a friend!
ALL: And as for our story,
Well, this is the end! (*Curtain*)

THE END

SOURDOUGH SALLY

Characters

SALLY CRANE, *who wants to be a sourdough*
MOTHER, *Mrs. Crane*
DAISY ⎫
EDITH ⎭ *Sally's girl friends*
BLACKBEARD ⎫
GRAYBEARD ⎪
BROWNBEARD ⎬ *"prospectors"*
YELLOWBEARD ⎪
REDBEARD ⎭
THORA ⎫
KOOTUK ⎭ *the Eskimo twins*
SOURDOUGH CHARLIE, *who struck it rich*
MISS COLLINS, *a teacher*

TIME: *The present. A spring day.*
SETTING: *The Crane living room in Alaska.*
AT RISE: *At center,* SALLY CRANE *is finishing a painting of the Alaskan flag, which is on a large easel. The flag has eight gold stars on a blue field, arranged to represent the Big Dipper and the North Star. Her* MOTHER *watches.*

MOTHER: That's a fine flag, Sally. Every star is perfect, and the Dipper is just right.
SALLY: Do you think Miss Collins will use it for the school play?

MOTHER: I hope so, dear.

SALLY: It's such a beautiful flag and so right for Alaska, the land of the North Star.

MOTHER: I can hardly believe you are the same Sally who was so homesick when we first came. Now you're a regular little sourdough.

SALLY: But I'm not a *real* sourdough. The others say I'm still a *Chee-cha-ko*, a newcomer!

MOTHER: You have lots of friends just the same.

SALLY: Oh, Mother, I do hope I am chosen to be Miss Alaska and say the poem about the flag. I know every word of it.

MOTHER: Maybe you will be chosen.

SALLY: But they are choosing the parts today, and I've been absent a whole week. I've missed all the fun and excitement of the spring break-up.

MOTHER: You even talk like a sourdough. A year ago you weren't the least bit interested in the ice breaking up.

SALLY: That's because I'd never lived through an Alaskan winter. Believe me, spring is something to celebrate up here. That's why we're having our play.

MOTHER: Well, I have a surprise for you. Since you are so much better, some of your friends will be stopping by after school today.

SALLY: That's great! Now I'll hear all the news. (*Doorbell*) I'll get it.

MOTHER: Better stay away from the door, Sally. I'll answer it. (*Admits* DAISY, EDITH *and* THORA) Come right in, girls. Sally is expecting you.

GIRLS (*Ad lib*): Hello, Sally. How do you feel? We've missed you.
SALLY: Oh, I feel fine now. Mother, these are my school friends, Edith Higgins, Daisy Grant, and Thora Katchatag.
MOTHER: I'm so glad you came. Sally has been lonely.
GIRLS: Good afternoon, Mrs. Crane.
SALLY: Do sit down and tell me all the news.
MOTHER: While you girls are chatting, I'll do some of my errands. I know you have plenty to talk about. (MOTHER *exits*.)
EDITH (*Seeing flag*): Oh, look at the Alaskan flag!
THORA (*Inspecting it*): It's beautiful. Miss Collins should see this.
DAISY: Who's the artist?
SALLY: I am. Do you think it's good enough to use in our spring program?
THORA: It's perfect.
SALLY: I can hardly wait to hear the news. Did you girls get parts in the play?
DAISY: I'm one of the Indian dancers.
EDITH: I'm only in the chorus, but Thora and Kootuk have speaking parts.
SALLY: How wonderful! Aren't you pleased?
THORA: I am, but Kootuk wanted to be a soldier. Since he and I are the only Eskimos in the class, Miss Collins wants us to be the Eskimo twins and tell about some of our customs.
DAISY: And guess what! Miss Collins wants them to

bring Seegoo so all the children can see a real sled dog. (*Doorbell*)

THORA: I hope that's Kootuk with the rest of the boys.

EDITH: Just wait till you see them. They have a surprise for you.

SALLY: Will you go to the door, Edith? I'm supposed to stay out of drafts.

DAISY: Miss Collins says this is going to be the best program we've ever had. Everybody is so excited. (EDITH *admits* KOOTUK.)

SALLY: Hello, Kootuk. I'm so glad to see you.

KOOTUK: Hello, Sally. You don't look a bit sick to me.

THORA: Where are the others?

KOOTUK: They stopped at the Trading Post. Mr. Smith has a grizzly bear down there. They wanted to see it.

SALLY: Oh, I've seen that old stuffed grizzly lots of times.

KOOTUK: You haven't seen this one, Sally. It's very much alive.

EDITH: A real, live grizzly bear?

SALLY: What is he going to do with it?

KOOTUK: Sell it to a circus or a zoo, I guess. Right now he has it in a cage outside the Post. (*Doorbell*) I'll bet that's the rest of the gang now. Wait till you see them! (KOOTUK *admits 6 boys dressed in jeans. Five, wearing beards of different colors, carry spades over their shoulders. The sixth one,* SOURDOUGH CHARLIE, *carries a pie pan. They march on stage to tune of*

"Clementine." They form a semicircle around SOURDOUGH CHARLIE *and sing.*)
BOYS:
In Alaska, in Alaska,
In the land of ice and snow,
Lived a miner, ninety-niner,
Making bread with sourdough.

Sourdough Charlie, Sourdough Charlie,
Sourdough Charlie won us fame.
Though he's lost and gone forever,
True Alaskans bear his name.

ALL: Meet Sourdough Charlie, the star of our show!
SOURDOUGH CHARLIE (*With a bow*): Howdy, Sally! Glad you're all well again!
SALLY: Thank you! So am I!
EDITH: How do you like their costumes?
THORA: And their song?
DAISY: And their beards?
SALLY: It's all great. And I love the beards, but why the different colors?
BLACKBEARD: So you can tell us apart. I'm Blackbeard.
SALLY: I thought Blackbeard was a pirate.
BLACKBEARD: Not in our play. We are all prospectors from the Gold Rush.
BROWNBEARD: I'm Brownbeard. I tell how gold was discovered in Alaska.
YELLOWBEARD: I'm Yellowbeard. I wanted to get rich so badly that even my beard turned to gold.

GRAYBEARD: I'm Graybeard, one of the old-timers. I carry the sourdough pot and explain how the prospectors baked their bread from the yeast they always carried in their packs.

REDBEARD: I'm Redbeard. I explain why true Alaskans are called sourdoughs to this very day.

SOURDOUGH CHARLIE: And I'm Sourdough Charlie, the guy who struck it rich!

BOYS (*Singing to the tune of "Clementine"*):
In the Yukon, in the Yukon,
Where the men all searched for gold,
Sourdough Charlie made a fortune,
So the story has been told.

Sourdough Charlie, Sourdough Charlie,
Sourdough Charlie won us fame.
Though he's lost and gone forever,
True Alaskans bear his name.
(GIRLS *applaud.*)

DAISY: I'm so glad you're coming back to school this week, Sally.

THORA: Miss Collins says we must practice every day.

SALLY (*Wistfully*): Are all the parts given out?

EDITH: Most of the speaking parts.

SALLY: Who is to be Miss Alaska and explain our state flag?

KOOTUK: Miss Collins hasn't decided yet.

SALLY: Thank goodness! Do you think I have a chance?

EDITH: You are a good speaker, Sally, but you've been here such a short time.

KOOTUK: You're still a *Chee-cha-ko*.
SALLY: I am not! I am not a *Chee-cha-ko!* We've lived here almost a year.
THORA: But you're not a sourdough.
SALLY: That's not fair! This is my state just as much as yours, even if I wasn't born here.
BLACKBEARD: None of us was born here except Thora and Kootuk.
GRAYBEARD: My folks came just three years ago.
SALLY: Then how come you're a sourdough and I'm not?
SOURDOUGH CHARLIE: Did you ever throw a stone in the Yukon?
SALLY: Sure I did, lots of times.
YELLOWBEARD: Did you ever rub noses with an Eskimo?
SALLY: What's that got to do with being a sourdough?
REDBEARD: Everybody knows you have to throw a stone in the Yukon, rub noses with an Eskimo, and pet a grizzly bear before you can become a sourdough.
SALLY: That's easy. Come on, Thora, let's rub noses.
THORA: Eskimos don't rub noses any more, Sally. We've outgrown that silly custom.
SALLY: Well, can't you do it with me, just this once?
THORA: O.K., but I feel mighty foolish! (*They rub noses.*)
SALLY: There! That makes me two-thirds of a sourdough right now.
KOOTUK: But you still have to pat a grizzly, and I wouldn't advise you to try that!

EDITH: Not if you want to stay all in one piece! A grizzly would tear you apart!

SALLY: But I want to be a sourdough more than anything else in the world.

DAISY: Forget it, Sally. The boys are just teasing you. Nobody pays any attention to that any more.

SALLY: But if I'm not a sourdough, I won't get to be Miss Alaska and recite the poem about the flag.

THORA: There are plenty of other parts.

BLACKBEARD: Somebody has to tell about the history of Alaska.

GRAYBEARD: How it was purchased by Secretary Seward from Russia in 1867.

YELLOWBEARD: And how everybody made fun of it and called Alaska "Seward's Folly" and "America's Ice Box."

EDITH: Miss Collins just taught us a new poem about being voted the forty-ninth state.

BROWNBEARD: Maybe we should recite it right now.

REDBEARD: We could use the practice.

SALLY: If you will excuse me, I'll get some refreshments. I know Mother baked some cookies this morning.

SOURDOUGH CHARLIE: Good! I never could work on an empty stomach, and I need to go over my speech of welcome.

SALLY: Go right ahead and practice. I'll join you in a jiffy. (*She exits.*)

SOURDOUGH CHARLIE: *Come on,* fellows, line up! (*The*

bearded PROSPECTORS *line up behind* SOURDOUGH
CHARLIE *as he recites.*)
Howdy folks!
And welcome be ye
To the forty-ninth state
In the land of the free.

'Tis a great land, Alaska,
And double in size
The big state of Texas,
The Westerners' prize.

Our winters are long,
And our summers are short,
But here we have fishing
And every great sport.

Our riches are many,
Our wealth is untold,
And people still come here
A-searching for gold.

Alaska, the Northland,
Of ice and of snow,
The land of the sled dog,
And real Eskimo!

Alaskans are brave,
And loyal and true,
In fact you will find us
Exactly like you!
(*Applause*)

KOOTUK: And now for the statehood poem. Let's all say it together.

ALL:
In nineteen hundred fifty-eight,
July the seventh was the date—
A new state joined your land and mine:
Alaska, number forty-nine!
(*During this poem* MOTHER *enters with* MISS COLLINS. *At close of poem they both applaud.*)

MISS COLLINS: Bravo! Bravo! I hope you all do as well the day of the program.

ALL (*Surprised*): Miss Collins! How did you get here?

MOTHER: I met her in town, and she says she has a special surprise for Sally. Where is Sally, by the way?

DAISY: She just went out to the kitchen, Mrs. Crane.

EDITH: She said she was going to get some cookies.

MOTHER: That's fine. I'll go help her fix something cold to drink. (MOTHER *exits.*)

MISS COLLINS: I hope none of you told Sally our secret.

KOOTUK: No, indeed. Wild horses wouldn't get it out of us.

MISS COLLINS: Good! I can hardly wait to see her face.

EDITH: And look, look, Miss Collins, Sally has painted a picture of the flag.

MISS COLLINS: It's lovely, and just the size we need for the program. (MOTHER *re-enters, upset.*)

MOTHER: Sally's not in the kitchen. What's happened to her?

SOURDOUGH CHARLIE: She said she was going for cookies.

MOTHER: But she's not there, and her coat is gone from the kitchen closet.

MISS COLLINS: Why would she leave the house when she has company?

THORA: Oh, dear me! You don't suppose—

MOTHER: Suppose what? What are you talking about, Thora? Do you know where Sally went?

THORA: Well, no, not exactly, but—

MISS COLLINS: Stop beating around the bush, Thora. If you have anything to say, say it. Mrs. Crane is worried.

KOOTUK: It's like this, Miss Collins. We were all teasing Sally about being a *Chee-cha-ko*, and some of the boys were telling her that old joke about what you have to do to be a sourdough.

MOTHER: Just what do you mean?

SOURDOUGH CHARLIE: Oh, it's all pretty silly, Mrs. Crane, and I didn't think Sally would take it seriously. There's an old saying that if you want to be a true sourdough, you have to throw a stone in the Yukon, rub noses with an Eskimo, and—and—

MOTHER: Well, go on.

SOURDOUGH CHARLIE: And pet a grizzly.

MOTHER: Pet a grizzly! Thank goodness there are no grizzlies around here, or she just might be foolish enough to try.

SOURDOUGH CHARLIE: That's the trouble, Mrs. Crane. We were telling her about the big grizzly down at the Trading Post.

MOTHER: Merciful heavens! You don't suppose that child has gone down there!

MISS COLLINS: Now don't be upset, Mrs. Crane. Sally is too sensible to do anything so dangerous.

MOTHER: But you don't know how badly she wants to be a sourdough. She'd try anything. I'm going down there right away.

MISS COLLINS: Use the telephone. It's quicker. Maybe Mr. Smith can stop her in time.

MOTHER: If she ever sticks her hand in that cage, she's sure to get badly hurt. (*At phone*) Operator, operator! Give me the Trading Post. Hurry, please; this is an emergency!

MISS COLLINS: You children should have known better. I'm ashamed of you!

REDBEARD: We never thought she'd fall for it.

MOTHER (*At phone*): Hello, Mr. Smith? Oh, Mr. Smith, this is Mrs. Crane. Have you seen my little girl down there? What? What's that? Oh, my goodness! (SALLY *enters, beaming with joy. She is wearing a coat and carries a letter in an envelope.*)

ALL: Sally! Sally!

MOTHER (*At phone*): Never mind, Mr. Smith. She's right here. She just came in. (*Hangs up*) Sally Crane, where have you been? You've scared the life out of us!

SALLY: I don't see why. I wore my coat, and the Trading Post isn't very far.

SOURDOUGH CHARLIE: Don't tell me you tried to pat that grizzly!

SALLY: I not only tried, I did it! Oh, hello, Miss Collins. I'm so glad you're here. You can read my letter from Mr. Smith to prove I really patted a grizzly.

MISS COLLINS (*Reading*): "This is to certify that Sally Crane patted a real, full-grown grizzly bear at the Trading Post on this last day of April, 1963. Signed, Preston R. Smith, Proprietor."

MOTHER: Sally! Sally! You might have been killed.

MISS COLLINS: That bear could have hurt you seriously.

SALLY: Oh, no, it couldn't, Miss Collins. It was quite dead!

ALL: Dead!

SALLY: You don't think for one minute I'd try to pat a live grizzly, do you? After all, there was nothing in your rules that said the grizzly had to be alive. I just patted that old stuffed one Mr. Smith has had for twenty years.

DAISY (*Laughing*): You really played a trick on us!

SALLY: And now you can't call me a *Chee-cha-ko* any more. I'm a real sourdough like the rest of you.

MISS COLLINS: What you don't know, Sally, is that you have been an honest-to-goodness sourdough for the past week.

SALLY: How? I don't understand.

MISS COLLINS: The real test of a sourdough is that he must live through an Alaskan winter from one spring ice break to another. When that ice began to melt last week, you and your whole family became official sourdoughs.

SALLY: But why didn't somebody tell me?

CHILDREN: It was a secret.

MISS COLLINS: The children voted that you are one of the most loyal Alaskans in our school and should, therefore, have the honor of making the closing speech about our flag.

SALLY: You mean I am to be Miss Alaska?

ALL: Yes, you are!

SALLY: Oh, I can hardly believe it! Oh, thank you! Thank you! This is the happiest day of my life.

MOTHER: That's wonderful, dear! And now I think it's high time I got those cookies. (*She exits.*)

MISS COLLINS: And I think it's high time for us to have a rehearsal. Sourdough Charlie, make your speech.

SOURDOUGH CHARLIE (*Stepping forward with a bow*): Ladies and gentlemen, as the final number of our spring program, we will have a tribute to the Alaskan state flag by Miss Alaska herself, otherwise known as Sourdough Sally!

SALLY (*Stepping up to painting of flag*): This beautiful flag which we all love and respect was designed by a thirteen-year-old Indian boy named Benny Benson. When Benny designed our flag, he was a seventh-grade pupil at the Mission School in Seward. His design was officially adopted by our legislature in 1927. Today our Alaskan flag takes its place with the flags of the other states which make up our grand and glorious union. So wherever this flag flies, Alaskans are reminded of their love of country and their pride in the last frontier.

Alaska's flag is filled with stars,

SOURDOUGH SALLY

The Dipper points the way
To where the North Star holds its place,
A steady, shining ray.
The North Star is a friendly guide
To sailors lost at sea,
To trappers lost in fields of snow,
And even you and me.
Alaska's flag, a beacon light,
A flag we all hold dear,
Its eight gold stars on field of blue,
Salute the last frontier.
(ALL *sing "God Bless America" as curtains close.*)

THE END

ALOHA, MOTHER

Characters

TAMMY	BETTY
GEORGE	TRUDY
JERRY	JANE
KAY	BOB
LINDA	JACK
KA-HI-KI	STEVE
SPEAKER	13 VISITING MOTHERS

SCENE 1

TIME: *The day before Mother's Day.*
SETTING: *A classroom.*
AT RISE: TAMMY, GEORGE, JERRY *and* KAY *are seated around a table, making plans for a Mother's Day party.*

TAMMY: The meeting of the Mother's Day Committee will please come to order.
JERRY: But where's the rest of the gang? There are two empty chairs.
KAY: Linda said she would be late, and I don't know if Ka-hi-ki is coming or not.
GEORGE: Ka-hi-ki! Did you ask *her?*
TAMMY: Of course I asked her. Miss Blair wants her to take part in everything we do so she will feel at home.

ALOHA, MOTHER

JERRY: She won't be inside the door before she starts telling us about Mother's Day in Hawaii.

GEORGE: You can count me out. I ought to be playing baseball anyhow. Come on, Jerry.

TAMMY: You ought to be ashamed. Ka-hi-ki is a lovely girl.

JERRY: But she's always telling us how much better everything is in Hawaii.

GEORGE: The climate's better in Hawaii, the flowers are bigger; even the pineapples are sweeter.

KAY: But that's because Hawaii is her home. You acted the same way when you moved from Georgia.

GEORGE: That was different. Georgia is part of the United States.

KAY: So is Hawaii. Don't you remember? Hawaii is our fiftieth state.

GEORGE: But it's so far away and everything is so different there. Anyway, Georgia was one of the thirteen original colonies.

LINDA (*Entering*): Hello, everybody. I hope I didn't miss anything.

TAMMY: We were just talking about Ka-hi-ki.

LINDA: Ka-hi-ki? Is she coming, too? I get so tired of hearing about Hawaii. But I like her anyway.

TAMMY: Some of her stories are very interesting . . . sort of strange and romantic like her name.

JERRY: Ka-hi-ki! That's some name!

LINDA: You boys should stop teasing her about it.

TAMMY: If we keep this up, we won't get our plans made for the Mother's Day party.

KAY: That's right. I think we should do something new and special.

GEORGE: Like what?

KAY: I can't think of anything. We had a picnic last year, and a regular party would mean our mothers do all the work.

KA-HI-KI (*Enters, carrying large suitcase*): Aloha!

LINDA, TAMMY *and* KAY: Aloha, Ka-hi-ki!

JERRY: Hello.

GEORGE: Hello, Katy.

KA-HI-KI: Don't call me Katy. My name is Ka-hi-ki!

TAMMY: Don't mind him, Ka-hi-ki. Sit down and help us plan our Mother's Day party. We need some new ideas.

KA-HI-KI: Back home in Hawaii, we always went to the beach on Mother's Day.

JERRY: I knew it! I knew it!

KA-HI-KI: What does he mean? How could he know it when I just told him?

GEORGE: He knew you would say something about what you did in Hawaii.

KA-HI-KI: And is that so bad?

TAMMY: Of course not. Everybody likes to talk about home.

GEORGE: This is your home now.

KA-HI-KI: But you don't make me feel at home here. You treat me like a stranger. You won't even say my name.

GEORGE: It's too hard.

KA-HI-KI: It is *not* too hard. Ka-hi-ki! Ka-hi-ki! Ka-hi-ki!
GEORGE: O.K. I'll call you Ka-hi-ki, if you stop talking about Hawaii all the time.
KA-HI-KI: But Hawaii's the most beautiful place in the world.
TAMMY: Why shouldn't Ka-hi-ki talk about Hawaii? We certainly heard enough about Georgia when you first came.
JERRY: And I remember you were going to sock me for calling you George.
KA-HI-KI: But isn't that his name?
JERRY: No. His real name is Dean. But we started calling him "Georgia George" and the name stuck. Now he likes it.
KA-HI-KI: I'd never like Katy. (*To* GEORGE) Why didn't you make them stop?
GEORGE: Oh, I don't know. I guess I got used to it. Besides, it sounded better after we became friends.
KA-HI-KI: When did you become friends?
GEORGE: I guess it was after I stopped boasting about Georgia.
JERRY: And after we found out we could learn a lot from old George.
KAY: Our room won the prize at the science fair with George's cotton project.
LINDA: And he helped me with a report on peanuts.
JERRY: He even showed me how to throw a baseball with a real Georgia twist.
TAMMY: I bet if we gave Ka-hi-ki a chance, she might

show us how to give our Mother's Day party a new twist.

KA-HI-KI: I did have an idea, but I'm afraid you wouldn't want to hear it because it's something we did in Hawaii.

ALL (*Ad lib*): Sure, we would. Why not? What is it? Tell us.

KA-HI-KI: Well, every year just about this time we had a Lei Day.

LINDA: Don't you mean a May Day?

KA-HI-KI: No, I mean a Lei Day. A lei is a wreath of flowers. (*Opens box and takes out a lei made of real or artificial flowers*) Look. I made one to show you.

GIRLS: Oh! Isn't it pretty!

GEORGE: What do you do with it?

KA-HI-KI: You put it around the neck of someone you love. In Hawaii the lei is a sign of friendship.

LINDA: We could all make them for our mothers.

KA-HI-KI: But first we could have a little program with some songs and dances.

LINDA: Would you teach us some Hawaiian dances?

KA-HI-KI: I'd love to.

JERRY: Can anyone in our class play a ukelele?

KA-HI-KI: It's easy. (*Takes ukelele from suitcase*) I've brought mine along. I'll show you some chords. (ALL *crowd around as* KA-HI-KI *strums a few chords.*)

KAY: This is fun.

TAMMY: I know our mothers will love it.

GEORGE: I think it's a great idea.

KA-HI-KI: Do you really mean it?

GEORGE: Sure, I do, Katy—I mean Ka-hi-ki.

KA-HI-KI: That's all right, George. You can call me Katy, if you want to. It's beginning to sound better already. (*Curtain falls.* SPEAKER *in Hawaiian costume steps out.*)

SPEAKER:
Americans say "Mother."
The English say it, too.
The German child says "Mutter," (*Moo-ter*)
The Chinese child says "Moo."

Romanians say "Mama."
In France the word is "Mère." (*Mare*)
No matter how you say it,
It's music everywhere.

In faraway Hawaii
"Makuahine" (*Mock-Waheeny*) is the word.
And mothers come a-running,
Whenever it is heard.

And so we call our mothers
To join us here today
At a Makuahine party
In the true Hawaiian way.

* * * * *

SCENE 2

TIME: *Mother's Day.*
SETTING: *The classroom.*

AT RISE: VISITING MOTHERS *are seated on chairs across the rear of stage. All the* CHILDREN *are present, seated in a semicircle on the floor and wearing Hawaiian costumes. Each wears a lei of real or artificial flowers. Ukeleles or autoharps may be used for accompaniment.*

SPEAKER: Since this is a true Hawaiian party, we wish to welcome our mothers in true Hawaiian style.

CHILDREN: Aloha, Makuahine.

SPEAKER: In Hawaii it is not enough to welcome one's guests with words, so we now welcome our mothers with a dance. (*Several girls may perform a simple Hawaiian dance to recorded music.*) Our next greeting will be in the language of the flowers. Our classmate, Ka-hi-ki, will explain.

KA-HI-KI (*Rising*): Since Hawaii is the land of flowers, we have used the brightest blossoms to honor our mothers. We have each made a lei of our favorite flowers to spell out a special message for our mothers. Betty will tell you what the pansy has to say.

BETTY (*Holding pansy*):
The pansy is for thoughtfulness,
And that's the word for mothers.
They seldom think about themselves,
But always work for others.

KA-HI-KI: Bob delivers the message of the violet.

BOB (*Holding violets*):
We chose the violet to say
How modest mothers are.

They never work for credit,
   Or try to be a star!
KA-HI-KI: Trudy presents the lily of the valley.
TRUDY (*Holding lilies of the valley*):
   The lily of the valley
   Is sweet as it can be.
   So it belongs to Mother
   'Cause she's so sweet to me!
KA-HI-KI: Jack brings the promise of the primrose.
JACK (*Holding primrose*):
   The primrose is for youthfulness.
   Its color is pure gold.
   We give it to our mother
   So she never will grow old.
KA-HI-KI: Jane will speak for the forget-me-not.
JANE (*Holding forget-me-nots*):
   The tiny, blue forget-me-not
   Is just the sweetest ever.
   And it belongs to Mother.
   Could we forget her? Never!
KA-HI-KI: Steve will have the last word.
STEVE (*Holding a rose*):
   This flower means love and beauty,
   As everybody knows.
   And so we give to Mother
   The biggest, brightest rose.
KA-HI-KI (*Addressing* MOTHERS):
   And now to you, our mothers dear,
   We each present a lei,
   A sign of love and gratitude,

Our gift for Mothers' Day.

CHILDREN (*Rise and sing to tune of "Farewell to Thee"*):
Fondly sing of mothers everywhere.
Our love for you we cannot tell.
May these blossoms bring such joy to you,
Mem'ries fond in your hearts will ever dwell.

Oh, Mother dear,
Oh, Mother dear,
To you we give this wreath of lovely flowers.
Each blossom sweet
The message will repeat
And tell our love for you!
(*As the song is played the second time,* CHILDREN *walk to rear of stage, where each stands behind his* MOTHER. *When the chorus is repeated, each puts lei around his* MOTHER'S *neck as curtain falls.*)

THE END

SO LONG AT THE FAIR

Characters

JOHNNY ARMSTRONG
BETSY ARMSTRONG
MRS. WEBSTER
PATTY WEBSTER
BILLY
PEGGY
BOBBY
POLICEMAN
4 BARKERS
CAROUSEL ATTENDANT
GYPSY
CHILDREN

SCENE 1

BEFORE CURTAIN: MRS. WEBSTER, BETSY, PATTY, BILLY, PEGGY, *and* BOBBY *are standing near a sign which says* BUS STOP. *Their arms are full of stuffed animals, balloons, and paper novelties such as are available at a fair. Some children may wear souvenir hats.*

BETSY (*Passing her balloon to* PATTY): Here, Patty. Please hold this for me. I want to take my shoes off. My feet hurt.

PATTY: No wonder! We've walked miles at the fair.

MRS. WEBSTER: Don't take your shoes off here, Betsy—not on the street!

BETSY: But my feet are killing me, Mrs. Webster.

PEGGY: I'd take mine off, but I know I'd never get them on again.

BOBBY: I'm hungry!

BILLY: Hungry? I'm starved. I could eat nails!
MRS. WEBSTER: How could you be hungry? You've done nothing but eat all day.
BOBBY: Only three hamburgers, two hot dogs and three bottles of soda.
BILLY: I don't call that a meal.
PATTY: Can't we go home now, Mother?
MRS. WEBSTER: You know we can't leave without Johnny.
PATTY: But where *is* Johnny? What could be keeping him?
MRS. WEBSTER: I can't imagine. But I'm worried about him.
ALL (*Singing to the tune of "What Can the Matter Be?"*):
"Oh, dear! What can the matter be?
Dear, dear! What can the matter be?
Oh, dear! What can the matter be?
Johnny's so long at the fair."
BOBBY: The last time I saw him he was getting off the merry-go-round.
PATTY: The last time I saw him he was eating a hot dog.
PEGGY: The last time I saw him he was riding the Ferris wheel.
BILLY: The last time I saw him he was watching the races.
MRS. WEBSTER: How about you, Betsy? Do you know where Johnny could be?
BETSY: I'm not sure. But I think he might be looking for something.

MRS. WEBSTER: Looking for something? Do you mean he has lost something?
BETSY: No. I think he was looking for a present.
ALL: A present?
BETSY: Yes, a present for me. (*She sings to the tune of "What Can the Matter Be?"*)
"He promised he'd buy me a fairing should please me,
And then for a kiss,
Oh, he vowed he would tease me,
He promised he'd buy me a bunch of blue ribbons,
To tie up my bonnie brown hair."
ALL:
"Oh, dear! What can the matter be?
Dear, dear! What can the matter be?
Oh, dear! What can the matter be?
Johnny's so long at the fair."
BETSY (*Singing*):
"He promised he'd bring me a basket of posies,
A garland of lilies, a garland of roses,
A little straw hat to set off the blue ribbons
That tie up my bonnie brown hair."
ALL (*Singing*):
"Oh, dear! What can the matter be?
Dear, dear! What can the matter be?
Oh, dear! What can the matter be?
Johnny's so long at the fair."
MRS. WEBSTER: I do hope he isn't lost.
BILLY: Johnny couldn't get lost on this fairground. He knows every inch of it.

PATTY: Maybe he sat down somewhere to rest and fell asleep.
BOBBY: Not Johnny. He never gets tired. (POLICEMAN *enters left and strolls across stage.*)
PEGGY: Here comes a policeman. Let's ask him.
MRS. WEBSTER: Good afternoon, officer. Have you seen a little boy about so high (*With gesture*), wearing a pair of blue jeans and a red sweater?
POLICEMAN: I've seen dozens of little boys like that, ma'am. What is his name? (*Makes notes in a pocket notebook*)
BETSY: His name is Johnny—Johnny Armstrong. He's my brother.
MRS. WEBSTER: And we're afraid he's lost.
POLICEMAN: I'll take a look around the grounds and see if I can find him.
MRS. WEBSTER: Maybe we should go with you.
POLICEMAN: No need for that, ma'am. Why don't you wait in the bus station, and I'll bring the young man here the minute I find him?
MRS. WEBSTER: That's a good idea. We're all tired. Come along, children. (MRS. WEBSTER *and children exit right.* POLICEMAN *consults his notebook as he walks left stage.*)
POLICEMAN: Johnny Armstrong. Blue jeans, red sweater. This will be like looking for a needle in a haystack, but I'll find him! (*As he exits left, curtains open on fair scene.*)

* * * * *

SCENE 2

SETTING: *Fairgrounds, with four brightly decorated booths.*
AT RISE: *At center stage there is a double ring of children playing the singing game, "Carousel." A* BARKER *stands behind each booth, and the* CAROUSEL ATTENDANT *stands beside the children's "merry-go-round."*

CHILDREN (*Singing "Carousel" as they play game*):
"Little children, sweet and gay,
Carousel is running.
It will run till evening.
Little ones a nickel, big ones a dime.
Hurry up, get your mate,
Or you'll surely be too late.
Ha, ha, ha, happy are we, Peterson and Henderson and Anderson and me!
Ha, ha, ha, happy are we, Peterson and Henderson and Anderson and me!"
CAROUSEL ATTENDANT: Everybody off! End of the ride! Line up for tickets. Little ones a nickel, big ones a dime. (*Children break up carousel formation. A few scatter to the four booths. Others buy tickets and form smaller circles for next game, which they play silently.* JOHNNY, *who is one of the carousel players, approaches* CAROUSEL ATTENDANT. JOHNNY *carries a little straw hat and some blue ribbons.*)
JOHNNY: Please, mister, may I have a fairing?

CAROUSEL ATTENDANT: Wait your turn. Get in line for your ticket.
JOHNNY: I don't want a ticket. I want a fairing.
CAROUSEL ATTENDANT: A fairing! I don't know what you're talking about.
BOY: Maybe he means the brass ring.
CAROUSEL ATTENDANT: We don't give any brass rings on this carousel.
JOHNNY: No, I don't mean a brass ring. I mean a fairing. I promised my sister I'd bring her one.
CAROUSEL ATTENDANT: Never heard of such a thing.
GIRL: Neither did I.
JOHNNY: I got the idea from a song we sing at school. I'm sure you get them at fairs.
BOY (*Pointing to booth right stage*): Why don't you try over there?
JOHNNY: Thanks, I will. (*Moves to first booth at extreme right.*)
1ST BARKER (*At first booth*): Right this way! Right this way, ladies and gentlemen. Right this way for the best buys at the fair.
JOHNNY (*To* 1ST BARKER): Say, mister, do you have any fairings?
1ST BARKER: Any what?
JOHNNY: Any fairings. I'd like to buy one.
1ST BARKER: Fairings, eh? Never heard of 'em, boy. (*Reciting or singing to tune of verse of "What Can the Matter Be?"*)
I've hot dogs and burgers
With mustard and pickles,

For only a dime,
Or the price of two nickels.
I've custard and ice cream
In forty-two flavors,
But nary a fairing have I.

JOHNNY: Oh, dear, it's getting later and later, and I *must* get a fairing before I leave. (*To* BOY *beside him*) Do you happen to know where I could get a fairing around here?

BOY: A fairing? Sounds like some kind of fish to me. If it's anything to eat, try the next booth. They have a little bit of everything.

JOHNNY: Thanks, I will. (*Moves to next booth*)

2ND BARKER: Hurry, hurry, hurry!
Get 'em while they're hot!
Hurry, hurry, hurry! The bite that hits the spot.
What can I do for you, young man?

JOHNNY: I'd like to buy a fairing, if you have any.

2ND BARKER: A fairing, eh? That's a new one on me, boy. (*Reciting or singing to tune of verse of "What Can the Matter Be?"*)

I've popcorn and peanuts,
And real cotton candy.
I've lemonade, soda,
And popsicles handy.
I've ginger ale, root beer,
Right here in the cooler,
But nary a fairing have I.

GIRL: Did I hear you ask for a fairing?

JOHNNY: Yes. Do you know where I can get one?

GIRL (*Pointing left*): Right over there at the booth next to the carousel. That man has all sorts of pretty things.

JOHNNY: Thanks, thanks a lot. (*Moves to booth next to carousel*)

3RD BARKER: Here's what you've been waiting for, ladies and gentlemen. Step right up and take your choice. First come, first served. Something for everybody—right this way.

JOHNNY: How much are your fairings, mister?

3RD BARKER: My what?

JOHNNY: Your fairings. I'd like to buy one.

3RD BARKER: Sorry, young man! You've come to the wrong place. (*Reciting or singing to tune of verse of "What Can the Matter Be?"*)

I've rings for your fingers,
And bracelets and lockets.
I've bright-colored aprons
With pretty patch pockets.
I've real leather wallets
To carry your money,
But nary a fairing have I.

JOHNNY: This is pretty discouraging, but I'm not going to give up. I'll try one more booth. (*Moves to last booth*)

4TH BARKER: Right this way, my little friends. Step right up for the snuggliest, cuddliest toys in the world. Hello, there, my young friend. How would you like this fine teddy bear?

JOHNNY: No, thanks, mister. I'm looking for a fairing.
4TH BARKER: Sorry, we just sold our last one, buddy. (*Singing to tune of verse of "What Can the Matter Be?"*)
I've teddy bears, pandas,
And dolls dressed in laces,
And poppets and puppets
With Mickey Mouse faces.
And here's Donald Duck
And a real alligator,
But nary a fairing have I.
JOHNNY: Well, I guess there's not a fairing to be had. I'll have to go home without one. (*As he turns to cross stage toward the right, he comes face to face with the* GYPSY, *who is entering.*)
GYPSY: Not so fast, my pretty gentleman! You can't leave the fair without hearing your fortune.
JOHNNY: I don't want to hear my fortune. I want to go home.
GYPSY: There is an air of mystery about you. You are in some kind of trouble.
JOHNNY: How did you know?
GYPSY: Ah, that is my secret. Just cross my palm with silver, and I'll tell you what is troubling you.
JOHNNY: I already know what is troubling me. I promised my sister I'd buy her a fairing, and I can't find a single one.
GYPSY: So that's the trouble. Well, it just so happens, my young friend, that I can help you.
JOHNNY: How?

GYPSY (*Extending her hand*): First, let me see your silver.
JOHNNY: But if I give you my money, I won't have any left for the fairing.
GYPSY: It's worth trying, isn't it?
JOHNNY: Oh, very well! (*Gives* GYPSY *a coin*)
GYPSY: Now let me see your hand. (*As* JOHNNY *extends his hand, and the* GYPSY *pretends to read his palm, the* POLICEMAN *enters.*)
POLICEMAN: Here, here! What is going on? (*To* GYPSY) I've told you fortune-telling is forbidden on this fairground.
JOHNNY: But she isn't telling my fortune, officer. She's just trying to help me find a fairing. I promised my sister I'd get her one.
POLICEMAN: A fairing, is it? And what does a gypsy fortune-teller know about fairings?
GYPSY: More than you'd think, officer. And I happen to have the very thing the young gentleman is looking for. (*Reaching into her pocket and bringing out a small charm on a silver chain*) Here, lad, you shall have your fairing.
JOHNNY (*In wonder*): Is this really a fairing? Are you sure?
GYPSY: It's a good luck charm my grandfather gave me many, many years ago.
JOHNNY: Oh, thank you, thank you. I am sure my sister will love it.
GYPSY: May it bring both of you the best of luck.
JOHNNY: I'm sure it will.

GYPSY: So you see, Mr. Policeman, I wasn't telling fortunes after all. I was just making an honest sale.

POLICEMAN: I'm sure it was the sight of my badge and uniform that turned you into an honest merchant. But don't let me catch you around here again.

GYPSY: No, sir! Not if I see you first, officer. (*Exits laughing*)

JOHNNY (*Looking at charm*): Do you really think it is a fairing, officer?

POLICEMAN: I suppose it is, sonny. A fairing is just a trinket, a sort of souvenir.

JOHNNY: It is? Gee whiz! If that's all it is, I could have bought almost any of these things they have for sale. I never really knew what the word meant.

POLICEMAN: Maybe you should buy a good dictionary. Say, does your name happen to be Johnny Armstrong?

JOHNNY: Sure. That's my name. But how did you know?

POLICEMAN: Then you'd better come along with me.

JOHNNY: But why? I haven't done anything wrong, have I?

POLICEMAN: Nothing but keep half a dozen people waiting for you. They think you're lost and sent me out to look for you.

JOHNNY: I never thought they'd be worried.

POLICEMAN: Don't you know you should never wander off by yourself at a fair? Always stay with your group.

JOHNNY: I'm sorry, officer. I'll go find them right away.

(MRS. WEBSTER *enters from right with* BETSY, PATTY, PEGGY, BILLY *and* BOBBY.)

BETSY: There's Johnny. There he is!

MRS. WEBSTER: Oh, thank goodness, officer, you've found him.

BILLY: I told you he wasn't lost.

BETSY: Oh, Johnny! You got my little straw hat and the bunch of blue ribbons!

JOHNNY (*Handing her the charm*): And here's your fairing. I hope you like it.

BETSY: It's beautiful.

PATTY: Where did you ever find it?

JOHNNY: It's a long story. I'll tell you about it on the way home in the bus.

MRS. WEBSTER: Where have you been, Johnny? What kept you so long?

JOHNNY: I was hunting for the fairing I promised Betsy.

MRS. WEBSTER: Let me see it. I've never heard of a fairing.

PATTY: We sing about it in school, Mother. You know the old song . . .

ALL (*Singing*):
"Oh, dear! What can the matter be?
Dear, dear! What can the matter be?
Oh, dear! What can the matter be?
Johnny's so long at the fair."

BETSY: "He promised to buy me a fairing to please me . . ."

JOHNNY: No, no! Don't sing it that way any more. The

policeman just told me that a fairing is really a trinket or a souvenir.

POLICEMAN: "Fairing" is an old English word. I doubt if many people use it any more.

PEGGY: The word "trinket" fits the music just as well.

BETSY: Well, I like "fairing," and if Johnny went to all this trouble to get me one, I'm going to keep right on singing the song the way it is.

BOBBY: At least, now we understand why Johnny was so long at the fair.

MRS. WEBSTER: If we don't hurry, we'll miss our bus. Come along, children. Thanks again, officer. (*Children exit singing "What Can the Matter Be?" as the curtain falls.*)

THE END

THE GLASS SLIPPERS

Characters

BUCKLE
KNUCKLE } *the Carefree Cobblers*
CHUCKLE
MOONEY, *the Maker of Glass Slippers*
MOTHER
OLDER DAUGHTER
YOUNGER DAUGHTER
CINDERELLA
OLD WOMAN, *Cinderella's Fairy Godmother*
PRINCE
2 HERALDS
8 CUSTOMERS

SCENE 1

TIME: *An afternoon, long, long ago.*
SETTING: *The workshop of the Carefree Cobblers.*
AT RISE: BUCKLE, KNUCKLE, *and* CHUCKLE *are rapping and tapping at their workbench.* MOONEY *is working at a small table which holds a basin of soapsuds and a pair of glass slippers. He is blowing bubbles from a long-stemmed pipe.* 8 CUSTOMERS *are standing behind the display counter at the center of the stage. As the*

THE GLASS SLIPPERS

curtain rises, they are singing "Shoemakers' Dance," with the folk dance motions.*

CUSTOMERS: Wind, wind, wind your thread,
And wind, wind, wind your thread,
And pull, and pull,
And pull it tight.
Wind, wind, wind your thread,
And wind, wind, wind, your thread,
And sew, and sew,
And sew it right.
Tap, tap, tap, tap on each heel.
Carefree Cobblers work with zeal.
(*They repeat. Then* MOTHER *enters with* 2 DAUGHTERS.)

MOTHER: Good morning! Are you the Carefree Cobblers?

CAREFREE COBBLERS: Yes, we are the Carefree Cobblers.

BUCKLE (*Rising with a bow*): I'm Buckle.

KNUCKLE (*Rising with a bow*): I'm Knuckle!

CHUCKLE (*Rising with a bow*): And I'm Chuckle.

MOTHER: I have heard you do very fine work. I would like to buy some slippers for my daughters.

BUCKLE: What kind of slippers do you want?

OLDER DAUGHTER: They must be very fine slippers.

YOUNGER DAUGHTER: We are going to wear them to the Prince's ball.

MOTHER: What kind of slippers do you have?

---

* The music to this song may be found in *Our Songs*, Book II, of "A Singing School" Series, C. C. Birchard & Co., Boston, Mass.

CAREFREE COBBLERS: We have all kinds.
BUCKLE: We have slippers of silver,
   And slippers of gold,
   And slippers of satin,
   All made to be sold.
KNUCKLE: We have slippers of wood,
   And slippers of straw!
   The prettiest slippers
   That ever you saw.
CHUCKLE: We have slippers for work
   And slippers for play,
   And you'll be surprised
   At how little you pay.
DAUGHTERS: We want dancing slippers.
BUCKLE: We have slippers of silk,
   And slippers of leather.
   They're light on your feet,
   Just as light as a feather.
KNUCKLE: So step to the counter,
   And give them a try.
   I'm sure you will find there
   A pair you will buy.
MOTHER: You girls go and look. (*Sitting on stool*) I'll sit here and rest. You may get whatever pleases you. (CHUCKLE *conducts* DAUGHTERS *to counter where they each select a pair of slippers*.) I'm so tired of shopping. We have been in every shop in town looking at party dresses. I want my daughters to be the most beautiful girls at the ball.

THE GLASS SLIPPERS

BUCKLE: Excuse me, ma'am, but don't you have another daughter at home?

MOTHER: Oh, no. I have only two girls.

KNUCKLE: There's a very sweet little girl who comes into the shop. I thought she was also your daughter.

MOTHER: Oh, you must mean Cinderella. She isn't going to the ball.

BUCKLE: That's too bad.

KNUCKLE: Doesn't she want to go?

MOTHER: I never asked her. But she must stay home and look after the house. Besides, she has no party clothes.

OLDER DAUGHTER (*With a pair of slippers*): Look, Mother. These gold ones will match my dress.

YOUNGER DAUGHTER: I am afraid these silver ones are a little small, but I am going to wear them anyway. They are so pretty.

MOONEY (*Approaching them with a glass slipper in his hand*): Wouldn't you young ladies like to try on one of *my* slippers?

MOTHER: Mercy me! Who is this fellow?

BUCKLE: This is our brother, Mooney.

KNUCKLE: Mooney, go back to your corner and don't bother the ladies.

MOONEY: But my slippers are so beautiful. There are no others like them in all the world.

OLDER DAUGHTER (*Examining slipper*): Look, Mother, the slipper is made of glass!

MOTHER: Made of glass! How perfectly silly!

YOUNGER DAUGHTER: And look how tiny! Not even a child could wear it.

MOTHER: Indeed, I am surprised you have such a fellow in your shop!
CHUCKLE: He is our brother, and if it makes him happy to work in glass, we let him go ahead.
MOTHER: Come along, girls. I am glad you found what you wanted. (KNUCKLE *and* BUCKLE *put slippers in boxes and give them to the* DAUGHTERS.)
DAUGHTERS: Thank you and good day to you.
CAREFREE COBBLERS *and* MOONEY: Good day to you. (MOTHER *and* DAUGHTERS *exit. Other* CUSTOMERS *select slippers and the* COBBLERS *put them in bags or boxes.*)
1ST CUSTOMER: I'll take the ones with the ribbon bows.
2ND CUSTOMER: I'll take the ones with the open toes.
3RD CUSTOMER: I'll take these with the high, high heel.
4TH CUSTOMER: I like the way these slippers feel.
5TH CUSTOMER: I like a shoe to be good and stout.
6TH CUSTOMER: I like the shoes that will not wear out.
7TH CUSTOMER: I like leather that is soft and fine.
8TH CUSTOMER: I like buckles that will really shine. (*All* CUSTOMERS *exit.*)
MOONEY: Oh, dear. I am so disappointed. Nobody even looked at my glass slippers. (*Returns slipper to his worktable*)
BUCKLE: We've told you that nobody wants a slipper made of glass.
KNUCKLE: They are uncomfortable.
CHUCKLE: And they would crack and break in no time.
MOONEY: But they are so beautiful. Look how they

sparkle in the light. (CINDERELLA *enters with a pair of worn-out shoes.*)

CINDERELLA: Good morning!

ALL: Good morning, ma'am, what can we do for you?

CINDERELLA (*Singing to the tune of "Partner Come and Dance with Me," from Humperdinck's "Hansel and Gretel."*):
Cobbler, Cobbler, mend my shoe,
Can you make it good as new?
Stitch and sew, mend the toe,
So that I may dancing go!
(*Gives them shoes*)

COBBLERS (*Pantomiming and singing*):
With our hammers, tap, tap, tap.
With our fingers, rap, rap, rap.
(*Handing them back to her*)
Here's your shoe, good as new,
And the best of luck to you.

CINDERELLA: Oh, thank you, thank you. How much is it?

CAREFREE COBBLERS: Not one cent. We are happy to do it for you.

MOONEY: You are Cinderella, aren't you?

CINDERELLA: Yes, I am, but how did you know?

MOONEY: I've often seen you in the shop.

BUCKLE: Your sisters were just here.

KNUCKLE: They were getting shoes for the ball.

CHUCKLE: Don't you want to go to the ball, too, Cinderella?

CINDERELLA: More than anything else in the world. But I have to stay at home.

MOONEY: Then why did you want your shoes fixed?

CINDERELLA: I can't wear them any more the way they are. And besides, if they should change their minds at the last minute and let me go, I want to be ready.

MOONEY: Would you like to see my wonderful glass slippers, Cinderella? (*Takes her to table and shows them to her*)

CINDERELLA: Oh, how lovely! These are the most beautiful slippers in the world. How I wish I could wear them.

MOONEY: I think they would fit you. You have such tiny feet. Would you like to try them on?

CINDERELLA: I'd love to, but I don't have time. I must be home before the others finish their shopping. Good day to you, and thank you for mending these poor, old shoes. (CINDERELLA *exits*.)

MOONEY: What a shame Cinderella can't go to the ball!

BUCKLE: She would be the prettiest girl there.

KNUCKLE: And the nicest!

CHUCKLE: And the sweetest!

MOONEY: And she could wear my beautiful glass slippers! (OLD WOMAN IN CLOAK *enters*.)

OLD WOMAN (*Stamping her cane on the floor*): Service! Service! How about a little service around here?

ALL: What can we do for you, ma'am?

OLD WOMAN: What do cobblers usually do for their customers? Sell them some shoes, of course.

BUCKLE: What kind of shoes would you like, ma'am?

KNUCKLE (*Holding up bedroom slippers*): These are very comfortable, ma'am. My grandmother wears this kind all the time!
OLD WOMAN: Who said anything about your grandmother? I want a pair of dancing slippers.
CHUCKLE (*To* KNUCKLE): You heard the lady, Knuckle. Show her some dancing slippers.
KNUCKLE: These satin ones are very pretty, and they have good, sensible heels.
OLD WOMAN: I don't want good, sensible heels.
KNUCKLE: How about this pair? They have nice, broad toes.
OLD WOMAN: I don't want nice, broad toes. I want the prettiest pair of dancing slippers in your shop. Don't you have anything in silver or gold?
COBBLERS: Silver or gold!
OLD WOMAN: Well, don't stand there gawking. Show me something in silver or gold.
BUCKLE: We just sold our last pair of gold slippers, ma'am.
KNUCKLE: And our last pair of silver.
CHUCKLE: We sold them to some young ladies who are going to the Prince's ball.
MOONEY: Are you going to the ball, ma'am?
OLD WOMAN: Who? Me? Don't be ridiculous. Why would an old woman like me be going to a ball? I want these slippers for a lonely, unhappy little girl who thinks she isn't going to the ball.
MOONEY: You must mean Cinderella.
OLD WOMAN: Yes, that is her name.

COBBLERS: Who are you?

OLD WOMAN: I am Cinderella's Fairy Godmother, and she's going to that ball, if it takes my last drop of magic to send her.

ALL (*Jumping up and down and clapping hands*): Hurray! Hurray! Hurray!

OLD WOMAN: Stop that dancing up and down and show me the finest slippers in your shop. There's no time to spare.

MOONEY (*Taking her by the hand*): Please, good, kind Fairy Godmother, please look at *my* slippers. I know they are just what Cinderella wants.

OLD WOMAN (*Looking at slippers*): Why, these slippers are made of glass. Not even I have heard of such a thing.

MOONEY: I have worked for many years on these slippers. No one else, not even my brothers, knows how they are made.

OLD WOMAN: Do you think she will like them?

MOONEY: She was just in here a few minutes ago, and looked at them.

BUCKLE: She said they were the most beautiful slippers in the world.

KNUCKLE: She said she'd give anything to wear them.

CHUCKLE: Her sisters have such big feet they could never get into them.

OLD WOMAN: That settles it. I'll take them! (MOONEY *wraps up the glass slippers.*)

MOONEY: How I should like to see Cinderella dancing in my glass slippers!

ALL: If only we could see our little friend at the ball.
OLD WOMAN: Meet me in the palace gardens at half past eight and I'll change you into fireflies. Then you can fly right up to the palace windows and see everything.
MOONEY: That will be wonderful!
BUCKLE: You won't forget to change us back again?
OLD WOMAN: Of course not. What kind of Fairy Godmother do you think I am, anyway?
ALL: We'll be there at half-past eight.
OLD WOMAN: I'll meet you by the palace gate! (*Curtain*)

* * * * *

SCENE 2

TIME: *The next morning.*
SETTING: *Same as Scene 1.*
AT RISE: *The* CAREFREE COBBLERS *and* MOONEY *are asleep at their worktables. There is a loud banging offstage.*

CINDERELLA (*Offstage*): Let me in! Let me in!
BUCKLE (*Yawning and stretching*): Ho-hum! What time is it?
KNUCKLE: It must be the middle of the night!
CHUCKLE: These late hours are killing me.
MOONEY: Someone is pounding at the door.
CINDERELLA (*Offstage*): Please, please, let me in!
MOONEY (*Jumping up and running to door*): It's Cin-

derella. (CINDERELLA *enters, carrying one glass slipper.*)
CINDERELLA: Oh, please, please, help me! The most terrible thing has happened.
ALL (*Jumping up*): What's the matter?
CINDERELLA: Oh, dear! I don't see how it happened, but I was having such a wonderful time, I forgot to look at the clock.
BUCKLE: What are you talking about?
CINDERELLA: It's such a long story and there isn't time to explain. Last night I went to the ball.
KNUCKLE: Yes, yes, we know.
CINDERELLA: My Fairy Godmother told me to be home by twelve, but I was late . . . and . . . oh, dear, I lost one of my beautiful glass slippers. Please, please, Mr. Mooney, can you make me another?
MOONEY: Make you another?
CINDERELLA: Yes, please. My beautiful slippers are all that I have to remember my wonderful night at the ball.
MOONEY: But it took me years to make those slippers.
CINDERELLA: But couldn't you hurry, please? (*More pounding at door*)
MOTHER (*Offstage*): Let me in! Open this door! Let me in!
CINDERELLA: Quick! I must hide. I don't want her to find me here. (*Crouches behind display table. One of the* COBBLERS *throws a long table cover over her.*)
MOTHER (*More pounding*): Let me in! Let me in at once! (BUCKLE *opens door for* MOTHER *and* DAUGH-

THE GLASS SLIPPERS

TERS. MOTHER *darts to* MOONEY'S *table*.) Where are those glass slippers that were here yesterday?

OLDER DAUGHTER: We must buy them at once.

YOUNGER DAUGHTER: Where are they? Where are they?

COBBLERS: They have been sold.

MOTHER: Sold! Impossible. Who would wear such things?

MOONEY: Yesterday you made fun of them. Why do you want them now?

MOTHER: I want them for my daughters.

OLDER DAUGHTER: Last night the Prince found a little glass slipper. He has announced that he will marry the girl who can wear it.

YOUNGER DAUGHTER: But she must have the mate to the slipper he found.

MOTHER: So if we can buy yours, each of my daughters will have a slipper.

OLDER DAUGHTER: I will take the right.

YOUNGER DAUGHTER: And I will take the left.

MOTHER: One of them will have to match up with the one the Prince has. (*Trumpets offstage*)

HERALDS (*Offstage*): Make way for the Prince! Make way for the Prince! (*Pounding at door*) Open this door. Open in the name of the Prince. (PRINCE *enters carrying glass slipper. He is attended by* 2 HERALDS.)

COBBLERS: All hail, Your Highness. (*Bow*)

MOTHER *and* DAUGHTERS: Your Highness! (*Curtsey*)

PRINCE (*Holding out slipper*): Did one of you cobblers make this glass slipper?

MOONEY: I did, sir. I made the slipper.

THE GLASS SLIPPERS

PRINCE: Then tell me who bought it. I command you to tell me at once.

MOONEY: An old lady bought it, Your Highness. A very, very old lady.

PRINCE: I don't believe it.

COBBLERS: He speaks the truth, Your Highness.

PRINCE: I have vowed to marry the young lady who can wear this slipper, but she must be able to show me the mate to it.

MOTHER: Please, sire. I am sure the slipper belongs to one of my daughters. Will you let them try it on?

PRINCE: Very well. (*Hands slipper to one of the* HERALDS. *He tries it on* OLDER DAUGHTER.)

1ST HERALD: She can't even get her big toe into it, Your Highness.

YOUNGER DAUGHTER: Please let me try.

2ND HERALD (*Taking slipper and trying it on* YOUNGER DAUGHTER): It's no use, Your Highness.

MOTHER: I am sure if you tried a little harder. . . .

PRINCE: I thought if the slippers were made here, you could lead me to their owner.

BUCKLE: I'm sure we can do that, Your Highness.

PRINCE: But he told me an old lady bought them.

KNUCKLE: So she did. But she did not wear them to the ball last night.

CHUCKLE: The young lady who wore them is right here in our shop.

COBBLERS (*Calling softly*): Cinderella! Cinderella! (CINDERELLA *emerges from hiding place.*)

MOTHER *and* DAUGHTERS (*In astonishment*): Cinderella!

PRINCE: My beautiful lady! (*Drops on one knee*) Quick, the slipper. (*Puts it on* CINDERELLA)
ALL: It fits! It fits!
CINDERELLA: And here, my Prince, is the other slipper.
PRINCE (*Rising and taking her by the hand*): On this very day the lovely Cinderella shall be my bride!
ALL (*Except* MOTHER *and* DAUGHTERS): Long live Cinderella!
MOTHER: Come, girls, we will leave at once! (MOTHER *and* DAUGHTERS *exit.*)
CINDERELLA: Please, dear Prince, may I ask a favor?
PRINCE: Anything your heart desires.
CINDERELLA: I ask only that these kindhearted cobblers become the royal shoemakers at the palace.
PRINCE: It shall be done. From now on, they will make all of the shoes for the court and our royal family.
MOONEY: But I can't make anything but glass slippers, Your Highness.
PRINCE: Then you shall be Cinderella's very own shoemaker. From this day forth, she will wear only glass slippers made by your hands.
COBBLERS: This calls for a song! (*They sing to the tune of "Fiddle-Dee-Dee."*)
Fiddle-dee-dee, fiddle-dee-dee,
We're all as happy as we can be.
Says the Prince, says he, "Will you marry me,
And live with me contentedly?"
Fiddle-dee-dee, fiddle-dee-dee,
We're all as happy as we can be! (*Curtain*)

THE END

THE MOUSE THAT SOARED

Characters

ORVIE MOUSE
MAMMA MOUSE
FRISKY ⎫
WHISKERS ⎬ *the "Three Blind Mice"*
RISKY ⎭
SCAMPER, *a mouse who plays the "Farmer's Wife"*
LONG TAIL ⎫
SHORT TAIL ⎪
NIBBLER ⎪
SCRIBBLER ⎬ *other mice*
FLUTTER ⎪
FURRY ⎪
SQUEAKY ⎪
SQUEALY ⎭
BILL ⎫ *boy rocketeers*
JAKE ⎭
THOMAS CAT
ANNOUNCER (*Offstage voice*)

SETTING: *Merry Mouse Meadow.*
AT RISE: *The game "Three Blind Mice" is in progress.* FRISKY, WHISKERS, *and* RISKY, *who are blindfolded, join hands and go around in a circle singing "Three Blind Mice."* SCAMPER, *as the "Farmer's Wife," brandishes a cardboard carving knife and tries to*

break through circle. When they finish song, "Farmer's Wife" chases "Three Blind Mice" as they break circle and run in all directions, until one is caught. During game, ORVIE *sits under tree, ignoring the others and pretending to read a torn scrap of newspaper. Other mice stand around stage and watch game.*

FRISKY: That was fun! Let's play again.
WHISKERS (*As he takes off blindfold*): Come on, Orvie, you play this time.
ORVIE: No, thanks. I want no part of that stupid game!
SCAMPER (*Offering* ORVIE *the carving knife*): But it's fun. Take my part.
ORVIE: No, thanks.
NIBBLER: Oh, come on, Orvie. We need your voice. You're such a good squeaker.
ORVIE: I wouldn't sing that disgusting song!
SCAMPER: Disgusting! What's disgusting about it?
ORVIE: Everything! It makes us mice look silly and stupid.
LONG TAIL: I never thought of that.
ORVIE: Well, think about it. Actually, mice are very clever creatures. We have to be to stay alive.
SHORT TAIL: Maybe we could play "Hickory Dickory Dock!"
ORVIE: That's almost as bad.
FURRY:
Hickory dickory dock,
The mouse ran up the clock.
The clock struck one,

The mouse ran down.
Hickory dickory dock!

RISKY: What's wrong with that?

ORVIE: Don't you see? The mouse was a coward. Afraid of a little old clock! He ran away.

WHISKERS: I never thought of that!

ORVIE: You're all too busy running away to think of anything. You're even afraid of old Thomas the Cat!

RISKY: Sh-h-h! Don't even mention him. He might hear you.

ORVIE: And what if he does? He's half blind and almost toothless. Yet you're all scared to death of him.

LONG TAIL: Mice are just naturally timid!

ORVIE: That's not true. Think of our great mouse heroes. Why doesn't anybody write songs about them?

SCRIBBLER: I don't know any mouse heroes.

ORVIE: Shame on you! What about our great ancestor who wasn't afraid of a lion?

SQUEAKY: Oh, I know about him. He even saved the lion's life.

ORVIE: And what about the brave mice who sailed with Columbus and came along with the Pilgrims on the *Mayflower*? Does anybody ever hear about them?

FURRY: No, never!

ORVIE: Take my own ancestor—Orville Mouse, the First.

SCRIBBLER: Tell us about him, Orvie. Maybe I could write a song about him.

ORVIE: He lived in the little bicycle shop where the

famous Wright brothers built the first airplane. He was named for Orville Wright himself.

FURRY: How exciting!

ORVIE: You just wait and see! One of these days I'm going to make all you mice sit up and take notice.

SQUEAKY: I'll bet you would be a real mouse hero, if only you had the chance.

SQUEALY: But nothing exciting ever happens here in Merry Mouse Meadow. (*There is a loud noise offstage. All the mice except* ORVIE *flee in terror.*)

ORVIE: Cowards! Cowards!

ALL (*As they creep back; ad lib*): What was that? What was that? (*Etc.*)

ORVIE: Don't you know?

FRISKY: It sounded like the end of the world.

ORVIE: It was a rocket taking off in the next field.

WHISKERS: A rocket! What rocket?

ORVIE: Don't you ever read the papers? Here, Scribbler. (*Hands him scrap of newspaper*) Read this.

SCRIBBLER (*Reading*): "The Junior Rocket Club meets every Saturday morning in Pleasant Acres near Merry Mouse Meadow where they have built a launching pad. The President of the Club told reporters they are planning to send up a mouse in their next experiment."

SQUEAKY: Run for your lives! Run for your lives!

ORVIE (*As they start to run off*): Stop! Stop! Where are you going?

SHORT TAIL: I don't know, but I'm getting out of here fast.

LONG TAIL: You heard what it said. They're looking for a mouse to go up in a rocket!

ORVIE: There's nothing to be afraid of. You're all perfectly safe.

SCAMPER: How do you know?

ORVIE: Because they're going to take *me*.

RISKY: You!

ORVIE: Yes, me! I am going to volunteer.

FURRY: What!

ORVIE: This is my big chance. Just think, I'll be the very first Mousetronaut!

NIBBLER: You wouldn't dare!

SCRIBBLER: You'll be blown to bits!

RISKY: What will your mother say?

ORVIE: She will be proud of me, and so will the rest of you when you see my name in headlines.

SCRIBBLER: "Orvie in orbit!" Yes, it has a wonderful sound.

WHISKERS: But you will be killed!

ORVIE: Nonsense! I'll live to tell my great-grandchildren about my adventure in space.

SCAMPER: You will bring honor and glory to Mouseland.

RISKY: Do you really think you can do it, Orvie?

ORVIE: I know I can, but I will need your help.

ALL (*Ad lib*): Tell us what to do, we'll help you . . . (*Etc.*)

ORVIE: Good! Now, first of all, I will need special equipment.

FLUTTER: I've heard there isn't any air in space. What will you breathe?

SQUEAKY: Couldn't we give him some cans of air to take along?

SQUEALY: It's not that simple. Orvie will need his own space suit.

NIBBLER: He will need a helmet.

SCRIBBLER: And gloves.

FURRY: And boots.

SQUEALY: What are we waiting for? Let's go round up the things he needs.

LONG TAIL: Come along, Orvie. You'll have to try them on for size. (*All* MICE *except* SCRIBBLER *and* NIBBLER *exit.*)

NIBBLER: Do you really think he can make it?

SCRIBBLER: Other animals have done it. Remember that monkey who went up in 1961? What was his name?

NIBBLER: His name was Enos. His picture was in all the papers at the time.

SCRIBBLER: If a monkey can do it, so can a mouse.

NIBBLER: Anything apes can do, mice can do better!

SCRIBBLER: Sh-h-h! I hear somebody coming.

NIBBLER: Quick! Let's hide. (NIBBLER *and* SCRIBBLER *hide, as* BILL *and* JAKE *enter.*)

JAKE: Everything is set for the big test flight. All we need is our mouse.

BILL: We'll catch one. There are traps all around the base.

JAKE: But they're still empty. Those mice are getting smarter every day.

BILL: Maybe we could catch a field mouse right here.
JAKE: What do you think you are, Bill, a cat?
BILL: There's just one thing that bothers me, Jake.
JAKE: What's that?
BILL: I want to bring our mouse back alive. I don't want him to burn up on the way down.
JAKE: That's always the big re-entry problem, but I think we have it licked. The mouse will be safe in his little nose cone, and he will come down by parachute.
BILL: Sh-h-h! (*Pointing*) Look! Look! Look over there.
JAKE: What? Where?
BILL: I thought I saw a mouse. Maybe we can sneak up on him.
JAKE: Oh, come on, Bill. We don't have time. We're due at the launching pad right now. Hurry up. (*As* JAKE *and* BILL *exit,* NIBBLER *and* SCRIBBLER *creep out.*)
NIBBLER: What was all that talk about burning up on the way down?
SCRIBBLER: It has something to do with what scientists call friction. A fast-moving object falling through the atmosphere can burn itself up. That's what happens to a falling star.
NIBBLER: Then it could happen to Orvie! We can't let him go!
SCRIBBLER: Simmer down. Every spaceman must face these dangers. But the scientists are finding new answers all the time.
NIBBLER: I hope those boys know what they're doing. Poor Orvie!

SCRIBBLER: Here he comes! And look! His mother is with him. (ORVIE *enters wearing a space suit. He is accompanied by* MAMMA MOUSE *and other* MICE.)
MAMMA MOUSE: Oh, Orvie, are you sure you're all right?
ORVIE: I'm fine, Mamma. Now, don't worry.
SHORT TAIL: We'll go with you to the launching pad.
LONG TAIL: We'll see you off.
SCRIBBLER: No, we'd better stay here.
NIBBLER: We just found out there are mousetraps all over the base.
SCAMPER: How will we know what happens to Orvie?
WHISKERS: We can listen on the radio.
FRISKY: I brought my transwhisker!
MAMMA MOUSE (*Throwing her arms around* ORVIE): Oh, Orvie! Orvie! I can't let you go!
ORVIE: Now, now, Mamma. Don't cry. When I come back, you'll be the proudest Mamma Mouse in all the world. Here, Squeaky, you look after her.
SQUEAKY: I'll take good care of her, Orvie.
ORVIE: And now I must be off. Thanks for all your help.
ALL: Good luck, Orvie. (ORVIE *exits, as* MICE *all wave and sing to the tune of* "*Good Night, Ladies.*")
Good luck, Orvie! Good luck, Orvie! Good luck, Orvie,
Come back here safe and sound.
MAMMA MOUSE: Oh, dear! I think I'm going to cry.
SQUEAKY: Now, now, Mamma Mouse. You must be brave.

RISKY: You come and sit by me, and we'll listen to the radio. (MICE *form semi-circle around* FRISKY *and radio.*)

FRISKY: It's too soon for any news.

FLUTTER: While we are waiting, I think we should plan a celebration for Orvie when he comes down.

FURRY: We'll give him a banquet.

SHORT TAIL: And call out the band!

LONG TAIL: We'll have music and speeches.

SCRIBBLER: I've already started a poem. Listen: It's called "Ode to Orville." (*Takes paper from pocket and reads.*)
Out by the Rocket Firing Pad
The Meadow Mousie stands.
The mouse a mighty mouse is he
With large and venturesome plans,
And the courage of his tiny heart
Is strong as iron bands!
(*All applaud.*)

SCAMPER: Let's hear the rest of it.

SCRIBBLER: That's as far as I can go till I see what happens.

WHISKERS: Turn on the radio now, Frisky. It must be close to launching time. (FRISKY *turns on the radio. There are static sounds from offstage. He pretends to listen closely.*)

FRISKY: I can't quite get the station, but I think they said they're starting the countdown.

ALL (*Singing to tune of "John Brown Had A Little Indian"*):

One little, two little, three little seconds,
Four little, five little, six little seconds,
Seven little, eight little, nine little seconds,
Ten little seconds to go!
Ten little, nine little, eight little seconds,
Seven little, six little, five little seconds,
Four little, three little, two little seconds,
One little second to go!
(*Loud crash and whistling sound from offstage.*)

ALL (*Ad lib*): He's off! He's off! (*They look up.*) Whee-ee! There goes Orvie! (*Etc.*)

MAMMA MOUSE (*Jumping up in a frenzy*): Orville! Orville Mouse! You come back here this very minute! Do you hear me?

SQUEAKY: There, there. Take it easy, Mamma Mouse.

MAMMA MOUSE: He'll be killed! I know he will! Oh dear! Oh dear!

FRISKY: Sh-h-h! I think I'm getting something on the radio. (*All crouch down and listen.*)

ANNOUNCER (*Offstage, on loudspeaker*): A perfect take-off! Everything is going according to plan, and all precautions have been taken to bring our mouse passenger safely back to earth.

SQUEALY: Hear that, Mamma Mouse? There's nothing to worry about.

LONG TAIL: Orvie is going to be a hero for sure.

SHORT TAIL: We must give him a medal.

FLUTTER: Where will we get one?

RISKY: I know! I know! Let's give him Thomas Cat's bell!

WHISKERS: Thomas Cat's bell! How would we get it?
RISKY: If Orvie can be a hero, so can we! We'll take it right off Tom's neck. All in favor?
ALL: Aye!
FURRY: Sh-h-h! I think I hear the cat coming. Quick, let's hide. (ALL *hide behind bushes, as* THOMAS CAT *enters.*)
THOMAS CAT: I smell something funny! Not a mouse in sight! (MICE *dash out and attack* THOMAS CAT. *In the scuffle, two of them sit on* THOMAS CAT, *as* SQUEALY *takes the bell from around his neck!*)
SQUEALY: We have it! We have it!
THOMAS CAT: Let me up! Let me up!
MICE: Promise to do us no harm.
THOMAS CAT: I promise. (*They let him up.*) Now what was that all about? Why did you take my bell?
NIBBLER: It's for Orvie.
SCRIBBLER: Orvie is a hero now. We want to give him a medal.
THOMAS CAT: Orvie has always been a hero. He was the only mouse who was never afraid of me. If you had told me the bell was for Orvie, I would have given it to you without all this fuss.
SCAMPER: Thanks, Thomas. You may join us at the radio for news of Orvie's return to earth.
THOMAS CAT: We don't need the radio for that. Orvie has already landed safe and sound.
MAMMA MOUSE: How do you know?
THOMAS CAT: I've just come from the field. Orvie is fit as a fiddle.

ALL: Hurrah! Hurrah! Hurrah!

THOMAS CAT: As soon as he has had his medical checkup, he'll be home.

FRISKY: Come on, everyone. We must get our band instruments and have a parade to welcome Orvie home.

MICE (*Ad lib*): Yes, let's. Come on, hurry! (*Etc.*) (FRISKY, WHISKERS, FURRY, FLUTTER, SQUEAKY, *and* SQUEALY *exit.*)

THOMAS CAT (*To* MICE *as they exit*): Bring me my fiddle. I want to take part in the celebration.

MAMMA MOUSE: Are you sure Orvie is all right?

THOMAS CAT: As right as rain, ma'am.

SCRIBBLER: Dear me. I must finish my poem. (*Takes pad of paper from pocket and begins to scribble rapidly.*)

MAMMA MOUSE (*Looking offstage*): Here they come with their instruments. (MICE *return with sheets of paper and rhythm instruments, including fiddle for* THOMAS CAT.)

FRISKY: We're all tuned up and ready to go with "Three Blind Mice."

RISKY: But Orvie hates that song.

FLUTTER: We made up some new words, and here's a copy for each of you. (*Gives sheet to each one.*)

MAMMA MOUSE (*Looking off left*): He's coming! He's coming! (*Running to meet* ORVIE *as he enters*) Oh, Orvie, Orvie! Welcome home!

ALL (*Singing to accompaniment of rhythm instruments*):
One brave mouse! One brave mouse!

See how he soars! See how he soars!
He soars right up in the morning light,
Away he goes like a flying kite!
Did ever you see such a wonderful sight
As one brave mouse!

ALL (*Ad lib*): Welcome home, Orvie! Are you all right? Congratulations! (*Etc.*)

ORVIE: Thank you. Thank you.

SCAMPER: As a small token of our admiration, we wish to present you with this medal. (*Hangs the bell around* ORVIE's *neck.*) May you wear it with pride and honor.

ORVIE: But this is Thomas Cat's bell. How did you get it?

THOMAS CAT: They mobbed me and took it by force.

ORVIE: But they've always been scared to death of you!

SCRIBBLER: Not any more, Orvie. Some of your courage must have rubbed off on us. All we needed was a hero to look up to. Listen! (*Reads poem*)
Our thanks to you, dear Orvie Mouse,
For the lesson you have taught.
In your brave deed each timid mouse
Found courage that he sought.
From this day forth, we sing your praise,
O mighty Mousetronaut!
(*Applause as curtain falls*)

THE END

SMOKEY WINS HIS STAR

Characters

7 ALL-STAR SAFETIES
SMOKEY THE BEAR
JOHNNY
FRED
TOM
BILLY
BOB
SALLY
BETTY
SHIRLEY
CINDY
MR. BATES

SCENE 1

TIME: *An autumn afternoon, after school.*
SETTING: *The stage is bare except for a large can labeled "Trash," at left.*
AT RISE: *The 7 ALL-STAR SAFETIES are lined up across the stage.*

7 SAFETIES (*Together*):
Seven little Safeties,
Standing in a row,
Guiding boys and girls to school,
As back and forth they go.
1ST SAFETY:
I'm the first, I'm Number One.
I guard you day and night.
My orders are to warn you
To watch the traffic light.

2ND SAFETY:
>   And I'm the next! I'm Number Two.
>   As you have plainly seen,
>   I let you cross the crossing,
>   Whenever lights are green!

3RD SAFETY:
>   And I'm the third. I'm Number Three.
>   I have to use my head,
>   And serve as a reminder
>   To *stop* when lights are red.

4TH SAFETY:
>   And I am next. I'm Number Four.
>   I'm always on my feet
>   To bid you play on sidewalks,
>   Instead of in the street.

5TH SAFETY:
>   And, as for me, I'm Number Five.
>   I'm always on the job
>   To make you walk in single file,
>   And never in a mob!

6TH SAFETY:
>   I'm Number Six, and I'm the one
>   To watch your head and heels,
>   When you go out on roller skates,
>   Or anything with wheels.

7TH SAFETY:
>   As Number Seven, I command
>   The schoolyard where you play;
>   I teach you all the Safety Rules,
>   And see that you obey!

ALL (*Singing to tune of "Sing a Song of Sixpence"*):
   Sing a song of safety,
   A song that's full of joy!
   Sing it, everybody,
   Each girl and boy!
   If you practice safety
   In all your work and play,
   You will all be safe and sound
   To play another day!
   (SMOKEY THE BEAR *enters*.)
SMOKEY: Hello, everybody. Do you mind if I join you?
ALL: Who are you?
SMOKEY: I am Smokey the Bear, and I would like to join your Safety Squad.
1ST SAFETY: Smokey the Bear?
2ND SAFETY: We don't know you!
3RD SAFETY: Smokey the Bear?
4TH SAFETY: Now what do *you* do?
SMOKEY: I help prevent forest fires. And I would like to join your Safety Patrol.
5TH SAFETY: Sorry! Sorry!
6TH SAFETY: We don't know who you are!
7TH SAFETY: You don't belong to us because
ALL: You do not have a *star*.
SMOKEY: But I work for safety, the same as you do.
1ST SAFETY: You don't understand. We are the All-Star Safety Squad!
2ND SAFETY: And you can't belong until you have a star.

SMOKEY: Please tell me where to get a star, and I'll get one right away.

3RD SAFETY: You can't just go out and *get* a star. You must *earn* it!

SMOKEY: How?

4TH SAFETY: By saving someone from great danger. That's how.

SMOKEY: But I've saved hundreds and hundreds of lives.

5TH SAFETY: Whose life did you ever save?

SMOKEY: Oh, I've saved deer and rabbits and bears and field mice . . .

ALL: Field mice! (*Laughing*) Ha, ha, ha! You can't win a star by saving field mice!

6TH SAFETY: You have to save *people!*

SMOKEY: But I've saved lots of people, too. Only last week I stopped a careless camper from starting a forest fire. He might have been killed.

7TH SAFETY: You still don't understand. To belong to our All-Star Safety Squad, you must save children—school children.

1ST SAFETY: And we don't have forest fires in school.

2ND SAFETY: So go on back to the woods where you belong, Mr. Bear.

SMOKEY: Not until I find out how to get a safety star.

3RD SAFETY: Very well. You may stand around and watch. But don't get in the way.

4TH SAFETY: We have work to do.

5TH SAFETY: And keep out of sight, so you won't frighten the children. (SMOKEY *hides behind trash can.*)

6TH SAFETY: The children are coming out of school now. See how orderly they are. (*All* CHILDREN *except* BOB *enter, single file. Some carry lunch baskets. One carries a thermos jug.*)

5TH SAFETY: No pushing or shoving! Stay in line!

JOHNNY: You don't have to remind me any more. Ever since you saved me from that bad fall on the stairs, I stay in line where I belong.

SMOKEY (*Peering around can*): Psst! Is that how you got your star, Number Five?

5TH SAFETY (*Nodding*): And Johnny is only one of many I saved from falling.

1ST SAFETY:
Be careful at the corner,
And watch the traffic light.

2ND SAFETY: Remember green is go ahead,

3RD SAFETY: And red is stop on sight!

CHILDREN: We'll be careful.

SALLY:
I know I'd be a sorry sight
Without that faithful traffic light.

BILLY:
I used to think that he was mean
To make me wait and wait for green.

BETTY:
I know I would be hurt or dead
If I should disobey the red!

1ST, 2ND *and* 3RD SAFETIES: That's how we got *our* stars, Mr. Bear.

FRED: Hurry up, Tom. Do you have the ball?

TOM: I have it. Want to catch? (*Starts to throw ball*)

FRED: Not here, Tom. The ball might roll into the street. Remember the Safety Squad is watching.

4TH SAFETY: I see you've learned your lesson well. Never play in the street.

FRED: You don't have to say that again . . . not after you saved me from being hit by a car.

7TH SAFETY: Hello, Shirley. How are you feeling?

SHIRLEY: Fine, thanks to you. I'll never stand up on a swing as long as I live, after what happened this afternoon.

7TH SAFETY: Good for you, Shirley. You know the playground rules. (BOB *enters wheeling a bicycle*.)

6TH SAFETY: Hi, Bob. Is that a new bike?

BOB: No, it's my old one, but Dad says it's as good as new since he had the brakes fixed. Thanks for telling me about it.

CINDY: How about giving me a ride on the handle bars, Bob?

BOB: Nothing doing. Do you want to break your neck?

6TH SAFETY: You're never too young to learn about safety on wheels.

BOB (*To* SAFETIES): Aren't you going to join us on our hike?

1ST SAFETY: Where are you going?

TOM: Out to Pine Grove for a picnic supper.

SALLY: We're going to build a fire and roast hot dogs and toast marshmallows.

1ST SAFETY: That sounds like fun. Let's go.

CHILDREN (*Exit, singing to tune of "Farmer in the Dell"*):
A-hiking we will go,
A-hiking we will go!
Up the hill, and down the hill,
A-hiking we will go!
2ND SAFETY (*Calling to* SMOKEY *as they move offstage*): Come along, Bear. The field mice may need you! (*The* SAFETIES *exit laughing.*)
SMOKEY (*Coming out from behind trash can*): I know they are making fun of me, but I'm going along just the same. A forest fire is no joke. (*Exits as curtain falls.*)

* * * * *

SCENE 2

TIME: *A little while later.*
SETTING: *A pine grove. There are a picnic table, a sign reading "Pine Grove" and some sticks, logs and dry leaves scattered about.*
AT RISE: SMOKEY *is alone, looking around. The* CHILDREN *are heard singing the hiking song offstage, then* CHILDREN *and 7* SAFETIES *enter.*

1ST SAFETY: Hello, Smokey. How did you get here ahead of us?
SMOKEY: I know all the short cuts.
JOHNNY (*Pointing*): Who is that?

SMOKEY: They are much too short. You would have to stand too close to the fire. And besides, these are not made of green wood. They would catch fire right away. You should find other sticks—green ones—or use long metal forks.

BETTY: I have some in my basket. I'll get them. (*Does so*)

SMOKEY: It would be better for the boys to roast the hot dogs. The girls' dresses might get too close to the blaze.

5TH SAFETY: Smokey is right. (*Taking one of the forks*) The boys will do the cooking. Are we all set? (SMOKEY *grabs his nose and howls as if in pain.*)

ALL: What's the matter? What's the matter?

SMOKEY:
My nose! My nose! It stings and scratches!
I think some boy is holding matches!

BOB: Of course we have matches. I have some and so does Fred.

TOM: I have some, too. How could we light a fire without matches?

SMOKEY: I knew it! I knew it! My nose is never wrong. It always hurts like this when boys have matches in their pockets. Get rid of them at once.

TOM: Where shall we put them?

SMOKEY: Put them out on the table where I can see them. (BOYS *put match boxes on table.*) My nose is feeling better already. Don't you know better than to carry matches?

FRED: We never carry them any other time.

TOM: It was only this once.

SMOKEY: That's what they all say! But it's too late once a fire has been started. Children should never, never, never, never, *never* carry matches.

BILLY: But how can we start our fire?

SMOKEY: I have news for you. You're not going to start any fire at all. Not in *my* woods!

JOHNNY: Why not?

BETTY: How can we cook our supper without a fire?

SMOKEY: I will not allow any children to build a fire unless a grown-up is present.

CINDY: We did ask Mr. Bates, our Safety Director, to come along. But I don't know where he is.

SMOKEY: You'll have to wait for him.

BOYS: But we're hungry!

GIRLS: We want to eat now!

FRED: Come on, fellows, what are we waiting for? I know how to light a fire, and I'm not afraid of this silly bear, either! (*Starts to take box of matches from table.* SMOKEY *growls and leaps on him.*)

ALL: Look out, Freddy! Look out! (SMOKEY *and* FRED *start to wrestle.* SMOKEY *gets* FRED *down and sits on him.*)

SMOKEY:
I'm Smokey the Bear! The woods are my home.
I live here in safety, and freely I roam.
My animal friends, whom I greatly admire,
Must not be endangered by smoke or by fire!

We welcome all humans, the young and the old,
But when you come here, you must do as you're told!
Is that clear?

ALL: That's clear, Smokey.

FRED: Let me up! Let me up!

SMOKEY (*Bouncing up and down*): Sit still! I like a soft seat. (MR. BATES *enters.*)

ALL: Mr. Bates! Mr. Bates!

MR. BATES: I'm sorry I'm late, boys and girls. Thank goodness, you waited for me! I was afraid you might try to start a fire before I got here. Say, that's a fine pile of wood! And you've placed it exactly right! No dry leaves could catch fire there.

1ST SAFETY: That was Smokey's idea.

MR. BATES: And you have your toasting forks ready. Long metal forks are safer than sticks.

3RD SAFETY: That was Smokey's idea.

MR. BATES: But best of all, you didn't try to light the fire yourselves. That's a job for a grown-up.

4TH SAFETY: That's what Smokey said.

MR. BATES: Smokey? Smokey who?

ALL: Smokey the Bear!

6TH SAFETY: Smokey saved us from doing a lot of silly things, Mr. Bates.

7TH SAFETY: He wanted to join our Safety Squad, but we laughed at him because he didn't have a star.

MR. BATES: Well, we can take care of that right now. Where is he?

FRED: Here he is! Here he is! Help! Help!

TOM: Mr. Bates, I would like you to meet Smokey the Bear.

SMOKEY: Excuse me for not getting up, Mr. Bates.

MR. BATES: Glad to see you, Smokey. (*To* CHILDREN) Smokey and I are old friends. What's the matter, partner? Have you been having trouble with one of my boys?

SMOKEY: This fellow didn't want to obey the rule about matches.

MR. BATES: I think you can let him up now, Smokey. (SMOKEY *lets* FRED *up*.)

FRED: I won't cause any more trouble, Mr. Bates. Not with Smokey around.

MR. BATES: I'm sure of that, Fred. Smokey knows how to lay down the law. And he makes grown-ups obey his safety rules the same as children. You ought to see him when he catches a careless smoker!

FRED: I'll never tangle with Smokey again!

MR. BATES: Now, Smokey, how would you like to join the All-Star Safety Squad!

SMOKEY: I'd love it, Mr. Bates. But I don't have a star.

MR. BATES (*Taking star from his pocket and pinning it on* SMOKEY): You do now. And you have earned it by teaching these boys and girls the first law of the forest!

ALL: *Be careful of fire in the woods!*

MR. BATES: And now, before I light our campfire, let's sing along with Smokey.

ALL (*Sing to the tune "Sing a Song of Sixpence"*):

Sing along with Smokey,
And make it good and strong.
Sing a song of Safety,
Sing loud and long.
In the town and country,
And everywhere you go,
There are always safety rules
That boys and girls should know.

7 SAFETIES: Three big cheers for Smokey the Bear!
ALL: Hurrah! Hurrah! Hurrah!

(*Curtain*)

THE END

MEET MR. MUFFIN

Characters

MR. MUFFIN		GRACE
MRS. MUFFIN		TRUDY
MARY		ELEANOR
MORRIS		TOM
MABEL		DICK
MICHAEL	*little*	HARRY
MARION	*Muffins*	DEBBY
MATTHEW		GEORGE
MILDRED		BAKER
MILES		

(MARY, MORRIS, MABEL, MICHAEL, MARION, MATTHEW, MILDRED, MILES are *little Muffins*; GRACE, TRUDY, ELEANOR, TOM, DICK, HARRY, DEBBY, GEORGE, BAKER are *children*)

SETTING: *A playground.*
AT RISE: GRACE, TRUDY, ELEANOR, TOM, DICK, HARRY, DEBBY *and* GEORGE *are singing.*

CHILDREN (*Singing to the tune of "The Muffin Man"*):
Oh, do you know the Muffin Man,
The Muffin Man, the Muffin Man?
Oh, do you know the Muffin Man
That lives in Drury Lane?

We've never seen the Muffin Man,
The Muffin Man, the Muffin Man,
We've never seen the Muffin Man
That lives in Drury Lane.

(MR. MUFFIN *enters on last line of song. He wears an old English costume—the traditional smock and tall Welsh hat. A wooden tray of muffins is suspended around his neck.*)

MR. MUFFIN: Here I am, boys and girls. What can I do for you?

CHILDREN: Who are you?

MR. MUFFIN: I'm Mr. Muffin, the man in your song.

GRACE: Are you really and truly the Muffin Man?

MR. MUFFIN: Here are the muffins to prove it. Mrs. Muffin baked them fresh this morning.

ELEANOR: And do you really live on Drury Lane?

MR. MUFFIN: Third house from the corner on the north side. The one with the picket fence.

TOM: I think you're fooling us. There's no street called Drury Lane in this whole town.

DICK: Why haven't we seen you before?

GEORGE: Why did you come today?

DEBBY: How did you know where to find us?

TRUDY: Did you make all those muffins yourself?

HARRY: Why are you wearing that funny suit?

MR. MUFFIN: I never heard so many questions in all my born days! (*To nearest child*) Here! Have a muffin! That's the best way to keep you quiet. (*Giving each child in turn a muffin*) Just keep your mouths full of muffins and let me do the talking. (*As he gives muffin to last child*) There! Aren't they good?

CHILDREN (*Now seated in a small half circle, nodding happily*): M-m-m!

MR. MUFFIN: Now I would like you to meet the rest of

the family. (*Gesturing right stage*) First of all, here is Mrs. Muffin.

MRS. MUFFIN (*Enters, wearing old-fashioned, full-skirted dress with an apron. She also wears toy spectacles and a ruffled cap. She is wiping her hands on her apron*): My goodness, Mortimer, my hands are covered with flour! I was right in the middle of mixing up another batch of muffins.

MR. MUFFIN: My dear, I want you to meet these delightful boys and girls. They were singing our song.

MRS. MUFFIN (*Dropping a curtsy*): It's a pleasure to meet you. I see Mortimer has already given you some of our muffins. Are you enjoying them?

CHILDREN (*Nodding enthusiastically*): M-m-m!

MR. MUFFIN: And now, I want you to meet our children, the little Muffins. (*As he calls the roll, each* LITTLE MUFFIN, *attired in chef's apron and hat and carrying a piece of equipment, enters and bows.*) Mary! Morris! Mabel! Michael! Marion! Matthew! Mildred! and Miles!

LITTLE MUFFINS (*Singing to the tune of "Here We Go Round the Mulberry Bush"*):
Eight little muffins, all in a row,
Watch how we mix the batter and dough.
Eight little muffins, all glad to know
You like your muffins each morning.

GRACE: Excuse me, Mr. Muffin. . . .

MR. MUFFIN: Quick! Quick! Have another muffin before you start asking questions!

GRACE: I only wanted to know what your little helpers do. Is there so much work to making muffins?
MRS. MUFFIN: Of course there is, if you want to make *good* muffins! And we don't make any other kind. Go ahead, children, tell them what you do.
MARY (*Shaking flour sifter*): I'm the flour sifter.
MORRIS (*Holding out muffin pan with hot potholder*): I'm the pan lifter!
MABEL (*Stirring in big bowl*): I'm the batter mixer!
MICHAEL (*Using large wrench*): I'm the oven fixer!
MARION (*Picking imaginary berries for basket*): I pick the berries!
MATTHEW (*Pantomiming action from small pail*): I pit the cherries!
MILDRED (*Writing in notebook*): I see there's no wasting!
MILES (*Tasting from big, wooden spoon*): And I do the tasting!
CHILDREN: M-m-m! He has the best job.
MRS. MUFFIN: They are all important. We couldn't get along without a single one.
LITTLE MUFFINS: Thank you! Thank you!
MRS. MUFFIN: And now back to work! All of you!
(LITTLE MUFFINS *exit*.)
TRUDY: I think *muffin* is such a funny word!
MR. MUFFIN: Funny indeed! Muffin is just the right word because a muffin is fluffy and muffy and puffy! I ought to know. I invented it.
DICK: I never tasted a muffin before, and I'm not quite sure what it is.

MEET MR. MUFFIN

MR. MUFFIN: It's not quite a cake, and not quite a roll.
MRS. MUFFIN: It could be a doughnut, minus the hole.
MR. MUFFIN: You eat it at luncheon, at dinner, or tea.
MRS. MUFFIN: Or toasted at breakfast, as good as can be.
MR. MUFFIN: You eat it with jam, or butter, or plain.
MRS. MUFFIN: "Delicious! Delicious!", you're bound to exclaim.
MR. MUFFIN: And sometimes a clever baker will hide.
MRS. MUFFIN: A handful of cherries or berries inside.
BOTH: So next time you eat one, so crusty and sweet,
Be sure to remember who gave you the treat!
(*Eight* LITTLE MUFFINS *re-enter, all crying.*)
LITTLE MUFFINS: Boo hoo! Boo hoo! Bad news for you!
MR. MUFFIN: What's the matter?
MRS. MUFFIN: Did you let the muffins burn?
LITTLE MUFFINS: Boo hoo! Boo hoo! What shall we do?
MR. MUFFIN: Stop crying and tell us what's wrong.
MARY: We have to go away.
MORRIS: We can't live here any longer.
MABEL: We'll have to leave Drury Lane.
MICHAEL: We're out of business.
MR. MUFFIN: Out of business! Impossible!
MRS. MUFFIN: Why? What has happened?
MARION: The children have stopped eating muffins!
MR. MUFFIN: Stopped eating muffins! I don't believe it!
MATTHEW: It's true, Father. The Baker Man just told us.
MILDRED: The Baker Man was very sad!
MILES: He brought us this order to close the shop.
MR. MUFFIN (*Reading from paper*):

I regret to inform you,
Alert you, and warn you
That baking of muffins must stop!
We have no more orders
From mothers and boarders,
And so you must close up your shop!
(*Looks up*)
This is dreadful! Just dreadful!

MRS. MUFFIN: I still don't believe it.

MR. MUFFIN: Tell the Baker Man to come here at once. I must speak with him. (LITTLE MUFFINS *exit*.)

MRS. MUFFIN: I never thought the children would turn against us!

TOM: They blame children for everything.

DICK: I don't see what we have to do with it.

HARRY: It's not our fault! (BAKER *enters. He is a tall boy who looks even taller because of his high, white baker's hat. He carries an empty baker's basket.*)

BAKER: Oh, yes, it is! It's all your fault! You children are eating so many sweets between meals that you're not hungry when you come to the table. You fill up on candy bars, ice cream and soda pop, and then you don't want your good bread and butter, your hot buttered toast, and your milk and muffins! Shame on you! (*Eight* LITTLE MUFFINS *re-enter, each one bearing a placard on a long stick. The placards read "Unfair!"* LITTLE MUFFINS *march in a circle, singing to the chorus of "Marching Through Georgia."*)

Unfair! Unfair! The children are unfair!
Unfair! Unfair! It's true and we declare!

Closing up our bakeries is more than we can bear, Why did you children turn against us?

ELEANOR: That is not true!

GRACE: We are not unfair!

GEORGE: You're just a lot of crazy, mixed-up muffins who don't know what you're talking about.

TRUDY: We always go by the rules!

BAKER: Not when it comes to eating. I can pick out someone right here who has broken Rule Number One for a five-star breakfast. Tommy, what did you eat for breakfast this morning?

TOMMY: A dish of cereal and a glass of milk.

BAKER: But what about fruit, eggs, and two pieces of toast?

LITTLE MUFFINS: Or two toasted muffins?

TOMMY: I was in a hurry. I forgot.

LITTLE MUFFINS: Unfair! Unfair!

BAKER: And you, Trudy, what became of that good sandwich your mother put in your lunch today?

TRUDY: I wasn't hungry.

BAKER: And you weren't hungry because you ate a candy bar during the morning.

LITTLE MUFFINS: Unfair! Unfair!

BAKER: And Debby's mother just told me she can't use any more bread, rolls, or muffins. They always go to waste.

DEBBY: I'm sorry, Mr. Baker. I guess I've been eating too many sweets between meals!

LITTLE MUFFINS: Unfair! Unfair!

MR. MUFFIN: I can see there's no hope. We will have to move to another town.
MRS. MUFFIN: And leave our dear little house in Drury Lane!
LITTLE MUFFINS: Unfair! Unfair!
CHILDREN: But we like muffins.
GRACE: And the Muffin Man is our favorite song.
ELEANOR: And our favorite singing game.
BAKER: Well, you've sung it for the last time.
MR. MUFFIN: If we have to go, our song goes with us.
DEBBY: Oh, please, Mr. Muffin, I am sure we could help you if you'd give us the chance.
HARRY: We promise to eat bread or rolls or muffins with every meal.
MR. MUFFIN: How about it? Is that a promise?
CHILDREN (*Raising right hands*): That's a promise.
BAKER: No more eating between meals?
CHILDREN: No more eating between meals!
MR. MUFFIN: What do you say, Mr. Baker? May we keep our shop open for another week?
BAKER: I think it's worth a try. These boys and girls seem to mean what they say.
MR. MUFFIN (*To* LITTLE MUFFINS): Then take those signs away and hurry back. I think we should have a song to seal the bargain. (LITTLE MUFFINS *exit with placards.*)
BAKER: Mr. Muffin and I will do our best to help you grow tall and strong.
MRS. MUFFIN: Dear me, I am so happy. I feel like dancing. (LITTLE MUFFINS *return.*)

MR. MUFFIN: Come, my dear, I will choose you as my partner. (*All join hands and sing "The Muffin Man."*)
Oh, now we know the Muffin Man, the Muffin Man, the Muffin Man,
Oh, now we know the Muffin Man who lives in Drury Lane.
And we will help the Muffin Man, the Muffin Man, the Muffin Man,
And we will help the Muffin Man, who lives in Drury Lane.
(*Curtain*)

THE END

THE ADMIRAL'S NIGHTMARE

Characters

CHRISTOPHER COLUMBUS, *Admiral of the Ocean Sea*
DON ALFREDO, *his friend*
FERDINAND ⎱ *his sons*
DIEGO ⎰
ALONZO, *a schoolboy of Cordoba*
MARIA, *a schoolgirl of Cordoba*
QUEEN ISABELLA OF SPAIN
FRANCESCA, *lady-in-waiting to the Queen*
THE 4 WINDS
SEA MONSTER
SAILORS

TIME: *An evening in 1492.*
SETTING: *The highest deck of the "Santa Maria," represented by a raised platform sturdy enough to hold Columbus, Alfredo, and a small folding canvas chair. A sheet fashioned into a sail forms the background. The main stage is empty except for a long, low table near left entrance.*
AT RISE: *The stage is dark, except for a spotlight on* COLUMBUS *who stands on the deck, hands behind his back, gazing out to sea.* ALFREDO *stands beside him. The* 4 WINDS *are under the table on main stage, unseen by audience.*

ALFREDO: Why do you stare into the darkness, Don Admiral? There is nothing to see at this hour.
COLUMBUS: My eyes are used to darkness, Alfredo, and

the moon gives enough light to see the hulk of the ship. With land so near at hand, I must keep close watch.

ALFREDO: But you have neither eaten nor slept for hours on end. Won't you rest a while, sir? It is two hours short of midnight.

COLUMBUS: I have forgotten sleep, Alfredo. I can rest only when we have gone ashore.

ALFREDO: But that might not be for days.

COLUMBUS: It could be any hour, Alfredo. Remember the land birds we saw and the sea grass floating on the water?

ALFREDO: I remember, sir. But I also remember how long it has been since you have taken food or rest. If you will not go to your cabin, you might at least rest a while in this chair I have carried out on deck.

COLUMBUS: That was good of you, Alfredo. You are a faithful friend. The others have turned against me. They call me a madman.

ALFREDO: They really love you, sir, and would follow you to the ends of the earth. But right now they are lonely and frightened. They know that our stores are running low, and they lack your courage. After all, three months at sea and no sight of land! Small wonder they demand to turn back.

COLUMBUS: Never, Alfredo, never! Let them swim back to Spain if they like. But as long as I am in command, we will sail westward. (*Breathing deeply*) Do you notice, Alfredo, the sea has a different smell? I am sure we are within sight of land right now.

ALFREDO: That's what you say every day, my Admiral. But every day we sail on and on. The others do not share your faith.

COLUMBUS: I know, I know. Even now they do not believe that the world is round and we will reach the Indies by sailing west.

ALFREDO: You have a noble dream, Don Admiral.

COLUMBUS: But a dream can turn into a nightmare, Alfredo. These last few terrible days have given me my share of doubts and demons.

ALFREDO: Please, sir, you are swaying on your feet. Pray, sit down before you fall.

COLUMBUS (*Sinking wearily into the chair*): Perhaps you are right, my friend. Perhaps you are right about that, and about other things. Sometimes when I am alone out here on the sea of darkness, I wonder if I really am a madman, to sail on and on in spite of all the warnings of the graybeards at home.

ALFREDO: You must not think such thoughts, sir.

COLUMBUS: How can I help it? I do not want my men to die. I want to live as much as any man aboard. I long to see my two sons and hold them in my arms.

ALFREDO: Think how proud Diego and Ferdinand will be when they see you again. You will be the hero of all Spain.

COLUMBUS: I wish I could see them now, this very minute.

ALFREDO: Close your eyes for a few minutes, Admiral. Sometimes our loved ones come to us in dreams.

COLUMBUS: I will take your advice, Alfredo. But only

for a few minutes. Rouse me if you see even the faintest sign of land.

ALFREDO: I will keep good watch, sir. You can depend on me.

COLUMBUS (*With a sigh*): Ah, how good it feels to rest! I did not know I was so tired.

ALFREDO (*Removing his cloak and spreading it over* COLUMBUS): The night is cold, sir. This will keep you warm and protect you from the spray. (*To himself*) He has overtaxed his strength. He is asleep already. (*To* COLUMBUS) Rest well, my Admiral, and pleasant dreams. (*As* ALFREDO *stands watch, the lights on the main stage come up slowly.* FERDINAND, DIEGO, MARIA, *and* ALONZO *enter left.*)

MARIA: Tell me, Diego, why do you and Ferdinand want to come down here to the river every day after school?

DIEGO: Because the river flows into the sea, and it makes us feel closer to our father.

ALONZO (*In a mocking sing-song*): Crazy, crazy Christopher Columbus!

FERDINAND (*Seizing him by the jacket*): You stop that kind of talk, Alonzo. Stop it at once.

DIEGO: Let him go, Ferdinand. He doesn't know any better.

FERDINAND: He knows well enough that our father is Admiral of the Ocean Sea, and the Queen herself gave him the title.

ALONZO: But he's crazy just the same. He thinks the world is round like an orange.

DIEGO: By this time he has proved that it's people like you who are the crazy ones.

ALONZO: By this time his ships have dropped off the edge of the world or been devoured by sea serpents.

FERDINAND (*Shaking him*): I warned you to be quiet. One more of your stupid remarks, and I'll blacken your eye.

DIEGO: Be careful, Ferdinand. We got a beating last week for fighting in the streets.

FREDINAND: Father should have taken us with him. He should never have left us in this wretched city of Cordoba.

DIEGO: Just wait till he comes home laden with the riches of Cathay. Then we'll show these peasants a thing or two!

ALONZO: You know you will never see your father again. He is food for the fishes by now.

MARIA (*Holding her ears*): I will not listen to such talk. You are a cruel, heartless boy, Alonzo.

ALONZO: And you are just a silly girl to be taken in by such foolishness.

MARIA: You wouldn't dare call the Queen a silly, foolish woman, and she had faith in Columbus.

ALONZO: I won't even waste my time arguing. I have better things to do. Besides, I don't want to be seen with these two idiots. They are as crazy as their father. (ALONZO *runs off left.*)

MARIA (*Putting her hand on* DIEGO's *arm*): I'm sorry, Diego. Alonzo has no manners.

FERDINAND: But he's right, Maria. Nobody wants to be

seen with us. Maybe you should find other companions.

MARIA: But you are my friends.

DIEGO: We have no friends, Maria. People just laugh at us, the way they did at Father.

FERDINAND: You'd better leave us. Besides, it's getting late. Your mother will be worried.

MARIA: Very well. I will go. But I really want to be your friend.

FERDINAND *and* DIEGO: Thank you, Maria.

MARIA: Goodbye. I'll see you tomorrow. (*Calling back as she exits left*) And don't pay any attention to that hateful Alonzo!

FERDINAND: Do you really think Father will return, Diego?

DIEGO: I don't know, little brother. It's been so long . . . so very long.

FERDINAND: But what if he doesn't come back? What will become of us?

DIEGO: I don't know, Ferdinand. I don't know.

FERDINAND: Perhaps the Queen would look after us.

DIEGO: The Queen has more important things to do than look after two luckless orphans.

FERDINAND: I don't want to be an orphan! Oh, Diego, let's stop at the church and say more prayers for Father's return. He *must* come back! He must! (*Stage lights dim, spot on* COLUMBUS)

COLUMBUS (*Twisting and turning in his chair, cries out as* FERDINAND *and* DIEGO *exit left*): Diego! Ferdinand! I will come back! I *will!*

ALFREDO (*Leaning over him and adjusting his cloak*): Just like a father! He is dreaming of his children. God grant he may return to them and to the Queen. (*Stage lights go up.* QUEEN ISABELLA *enters followed by* FRANCESCA, *her lady-in-waiting. The* QUEEN *holds a necklace in her hand.* FRANCESCA *carries a crystal ball.*)

ISABELLA: Just look, Francesca. Isn't it the most beautiful necklace you ever saw?

FRANCESCA: It is lovely, Your Highness, but think of the money!

ISABELLA: Money, money, money! That's all I hear.

FRANCESCA: But the state treasury is very low.

ISABELLA: And my jewel box is even lower. Surely the Queen of Spain can buy a few jewels.

FRANCESCA: If you will excuse my saying so, Your Majesty had plenty of jewels when that madman, Columbus, first came to this court.

ISABELLA: You are right, Francesca, but any day now he may return with great riches from the East.

FRANCESCA: Alas, Your Majesty still hopes for his return. You refuse to believe the truth.

ISABELLA: And what is the truth, Francesca?

FRANCESCA: His ships are lost—his men all perished in the Sea of Darkness.

ISABELLA: How can you be so sure?

FRANCESCA: With my own eyes I have seen it.

ISABELLA: But that is impossible.

FRANCESCA (*Holding out crystal ball*): See for yourself, Your Majesty. Gaze into my crystal ball and tell me what you see.

ISABELLA: No, no, I will not look.

FRANCESCA: You *must* look, Your Majesty. You cannot fool yourself any longer. Columbus and his men are lost.

ISABELLA (*Looking into glass ball*): No! No! I cannot believe it. Take it away! Take it away! It is a fearful sight!

FRANCESCA: What do you see, my lady?

ISABELLA: The wind . . . the waves . . . the terrible storm! Oh, the poor sailors! They are lost! They are lost! I must tell the King! (*She runs off left followed by* FRANCESCA. *Lights dim, spot on* COLUMBUS.)

COLUMBUS (*Moaning*): Lost! Lost! We are lost! Help! Help! My ships! My ships!

ALFREDO (*Bending over him*): Sleep gently, sir. Let no bad dreams disturb you. You are safe on your own deck. (*Stage lights go up as* 4 WINDS *rise from behind the long table where they have been hiding.* WEST WIND, NORTH WIND, *and* EAST WIND *each place a model ship on the table. Each ship bears a flag with labels of "Nina," "Pinta," and "Santa Maria" respectively.*)

4 WINDS: Blow, blow, blow!
Blow fast and then blow slow!
North Wind, South Wind,
East Wind, West,
No ship that's built
Can stand the test!

NORTH WIND: Let's put an end to this foolishness.
EAST WIND: It's time we taught this madman a lesson.
SOUTH WIND: How dare he call himself the Admiral of the Ocean Sea?
WEST WIND: We rule the sea! Let no man set himself to conquer us, not even Columbus.
NORTH WIND: West Wind, you have blown long enough. Let me destroy his ships and make an end of his madness.
SOUTH WIND: No, no, let me! Let me!
EAST WIND: Let me send a hurricane. That will destroy them all.
WEST WIND: The *Pinta* is the fastest ship of the three. See how it flies ahead of the rest. One good blow and we could topple it over the edge of the world.
ALL: A fine idea.
NORTH WIND: I'll give the signal. One, two, three! All together—*blow!* (*The* WINDS *lean over the "Pinta" and blow with all their might.* WEST WIND *pulls a string which sends the "Pinta" crashing over the edge of the table. The* WINDS *howl with glee.* COLUMBUS *cries out.*)
COLUMBUS: Help! Help! The *Pinta!* The *Pinta!* She's lost! She's lost!
ALFREDO (*Soothingly*): Quiet, Don Admiral, quiet!
EAST WIND: Now for the next one! Get ready, get set, blow! (*Before they can blow,* SEA MONSTER *enters. Note: The monster is a living chain of children with their hands linked around each other's waists. Their bodies are concealed by a green covering. The first*

THE ADMIRAL'S NIGHTMARE

child is the head, his outstretched arms forming the jaws. The last child wears a long tail which he lashes about.)

SEA MONSTER: Wait! Wait! The next one belongs to me!

EAST WIND: I've been wondering where you were.

NORTH WIND: It's about time you got here.

WEST WIND: Why were you so slow?

SEA MONSTER: I've been following these ships for days, but they were too fast for me!

SOUTH WIND: You are too late. The ships belong to us.

SEA MONSTER: But I have not eaten for weeks, and these sailors will make a tasty morsel!

EAST WIND: Oh, let the sea monster have them. It will be fun to see him gobble up the *Nina* with all hands on board.

SEA MONSTER: Thank you. Thank you. Umm! What a mouthful! (*The* SEA MONSTER *approaches the table, and scoops up the model of the "Nina" as sound of crunching wood is heard.*)

COLUMBUS (*Trying to rise*): The monster! The monster! He is devouring the *Nina!*

ALFREDO (*Pushing him back in the chair*): Sh-h-h! It's only a dream, sir. Go back to sleep. (COLUMBUS *sighs and relaxes.*)

EAST WIND: Now for the *Santa Maria!* The biggest prize of all! Columbus himself is aboard.

SEA MONSTER: Columbus! Let me have him! He never believed I was real.

SOUTH WIND: You've had your share. This one belongs to us.

NORTH WIND: Look at the sailors! How terrified they are!

WEST WIND: See how they beg for mercy! (3 SAILORS *enter with wooden swords and daggers.*)

1ST SAILOR: Spare us! Spare us, oh mighty winds!

2ND SAILOR: Have mercy, O Monster of the Deep.

3RD SAILOR: Pity! Pity! Have pity upon us!

1ST SAILOR: We would never have come here of our own free will.

2ND SAILOR: It was Columbus who forced us into this venture.

3RD SAILOR: He would not listen to us. He laughed at our fears.

1ST SAILOR: We begged him to turn back, but he threatened to kill us if we did not obey.

2ND SAILOR: Now we are going to kill him.

WINDS: You are going to murder your leader?

SEA MONSTER: I would like to see this!

EAST WIND: What are your plans?

3RD SAILOR: This very moment he is sleeping on the deck with only Alfredo on guard.

1ST SAILOR: We will sneak up behind them.

2ND SAILOR: I will take care of Alfredo.

3RD SAILOR: And the rest of us will make an end of the Admiral of the Ocean Sea.

1ST SAILOR: We will toss him overboard.

SEA MONSTER: Excellent! Excellent! Then I will get him after all.

EAST WIND: This may be fine sport.
SOUTH WIND: We'll let them carry out their plan.
NORTH WIND: We must blow gently while they are at work.
WEST WIND: It would not do to wake him now. (*The* SAILORS *creep stealthily forward and start to climb up on the deck where* COLUMBUS *is sleeping. Just as the* 1ST SAILOR *raises himself over the edge,* COLUMBUS *springs to his feet with drawn sword.*)
COLUMBUS: Mutiny! Mutiny! To arms! To arms! (*The* SAILORS *scramble off right, the* WINDS *and* MONSTER *scurry off in both directions.*) To arms, Alfredo! There's mutiny aboard!
ALFREDO: Calm yourself, sir. 'Tis but a dream. We are alone here on the deck and all is well.
COLUMBUS: But I saw them. They were almost upon me.
ALFREDO: You were dreaming, sir. You must have had a nightmare. See for yourself. There is no one else about.
COLUMBUS (*Stretching and rubbing his eyes*): But it was all so real! The *Pinta!* The *Nina!* They were destroyed before my very eyes. The sea monster! Those winds! Those terrible winds!
ALFREDO: The sea is smooth as glass, my Admiral. There is hardly a ripple on the surface. Here, take a look . . . (*Moves aside and* COLUMBUS *looks ahead*)
COLUMBUS: Yes, yes, I see. It must have been a dream . . . a long and terrible dream, made up of all my secret fears. But look, look, Alfredo!

ALFREDO: Where, sir? Where?

COLUMBUS: Out there, a bit to starboard. Alfredo, can I believe my eyes? It seems as if a light is moving in the darkness.

ALFREDO: I don't see anything, sir.

COLUMBUS: Look sharply, a bit more to your left. Tell me, what do you see?

ALFREDO: My faith, sir, you are right. It is a light. A fire is blazing fairly close at hand!

COLUMBUS: By all the saints, it is a bonfire burning in the night.

ALFREDO: But that is impossible, sir. A fire cannot be burning on the water.

COLUMBUS: It is not burning on the water, Alfredo. It is burning on the land! Land! Land! Don't you know what that means, my friend?

ALFREDO: Land at last! Oh, Don Admiral, let me rouse the sailors and fire the cannon!

COLUMBUS: No, no, Alfredo! I forbid it. There have been too many false warnings, too many disappointments. Let us wait until morning.

ALFREDO: But this time we are sure. This time it is no mistake.

COLUMBUS (*After a pause*): Yes, you are right, Alfredo. Let us call the men. They deserve to share the good news with us, after the many bitter disappointments. We shall all kneel together in the darkness and offer our thanks to God for his mercy and protection.

ALFREDO (*Shouting*): Land! Land! Sailors, men, come

out on deck! We are saved! We are saved! (SAILORS *rush onstage noisily*.)
SAILORS (*Ad lib*): Is it really true? Where? Where is the land? It's a wonder we're still alive! (*Etc.*)
COLUMBUS: Yes, my brave crew, the long voyage is ended and land is in sight. The nightmare is over. Let us give thanks.
ALL (*Kneeling, sing to the tune of "Old Hundredth"*):
Oh, blessed be the light of day,
And he who sends the night away.
Our thanks to thee for thy great love,
All praise to thee, the Lord above.
(*Curtain*)

THE END

WHICH WAY TO HALLOWEEN?

Characters

MISS WARNER, *a teacher*	PAT, *an Irish girl*
WANDA WITCH	MIKE, *an Irish boy*
MAMMA WITCH	MARCH WIND
PILGRIM BOY	APRIL FOOL
PILGRIM GIRL	MOTHER
2 INDIAN BOYS	BRIDE
SANTA CLAUS	6 PARADE GIRLS
4 ELVES	POLICEMAN
FATHER TIME	TRUDY
LITTLE NEW YEAR	LOIS
CUPID	ELEANOR

TIME: *The day before Thanksgiving.*
SETTING: *The stage is bare except for one bench.*
AT RISE: MISS WARNER *is rehearsing 4 children for a Thanksgiving program. The* PILGRIM BOY *holds a pumpkin; the* PILGRIM GIRL *holds a turkey platter. One* INDIAN BOY *holds an ear of corn, the other* INDIAN BOY *a peace pipe.*

MISS WARNER: Now, children, you can do better than that. Let's try again. This time make it louder and slower.
ALL: Yes, Miss Warner.
MISS WARNER: Go ahead, Johnny. You're first.

PILGRIM BOY:
> I bear this jolly pumpkin
> To welcome you today
> To join with us in watching
> Our own Thanksgiving play.

PILGRIM GIRL:
> The turkey on the platter
> Looks good enough to eat,
> But you will find our program
> A real Thanksgiving treat.

1ST INDIAN:
> Me heap big Injun Chieftain.
> Upon Thanksgiving morn
> Me bring 'em early settlers
> An ear of Injun corn.

2ND INDIAN:
> Me faithful friend of Paleface.
> Our friendship will not cease
> Because today white brother
> Will smoke the pipe of peace!

MISS WARNER: That was very good, very good indeed. You may go now.

PILGRIM BOY: May we take off these costumes, Miss Warner? My collar scratches.

MISS WARNER: Put them away carefully so they will be ready for the play this afternoon. (WANDA WITCH *enters, dragging her broomstick and crying.*)

WANDA:
> Boo hoo. Boo hoo.
> I don't know what to do!

Alack-a-day! I've lost my way.
I need some help from you.

MISS WARNER: Who are you, little girl? And what are you doing here in that costume?

PILGRIM GIRL: There aren't any witches in our play.

WANDA: My name is Wanda. I am really truly a witch, and I have lost my way.

1ST INDIAN: Lost your way where?

2ND INDIAN: Where are you going?

WANDA: I went to a Halloween party and stayed too late. All the others went home without me, and I can't find my way back.

MISS WARNER: But Halloween was a month ago. I'm afraid you are trying to be funny!

WANDA: I don't feel a bit funny. I feel very sad and scared. I want to go home.

MISS WARNER: This is no time to be dressed up for Halloween. Tomorrow is Thanksgiving Day, and we must give our play this afternoon. Come along, children. (*Exits;* CHILDREN *follow.*)

WANDA: What will I do? No one will help me.

PILGRIM GIRL (*Returning to stage*): I feel sorry for you, Wanda. I would like to help you.

WANDA: Then please show me the way to go home— back to Halloween.

PILGRIM GIRL: I can't do that because I don't know the way back to Halloween. But I do know someone who will help you.

WANDA: Who? Who will help a poor little lost witch?

PILGRIM GIRL: The jolliest, kindest man in all the world will be coming along here in just a little while. Why don't you wait for him?
WANDA: Who is he? What's his name?
PILGRIM GIRL: His name is Santa Claus, and he helps all children, everywhere, to get what they want.
WANDA: Oh, thank you! Thank you! I'll sit right here and wait. (*Sits on bench as* PILGRIM GIRL *exits*)
Oh me, oh my!
I have to cry!
And wipe my eyes because,
I'm so dismayed and so afraid,
To meet this Santa Claus!
(*"Jingle Bells" is heard offstage, and* SANTA CLAUS *enters, carrying pack of toys. He is attended by 4* ELVES.)
ELVES (*Singing*):
Jingle bells, jingle bells, jingle all the way,
Santa Claus is coming soon! Hurrah for Christmas Day!
SANTA: Merry Christmas, one and all! Hello, little girl. Who are you and what do you want old Santa to bring you this year?
WANDA: My name is Wanda Witch, and I want you to show me the way to go home.
1ST ELF: A witch! Christmas is no time for witches!
2ND ELF: Let's be on our way, Santa.
SANTA: Wait a minute. What kind of witch are you, my dear?

WANDA: I am a Halloween Witch. Oh, please, Santa, help me get back to Halloween. A little girl told me you always give children what they want.

SANTA: So I do. So I do. And I will help you.

3RD ELF: We don't have time, Santa. We're late now.

SANTA: You come along with me, child. I will give you a lift in my sleigh.

4TH ELF: But it's overloaded now! The reindeer can hardly pull it.

SANTA: There's always room for one more. Come along, Wanda. I'll take you as far as January.

WANDA: Oh, thank you! Thank you, Santa Claus. (WANDA, SANTA *and* ELVES *exit right. There is a pause during which offstage bells strike twelve.* FATHER TIME *enters pushing baby carriage with* LITTLE NEW YEAR *inside.*)

FATHER TIME: I hate to leave you, Little New Year, but the clock has just struck twelve. So I must be on my way. Will you be all right?

LITTLE NEW YEAR (*From carriage*): Of course, Father Time, I can get along.

FATHER TIME: I'll be back in 365 days. Good luck to you. (*Exit* FATHER TIME.)

LITTLE NEW YEAR: Brrr! It's cold out here. (*Shakes a rattle or New Year's noisemaker*) Maybe I can warm things up a bit.

WANDA (*Entering left and waving offstage*): Goodbye, Santa, and thank you. (*Turns around and sees baby carriage*) Look! A baby! Somebody has gone off and left it all alone! (*Peering into coach*) Poor baby, I wonder who you are.

LITTLE NEW YEAR: I am not a "poor baby" at all. I am a very special baby!

WANDA: My goodness, you can talk!

LITTLE NEW YEAR: Of course I can talk. I told you I was a very special baby. I am the Little New Year. Now, who are you?

WANDA: My name is Wanda Witch. I'm looking for the way back to Halloween. But you're too little to help me.

LITTLE NEW YEAR: Is that so? Listen to me, Wanda. I will tell you how we can help each other.

WANDA: I'll be glad to help you. I love babies.

LITTLE NEW YEAR: I can talk, but I haven't learned to walk yet. If you'll push me into February, I'll introduce you to someone who can really help you.

WANDA: That's fine. Which way do we go?

LITTLE NEW YEAR (*Pointing offstage right*): That way. That's the way to February.

WANDA (*Putting broomstick in baby coach*): Here, you hold my broomstick, and off we go. (*They exit right, as* CUPID, *with bow and arrow, dances on left and does a few ballet steps. At end of dance,* WANDA *enters left, leading* LITTLE NEW YEAR *by the hand.*)

WANDA: I never thought you would learn to walk so soon, Little New Year.

LITTLE NEW YEAR: Thanks for helping me into the middle of February. And here is your next helper.

His name is Dan Cupid. Dan, I'd like you to meet my friend, Wanda Witch.

CUPID: A witch! A witch!

LITTLE NEW YEAR: Stop staring and come and shake hands. (*As* WANDA *and* CUPID *shake hands*) I want you to be friends.

CUPID: Hello, Wanda. You are a very pretty little witch. What can I do for you?

WANDA: Can you help me find my way back to Halloween?

CUPID: Just watch this, Wanda. (*Shoots arrow offstage left. A yell is heard.*)

WANDA: Oh, dear! You hit somebody.

CUPID: Sure I did. I never miss my mark. But my arrows never hurt people. They just make them fall in love. (*Gives* WANDA *big heart*) Here is my calling card. Just give it to the next person you meet and he will help you.

LITTLE NEW YEAR: You come with me, Cupid. I need you for St. Valentine's Day.

WANDA: Goodbye and thank you both. (CUPID *and* LITTLE NEW YEAR *exit right as* PAT *and* MIKE, *dressed in Irish costumes, enter left.*)

PAT *and* MIKE:
We're Pat and Mike.
We look alike.

WANDA: I don't think you look a bit alike. Why are you dressed all in green?

PAT *and* MIKE:
Begorra, bejabbers and hip, hip hurray!

We're wearing the green for Saint Patrick's day.
PAT: And why are you dressed all in black?
WANDA: Because I'm a witch and witches always wear black.
MIKE: A witch! A witch!
PAT: A wicked little witch!
WANDA: I am not a wicked witch. I am a very good witch, only I can't find my way back to Halloween. I'd like you to help me.
PAT: Don't do it, Mike. I think she was the one who shot you with that arrow.
WANDA: No, I'm not. That was Dan Cupid. Here—here is his calling card. (*Hands* MIKE *the Valentine heart*)
MIKE: Look, Pat. See what it says.
PAT (*Reading*): Be my valentine.
MIKE: We can't be your valentine today, little witch. But we'd love to help you.
PAT: I'll give you my shamrock to bring you luck. (*Gives it to her.*)
MIKE: And we can ask the March Wind to blow you on your way.
PAT: He is so strong that he can blow you right into April.
PAT *and* MIKE:
Huffo-Puffo, March Wind, blow!
Huffo-Puffo—here you go!
(MARCH WIND *rushes in waving two huge palm leaf fans and making a swooshing noise. He blows* WANDA *offstage right.*)
PAT *and* MIKE (*Clapping their hands*): Bravo! Bravo!

MARCH WIND: And now it's your turn. (*Blows* PAT *and* MIKE *off right, then follows, as* APRIL FOOL *enters left. He is whistling and twirling a purse tied to a string. He places the purse on the floor, loosens the string and perches on bench. Only when he turns around does the audience see a sign on his back,* "April Fool!" WANDA *enters left and sees purse.*)

WANDA: Oh, look. Someone lost a purse. (*As she leans over to pick it up,* APRIL FOOL *jerks the string.*)

APRIL FOOL: April fool! April fool!

WANDA: You think you're pretty smart, don't you?

APRIL FOOL: Of course I do. I was smart enough to fool you, wasn't I?

WANDA: Then maybe you'll be smart enough to show me the way back to Halloween.

APRIL FOOL: Oh, sure. That's easy. (*Pointing right*) Just go down this way, turn left, walk three blocks, turn right, walk six blocks, turn two somersaults and there you are!

WANDA: Oh, thank you! Thank you.

APRIL FOOL: You can't miss it! (*Doubles up with laughter as* WANDA *runs off right*) April fool! April fool! (*While he is laughing,* MOTHER *enters left.*)

MOTHER: Aren't you ashamed, you naughty boy! Fooling a little girl like that!

APRIL FOOL: She's not a little girl. She's a witch. And besides, it's my business to fool people.

MOTHER: But only for one day. You've had your fun. Now leave us in peace for another year. This is

Mother's Day, when all children try extra hard to behave themselves.

APRIL FOOL: Oh, I can behave when I want to. (*Gets up and offers her the bench*) Sit here, Mother. I promise to be good for the rest of the year.

MOTHER: Thank you and goodbye.

APRIL FOOL: Goodbye, and happy Mother's Day. (*Exits right*)

MOTHER: Poor little witch. I hope she comes back so I can help her. (WANDA *enters crying.*)

WANDA: I'm so tired I don't know what to do. My feet hurt and I want my mother.

MOTHER: Come over here, dear, and sit down. Perhaps I can help you.

WANDA (*Sitting beside* MOTHER): I can't find my way back to Halloween.

MOTHER: Halloween is a long, long way from here. But there are lots of good people in the world who will help you find it.

WANDA: I can't walk another step.

MOTHER (*Getting up*): Then lie down here and rest. Just shut your eyes and when you open them it will be June.

WANDA (*Lies down and yawns*): I'm so sleepy.

MOTHER: Then go to sleep. (*Leans over and kisses* WANDA) And happy dreams. (*Tiptoes off right as* BRIDE *enters left carrying a bouquet.*)

BRIDE: All of the girls are waiting for me to throw my bouquet, but I'm going to fool them. (*Sees* WANDA *sleeping*) Why, there's a little witch, fast asleep.

(*Places bouquet beside her*) Won't she be surprised to wake up and find a bouquet from a June bride? Perhaps it will bring her love and happiness.

VOICES (*Offstage*): Where's the bride? Where's the bride?

BRIDE: Here I am! Here I am! I'll be with you in a second. (*Exits left*)

WANDA (*Waking up and stretching*): Oh, I had such a good nap. (*Sees flowers*) And what beautiful flowers! (*Smelling*) Umm! They smell so sweet. (*Springs to her feet as bugle and roll of drums sound offstage.*) What's that? What's that? (6 PARADE GIRLS *march in wearing three-cornered paper hats and carrying flags. They line up and sing "Yankee Doodle."* WANDA *applauds from bench.*) Thank you! Thank you! Were you singing that song for me?

1ST PARADE GIRL: Of course not. We were singing it for the Fourth of July.

2ND PARADE GIRL: If you want to be in the parade, you should be wearing red, white and blue.

WANDA: I have to wear black because I'm a witch. But I'd like to march along with you.

3RD PARADE GIRL: We can't have a witch in a Fourth of July parade.

4TH PARADE GIRL: Witches march in Halloween parades.

WANDA: Halloween! That's where I'm going. Oh, please let me march along with you.

5TH PARADE GIRL: Let her come. It will be something different.

6TH PARADE GIRL: She can walk at the end of the line and carry her flowers.

1ST PARADE GIRL: Attention! Mark time! One, two, three, four! Forward, march! (GIRLS *march off right with* WANDA *following at end of line.* POLICEMAN *enters left and paces up and down.*)

POLICEMAN: Heigh ho! Things are too quiet. August is the dullest month of the year. I'd like a little excitement. (*As* WANDA *enters*) Hello, little girl. Isn't August a bit early to dress up for Halloween?

WANDA: Oh, dear, kind Mr. Policeman, will you show me the way back to Halloween? I've lost my way and policemen always help lost children.

POLICEMAN: If you're really lost, you'd better come down to the station house with me. I'll buy you an ice cream cone and we'll try to get in touch with your folks.

WANDA: Oh, thank you. I'm sure they're worried about me.

POLICEMAN: Then come along. (POLICEMAN *and* WANDA *exit right as* TRUDY, LOIS *and* ELEANOR *enter left carrying school books, and walk slowly across stage.*)

TRUDY: I'm so excited about going back to school.

LOIS: I wonder what our new teacher will be like.

ELEANOR: I hope she lets us have a Halloween party.

WANDA (*Running in from left*): Wait! Wait! Oh, please wait for me.

LOIS: Who are you?

TRUDY: You can't go to school dressed up like that.

ELEANOR: Were you in our class last year? I don't remember you.

WANDA: No, but I heard you talking about a Halloween party and that's where I want to go.

LOIS: But this is only September.

ELEANOR: Halloween is not until *next* month.

WANDA: I'll wait. And I promise I'll be as good as gold.

TRUDY: Oh, let her come along if she wants to.

ELEANOR: I don't know what the teacher will say.

LOIS: Come along, little girl. (*They exit right.* PILGRIM BOY *and* GIRL *in Halloween masks enter left with* MISS WARNER.)

MISS WARNER: I'm so glad you children came early for the Halloween party. How nice you look.

PILGRIM GIRL: My mother was glad I had this costume left over from the Thanksgiving play.

MISS WARNER: You can help with the grand march. The music is about to begin. (*March music is heard from offstage.* ALL *except* WANDA *enter, two by two, wearing Halloween masks and costumes, or sheets, and march to music.* MAMMA WITCH *rushes in.*)

MAMMA WITCH: Stop the music! Stop the music! (*Music stops.*)

MISS WARNER: What's the matter?

MAMMA WITCH: I am looking for a little witch about so high. She has been lost ever since last Halloween. Has anyone seen her?

ALL: That must be Wanda.

MISS WARNER: I saw her last Thanksgiving.

SANTA: I saw her at Christmas.

LOIS: I saw her the first day of school.
TRUDY: I thought she'd be sure to come to the party.
ALL (*Looking offstage*): Here she comes now!
WANDA (*Running in left*): Here I am! Oh, Mamma, Mamma, I've found you at last.
MAMMA WITCH: Where on earth have you been? I've been worried sick.
WANDA: It's a long story, Mamma. I'll tell you all about it when we get home. All of these nice people helped me find my way back to Halloween.
MISS WARNER: You are both welcome to stay for the party.
WANDA: Thank you very much, but I just want to go home. Let's get on our broomsticks, Mamma.
MAMMA WITCH: Just a minute, Wanda. I have something to say to these boys and girls.
When Halloween comes and you go to a party,
Be sure to have fun and be happy and hearty.
But think of poor Wanda's sad fortune and fate,
And never, no, never, decide to stay late.
When the party is over, remember this rhyme,
And always be sure that you go home on time!
WANDA *and* MAMMA WITCH (*Singing to the tune of* "*Good Night, Ladies*"):
Good night, ladies,
Good night, gentlemen,
Good night, everyone,
We're going to leave you now.
(*To the tune of* "*Merrily We Roll Along.*")
Merrily we'll fly away, fly away, fly away,

Merrily we'll fly away for Happy Halloween.
ALL (*Singing to same tunes*):
   Good night, Wanda,
   Good night, Mamma,
   Good night, Wanda,
   Come back again next year.
   Merrily you'll fly away, fly away, fly away,
   Merrily you'll fly away,
   But come again next year.
   (*Curtain*)

THE END

THE RUNAWAY UNICORN

Characters

THE UNICORN KEEPER
ROBIN HOOD
WILL SCARLET
LITTLE JOHN
ALICE IN WONDERLAND
PINOCCHIO
PETER RABBIT
JACK (*of beanstalk fame*)
SNOW WHITE
THE SEVEN DWARFS
MOTHER GOOSE
HANSEL
GRETEL
THE WIZARD OF OZ
LINDA BORDEN
LEWIS BORDEN
THE UNICORN

SETTING: *Storybook Lane, in Bookland. On the stage are nine cardboard replicas of books, each one large enough to conceal a child. They are:* ROBIN HOOD, ALICE IN WONDERLAND, PINOCCHIO, PETER RABBIT, MOTHER GOOSE, HANSEL AND GRETEL, SNOW WHITE, JACK AND THE BEANSTALK, *and* THE WIZARD OF OZ.
AT RISE: *The* STORYBOOK CHARACTERS *are hidden behind their books.* WILL SCARLET *and* LITTLE JOHN *also stand behind the* ROBIN HOOD *book. The* UNICORN KEEPER *runs on stage from right.*

UNICORN KEEPER: Help! Help! The Unicorn has run away. Help! Help! We must find him at once! (*Each book character steps out from behind his book.*)
ROBIN HOOD: Are you sure he's gone?

UNICORN KEEPER: I've looked all through Bookland for him. He's not anywhere on Storybook Lane.

ALICE: Did you look in Poetry Park? He sometimes goes there in the afternoon.

UNICORN KEEPER: He's not there now!

GRETEL: Oh, dear! Maybe he's lost in the haunted wood!

SNOW WHITE: Maybe he tried to climb the magic mountain.

PINOCCHIO: Maybe he started to swim to Treasure Island.

MOTHER GOOSE: You were never strict enough with him. The Old Woman in the Shoe would know what to do with him.

HANSEL: Yes, I know. She'd give him some broth without any bread, then give him a spanking and send him to bed!

UNICORN KEEPER: But she'd have to find him first, and I don't even know where to look for him.

PETER RABBIT: Why do you think he ran away? Was he in any trouble?

UNICORN KEEPER: Not that I know of, but yesterday he wouldn't eat his dinner.

ALICE: He's been very sad lately.

SNOW WHITE: He wouldn't even play with me this morning.

MOTHER GOOSE: He looked to me as if he might be catching a cold.

GRETEL: Poor little Unicorn. He's probably frightened and can't find his way home.

MOTHER GOOSE: He had no business running away in the first place.
ALICE: But it's getting late. We must find him before dark.
ROBIN HOOD: We should form a searching party.
ALICE: I'll take a look Through the Looking Glass and I'll ask the White Rabbit to search through Wonderland. (*Exits*)
PETER RABBIT: I'll take a look through Mr. McGregor's garden. He might be hiding under a watering can. (*Exits*)
JACK: I'll climb up my beanstalk and have a look around. (*Exits*)
PINOCCHIO: I'll ask the Fairy with the Blue Hair to help us find him. She always knows the truth about everything. (*Exits*)
HANSEL: Gretel and I will walk through the woods.
GRETEL: Maybe he's hiding in the Gingerbread House. (*Both exit.*)
SNOW WHITE: I'll ask the Seven Dwarfs to join our searching party. (*Exits*)
MOTHER GOOSE: I'd like to help, but I have no one to send. Simple Simon is much too simple. Miss Muffet is afraid of everything, even spiders, and Humpty Dumpty is in no shape to go anywhere.
ROBIN HOOD: Never mind, Mother Goose. You stay here and look after things. I'll take Will Scarlet and Little John, two of my very best men. The minute we find him, I'll blow my hunting horn. (*Exits left as* SNOW

WHITE *re-enters right with the* SEVEN DWARFS. *They cross the stage singing to tune of "Heigh-Ho."*)

DWARFS:
> Search high and low,
> It's off to look we go,
> We'll keep on looking all day long,
> Heigh-ho, heigh-ho,
> Heigh-ho, heigh-ho,
> We're looking high and low!
> And we will find him, this we know
> With a heigh, heigh-ho!

UNICORN KEEPER: Everybody is so kind and helpful! I'm sure they'll find him.

WIZARD OF OZ: Oh, no, they won't! They won't find him at all.

UNICORN KEEPER: What makes you say such a thing?

WIZARD OF OZ: Because I'm a Wizard, that's why. I know all about catching unicorns.

UNICORN KEEPER: Then why didn't you say so?

WIZARD OF OZ: Nobody asked me. When people ask me no questions, I give them no answers.

UNICORN KEEPER: Oh, dear, kind, wise Wizard of Oz, I'm asking you now. Do you know where the Unicorn is?

WIZARD OF OZ: No, of course not. Nobody knows that, but I do know how to catch him and bring him back.

UNICORN KEEPER: How?

WIZARD OF OZ: Unicorns are very strange creatures.

UNICORN KEEPER: Yes, yes, I know.

WIZARD OF OZ: In the first place, they are very shy.

UNICORN KEEPER: Yes, yes, I know.
WIZARD OF OZ: In the second place, they are very, very clever.
UNICORN KEEPER: Yes, yes, I know.
WIZARD OF OZ: And in the third place, they can run very, very fast.
UNICORN KEEPER: Yes, yes, I know.
WIZARD OF OZ: Stop saying, "Yes, yes, I know!" If you know so much, why don't you catch him yourself?
UNICORN KEEPER: Please excuse me, Mr. Wizard. I don't pretend to know as much as you do about unicorns or anything else. Just tell me what to do.
WIZARD OF OZ: You must set a Unicorn trap!
UNICORN KEEPER: Oh, no! A trap is so cruel! I wouldn't want to hurt him.
WIZARD OF OZ: Who said anything about hurting him? This is a very tender trap, indeed.
UNICORN KEEPER: Very well. How do we begin?
WIZARD OF OZ: We will need a real, live little girl—not a story-book child, but a real one.
UNICORN KEEPER: There are no real children here. Where will we find a little girl?
WIZARD OF OZ: In the library, of course. I happen to know there is one right there this very minute.
UNICORN KEEPER: How can we bring her here to Bookland?
WIZARD OF OZ: Shut your eyes while I make some magic that will bring her here at once.
UNICORN KEEPER (*Shutting eyes*): My eyes are shut tight.

WIZARD OF OZ (*Suiting actions to words*):
I turn me round and round about!
I put my hat on inside out!
I pull my whiskers, one, two, three!
Now open your eyes, and here she'll be!
(LINDA *and* LEWIS *enter.*)

UNICORN KEEPER (*In surprise*): You did it! You did it! But look! There are two children instead of one!

WIZARD OF OZ: I must have turned around too many times. But no matter!

LINDA: How do you do. I don't believe we have ever met.

LEWIS: This isn't the library. How did we get here?

UNICORN KEEPER: This is Bookland, my little dears, and you are on Storybook Lane.

WIZARD OF OZ: I am the Wizard of Oz, who brought you here, and this is the Unicorn Keeper. He is in great trouble, and we want you to help him.

LINDA: I'm sorry to hear about the trouble. My name is Linda Borden.

LEWIS: And I am her brother, Lewis. What do you want us to do?

WIZARD OF OZ: We don't want *you* to do anything, but we want Linda to help us catch a runaway Unicorn.

LINDA *and* **LEWIS:** A runaway Unicorn!

LINDA: I don't even know what a unicorn is.

UNICORN KEEPER: The Unicorn is the most beautiful beast in Bookland.

WIZARD OF OZ: He has the legs of a deer . . .

THE RUNAWAY UNICORN   153

UNICORN KEEPER: The tail of a lion . . .
WIZARD OF OZ: And the head and body of a horse!
UNICORN KEEPER: And he has one, big, long horn growing from the middle of his forehead.
LINDA: He sounds dangerous!
WIZARD OF OZ: Nonsense! He's as gentle as a lamb!
LINDA: What must I do?
WIZARD OF OZ: Just stand right here and wait till he comes.
LEWIS: How do you know he will come?
WIZARD OF OZ: Because this is the only way to catch a unicorn. If a lovely little girl stands all alone, the Unicorn will come and lie down at her feet.
UNICORN KEEPER: Please, little girl, will you do it?
LEWIS: Go ahead, Linda. It won't hurt you.
WIZARD OF OZ: The rest of us will be nearby.
LINDA: Very well. I'll do it!
UNICORN KEEPER *and* WIZARD OF OZ: Good! Good!
WIZARD OF OZ: Now get the child something to read while she's waiting. We don't want her to get nervous.
UNICORN KEEPER: I know the very thing. (*Calling*) Mother Goose! Mother Goose! Come quickly and bring your book of rhymes.
MOTHER GOOSE (*Entering with book*): I always have it handy on the parlor table. Who wants it?
UNICORN KEEPER: This is Linda Borden. She is going to help us get our Unicorn back.
MOTHER GOOSE: That's very nice of her. And what about this boy?

WIZARD OF OZ: This is her brother Lewis. We want to wait in your house until the Unicorn returns.

MOTHER GOOSE: Come right in, and I'll see what Mother Hubbard has in her cupboard for this little boy. (*Handing* LINDA *the book*) Here you are, child. The story of the Unicorn is on page ten. (*All except* LINDA *exit behind Mother Goose House.*)

LINDA: I'm not so sure I like this. (*Looking at book*) Oh, here is a picture of a unicorn, and he's just as beautiful as they said he was. His body is white, his head is red and his eyes are blue. Ooooh! What a lovely horn—black in the middle and red at the tip. In the picture he is fighting with a lion. I bet the story is exciting. (*Reading*)
"The Lion and the Unicorn
Were fighting for the crown,
The Lion beat the Unicorn
All round the town."

Dear me! That's too bad. I guess that's why he ran away. (*Reading on*)

"Some gave them white bread,
And some gave them brown,
Some gave them plum cake,
And sent them out of town."
(*As she reads, the* UNICORN *enters and lies at her feet.*)
And after that, he must have come here to live.

UNICORN: That's right, beautiful lady. That's just what I did.

LINDA: The Unicorn! He's back! He's back! (*Enter*

MOTHER GOOSE, UNICORN KEEPER, WIZARD OF OZ *and* LEWIS.)

WIZARD OF OZ: It worked like a charm!

UNICORN KEEPER: My beautiful Unicorn is back, safe and sound!

LEWIS: What a wonderful creature! (ROBIN HOOD *enters with* WILL SCARLET *and* LITTLE JOHN.)

ROBIN HOOD: We searched the greenwood, but he wasn't there.

WILL SCARLET: We looked behind every bush and tree!

LITTLE JOHN: Quick, Master Robin, blow your horn! There he is!

ROBIN HOOD: He's back! He's back! The search is over! (*As* ROBIN HOOD *blows his horn, all the searchers enter.*)

ALICE: I couldn't find him anywhere in Wonderland or Through the Looking Glass.

HANSEL AND GRETEL: He wasn't in the Gingerbread House.

JACK: I couldn't even spot him from my beanstalk.

PETER RABBIT: And he wasn't in Mr. McGregor's garden!

PINOCCHIO: Even the Fairy with the Blue Hair couldn't help me find him.

SNOW WHITE (*Entering with* DWARFS *who sing to tune of "Heigh-Ho"*):

> Not high, not low,
> We simply do not know
> Just where that Unicorn did go,
> Did go, did go.

> Heigh-ho, heigh-ho,
> Now we are feeling low,
> He positively can't be found
> Not high, not low!

SNOW WHITE: Bless my stars! Here he is!

DWARFS: He's here, he's here.

PINOCCHIO: But I want to know where he's been.

JACK: And why did he run away?

UNICORN KEEPER: Tell us, my pretty pet. Where have you been?

UNICORN: I've been to my secret hiding place, and where it is, I'll never, never, never tell.

LEWIS: I don't blame him. Everybody should have a secret hiding place.

UNICORN KEEPER: But why did you run away and scare us half to death?

UNICORN: I'm sorry you were so worried, but I can't tell you why I ran away.

LINDA (*Putting her arm around the* UNICORN'S *neck*): Was it because that bad old lion beat you all around the town? (UNICORN *shakes his head.*) Please, you nice Unicorn, you can tell me.

UNICORN: All right. But I must whisper in your ear. (*Whispers to* LINDA)

MOTHER GOOSE: What did he say?

LINDA (*To* UNICORN): Is it all right to tell? (UNICORN *nods "yes" and* LINDA *turns to book characters.*) He says he ran away because he found out he isn't real!

UNICORN KEEPER: What does he mean?

WIZARD OF OZ: How did he discover this?

LINDA (*Consulting with* UNICORN): How did you find out? (UNICORN *whispers.*) He says he looked himself up in the dictionary, and it said a unicorn is a fabled creature of olden time.
UNICORN KEEPER: What does that mean?
LEWIS: That means he is just a creature out of a storybook.
BOOK CHARACTERS: But so are we. None of us is real!
PINOCCHIO: I am just a puppet carved from a block of wood.
PETER RABBIT: I was made up by a lady named Beatrix Potter.
JACK: I came right out of a fairy tale.
HANSEL AND GRETEL: We are also make-believe.
ROBIN HOOD: Most of my adventures were made up!
WILL SCARLET AND LITTLE JOHN: We're not real, either.
MOTHER GOOSE: Neither am I, but I never lose any sleep over it!
WIZARD OF OZ: Even I, the great Wizard of Oz, stepped right out of a storybook.
LEWIS: So what? Even if you did step out of a storybook, you're real enough.
UNICORN: What do you mean?
LINDA: All of you are real. Mother Goose is real, and Pinocchio is real, and Snow White is real.
UNICORN: I don't understand.
LINDA: You are real to all of the children who read about you in books.
LEWIS: Because they read about you, they believe in you and love you, and that makes you real.

UNICORN: Is that the truth?

LEWIS AND LINDA (*Crossing hearts*): Cross our hearts!

LEWIS: Santa Claus is real because children believe in him.

LINDA: And so is the Easter Bunny, and so are the elves, and the fairies, and the brownies, and the pixies, and so are you, you foolish little Unicorn. You're just as real as anybody.

WIZARD OF OZ: You two are very clever children, very clever, indeed.

LEWIS: That's because we spend so much time in the library.

LINDA: And read so many books.

UNICORN: Then you mean that as long as children read about us and believe in us, we will be real?

LINDA: That's just the way it is. When we go home, we're going to tell all our friends to read about you and Mother Goose, and Hansel and Gretel, and Snow White and Jack and the Beanstalk.

LEWIS: And Robin Hood and Pinocchio and Peter Rabbit and the Wizard of Oz!

UNICORN: And me! Don't forget me! (MOTHER GOOSE *steps offstage.*)

LINDA (*Hugging him*): We'll never forget you. We'll read about you over and over and over again, so you will stay alive in our hearts.

UNICORN: I'm so happy! I'll never run away again! (MOTHER GOOSE *comes back carrying a crown.*)

MOTHER GOOSE: To show you how glad we are to have you home again, I have a present for you. (*Puts*

crown on UNICORN's *head*) Now you have nothing to fight about! You have a crown of your very own.
UNICORN: Thank you! Thank you!
MOTHER GOOSE: From now on, I want another verse printed in my book:
The Lion and the Unicorn
Were fighting for the crown,
But our friendly Unicorn
Is ruler of the town!
ALL: Long live King Unicorn! Hurray! Hurray! Hurray! (*Curtain*)

THE END

THE PARROT AND THE PIRATES

Characters

CAPTAIN KIDD
CAPTAIN CUTLASS
CAPTAIN CUTTHROAT
CAPTAIN CUSTARD
DAVY JONES
JOLLY ROGER
} *pirates*

CAPTAIN RAMROD
SOLDIERS
VOICE OF PARROT

SETTING: *A tropical island. There are palm trees at right and left, and a large artificial parrot sits on a perch which hangs on a low branch of one of the trees.*

AT RISE: CAPTAIN CUTLASS, CAPTAIN CUTTHROAT, DAVY JONES, *and* JOLLY ROGER *are digging at a large rocky mound at center of stage.* CAPTAIN CUSTARD *leans on shovel and holds a book in one hand and reads. Occasionally he lifts shovel of dirt as he continues to read.* CAPTAIN KIDD *is relaxing under a palm tree.*

CAPTAIN KIDD (*To audience*):
I'm Captain Kidd.
A treasure I hid,
And now I've forgotten the spot!
I've dug up the ground

For miles all around.
I've dug all the places it's not!
These rascals you see
   (*Pointing to others*)
Were comrades with me.
They helped me to bury the loot.
They do as they're told,
But when they find gold,
I'll give them the toe of my boot.
   (*Illustrates with kick*)
While they use the spade,
I'll sit in the shade,
And maybe I'll take a wee nap.
But if I decide
More treasure to hide,
I'll remember to draw a good map!
   (CAPTAIN KIDD *settles down for a nap.*)
VOICE OF THE PARROT (*Squawking offstage*):
   Pieces of eight! Pieces of eight!
   Come and get 'em before it's too late!
   Pieces of eight! Pieces of eight!
   Come and get 'em before it's too late.
CAPTAIN KIDD (*Sits up; annoyed at being disturbed*):
   That horrible bird
   Whose voice you just heard
   Is making me one nervous wreck!
   If he doesn't keep still,
   I swear that I will
   Go wring his feathered old neck!

Custard! Captain Custard! Can't you do something about that wretched bird?

CAPTAIN CUSTARD (*Approaching* CAPTAIN KIDD): I'm sorry, sir. Did Bony disturb you?

CAPTAIN KIDD: Disturb me? He's driving me crazy. Get him out of here.

CAPTAIN CUSTARD: I really don't know where to put him, sir! And he's so interested in the digging!

CAPTAIN KIDD: Take him down to the beach! Drown him!

CAPTAIN CUSTARD (*Politely*): Oh, I couldn't do that, sir. Bony is more than a pet, sir. He's like one of my family.

CAPTAIN KIDD: I agree with you that he's more than a pet. He's a pest! Now take him away from here. Get rid of him at once. That's an order.

CAPTAIN CUSTARD: Very well, sir.

VOICE OF PARROT (*Offstage*):
Pieces of eight! Pieces of eight!
Come and get 'em before it's too late!

CAPTAIN CUSTARD (*Picking parrot up from perch and putting bird on his shoulder*): Come along, old boy. We mustn't disturb the captain. I'll take you down to the beach where it's nice and quiet. (*Exits with parrot*)

CAPTAIN KIDD: Now maybe I can get some sleep. (*Settles himself again for a nap.*)

CAPTAIN CUTTHROAT (*Throwing down his shovel*): It's no use, mates. This is not the right spot.

JOLLY ROGER: But where shall we dig next, Captain

Cutthroat? We'll soon have holes all over the island.
CAPTAIN CUTTHROAT: I'm sure I don't know, Roger. But I'm through for the day. It's too hot to dig any more. (*Sits down and mops his face with bandanna.*)
DAVY JONES: Captain Kidd won't like it if we stop so soon.
CAPTAIN CUTLASS: Don't worry about Captain Kidd, Davy. He's fast asleep. (*Stretching and yawning*) I could do with forty winks myself!
DAVY JONES: But Captain Custard is sure this is the right spot.
CAPTAIN CUTLASS (*Laughing*): Captain Custard! Don't believe anything he says. (*Contemptuously*) He probably got his idea from one of his precious books.
DAVY JONES: You're right, Captain Cutlass. I go along with you and Captain Cutthroat. (*Throws down shovel*) I quit. (CAPTAIN CUSTARD *enters without bird.*)
CAPTAIN CUSTARD: What's this? What's this? Up and at it, men, while it's still daylight.
CAPTAIN CUTTHROAT: It's too hot.
JOLLY ROGER: My back hurts!
DAVY JONES: I'm getting a sunstroke!
CAPTAIN CUSTARD: I'm ashamed of you! Now pick up those shovels and get to work.
CAPTAIN CUTLASS (*Rising*): Who's giving the orders around here, Custard? I thought Captain Kidd was in command.
CAPTAIN CUSTARD: Sure, he is, but you can't quit now. It's only a few more feet.

CAPTAIN CUTLASS: That's what you said yesterday!
CAPTAIN CUSTARD: Very well! If that's the way you feel, I shall have to go on by myself!
CAPTAIN CUTTHROAT: Go ahead!
JOLLY ROGER: Go ahead and dig all the way to China!
DAVY JONES: You'll never find the treasure!
CAPTAIN CUSTARD: Oh, yes, I will. You just wait and see.
CAPTAIN CUTLASS: And what if you do find it? What makes you think Captain Kidd would ever let you get off this island with a single gold piece?
CAPTAIN CUSTARD: Because he says we share and share alike, and the Captain is an honest pirate!
ALL (*Roaring with laughter*): Ho! Ho! Ho! An honest pirate!
CAPTAIN CUTTHROAT: There is no such thing as an honest pirate.
CAPTAIN CUSTARD: *I* am an honest pirate, and I'll prove it to you. When I find this treasure, every man will get what's coming to him.
JOLLY ROGER: You don't even talk like a pirate.
DAVY JONES: Captain Custard! That isn't a real pirate name!
CAPTAIN CUSTARD: It's my name, and I'm a real pirate.
CAPTAIN CUTLASS: I don't believe it. I don't believe you're a real pirate at all!
CAPTAIN CUTTHROAT: What's the good of arguing? It's too hot.
CAPTAIN CUTLASS: I agree. I'd like a good long drink of coconut milk.
DAVY JONES: So would I.

JOLLY ROGER: Me, too, and I know the very tree. Come along. I'll show you. (*Exits with* CAPTAIN CUTTHROAT, CAPTAIN CUTLASS, *and* DAVY JONES)

CAPTAIN CUSTARD: Aha! The joke's on them! They don't know I have *this*. (*Takes map from pocket*) The night we buried the treasure, I made a very careful map! I marked every bush and tree, and counted the number of paces from the shore line. And right here is the very spot! (CAPTAIN KIDD *wakes up, and seeing* CAPTAIN CUSTARD *with the map, moves toward him.*)

CAPTAIN KIDD: Where did you get that map, you dog?

CAPTAIN CUSTARD: Captain Kidd! How you startled me!

CAPTAIN KIDD: Hand it over!

CAPTAIN CUSTARD: Come now, Captain, it's share and share alike!

CAPTAIN KIDD (*Drawing sword*): I order you to give me that map, or I'll run you through!

CAPTAIN CUSTARD: No bloodshed, please! (*Handing him map*) Take it and welcome. (CAPTAIN CUTTHROAT, CAPTAIN CUTLASS, JOLLY ROGER, *and* DAVY JONES *return, each with a coconut shell.*)

PIRATES (*Singing*):
Four good men on a dead man's chest!
Yo-ho-ho and a fee-fie-fum!
Look what the hangman has done with the rest!
Yo-ho-ho and a fee-fie-fum!

CAPTAIN CUTLASS (*Offering shell to* CAPTAIN KIDD): Have some coconut milk, Captain. Best I've ever tasted.

CAPTAIN KIDD: I have something sweeter than coconut milk, my hearties! Look! (*Shows map.*) A map of the island! And see! X marks the spot where the treasure is buried. (*Points to* CAPTAIN CUSTARD) That dog had it all the time!

CAPTAIN CUTLASS: Death to the traitor!

CAPTAIN KIDD: We'll deal with him later. (*To* DAVY JONES *and* JOLLY ROGER) Tie him up, lads! (JOLLY ROGER *and* DAVY JONES *tie* CAPTAIN CUSTARD *to tree.*)

CAPTAIN CUTLASS: Be gentle with him, lads!

CAPTAIN CUTTHROAT: He was such an honest pirate!

CAPTAIN CUSTARD (*As they pull ropes*): Ouch! Ouch! I can't breathe!

DAVY JONES: You promised us we'd get what's coming to us!

JOLLY ROGER: Now we'll give you what's coming to you!

CAPTAIN KIDD: The map shows this is the right spot.

CAPTAIN CUTLASS: Quick, men. A few more feet and we'll strike gold!

CAPTAIN CUSTARD: I told you so, but you wouldn't listen. (DAVY JONES *and* JOLLY ROGER *help dig.*)

CAPTAIN CUTTHROAT: Careful! My spade struck something hard!

CAPTAIN KIDD: It's the treasure chest! (*All drop to ground and dig with their hands.*)

ALL: There it is! There it is! (*Lift chest into view*)

CAPTAIN KIDD (*Lifting lid*): There it is, lads. Help yourselves. (*As all dive in,* CAPTAIN KIDD *draws sword. When they turn, each man holding two bags of gold,*

CAPTAIN KIDD *brandishes his weapon.*) Thank you for picking up those heavy bags! Now, forward march!
DAVY JONES: What's the rush?
JOLLY ROGER: I want to count my gold.
CAPTAIN KIDD: It's *my* gold, you simpleton! And I will do the counting after you have loaded it on the ship!
JOLLY ROGER: But we are partners.
CAPTAIN KIDD: Not any more! You are of no further use to me!
JOLLY ROGER: Help! Help!
DAVY JONES: He's going to murder us! Help! Help!
CAPTAIN KIDD: Not right away! I need you to carry those bags down to the beach! Now march!
CAPTAIN CUSTARD: What about me? What about me?
CAPTAIN KIDD: As for you, Captain Custard, if you ever work yourself loose, you may have the empty treasure chest as a present from me! By that time, I'll be safe at sea, and these wretches will be where they can tell no tales. (*Offstage beat of drum is heard.*)
CAPTAIN CUTLASS: Listen! What's that?
CAPTAIN CUTTHROAT: Sounds like a drum!
CAPTAIN KIDD: But there's no one else on the island.
VOICE OF PARROT (*Offstage*):
Pieces of eight! Pieces of eight!
Come and get 'em before it's too late!
CAPTAIN KIDD: It's that cursed parrot! I'll get him yet!
(*As* CAPTAIN KIDD *starts forward,* CAPTAIN RAMROD *enters with parrot on his shoulder. He is followed by* 6 SOLDIERS *with muskets.*)
CAPTAIN RAMROD: Halt! Halt! In the King's name!

CAPTAIN KIDD: Who are you? Where did you come from?

CAPTAIN RAMROD: I am Captain Ramrod of the *Flying Dragon*, and these men are in his Majesty's service. We demand your surrender.

1ST SOLDIER: Surrender in the name of the King!

CAPTAIN KIDD (*Drawing his sword*): We'll fight to the last ditch!

CAPTAIN CUTTHROAT (*Obviously frightened*): Bu-bu-but they have gu-gu-guns!

CAPTAIN CUTLASS: Swords are no use against gunpowder!

DAVY JONES: They'll blow us to bits!

JOLLY ROGER (*Throwing up his hands*): I surrender! I surrender!

CAPTAIN KIDD: You cowards!

CAPTAIN RAMROD: Hand over your sword, Kidd! (*Takes sword*) Take the treasure, men, and march these rascals to the boats. (SOLDIERS *round up treasure bags and line up pirates.*)

CAPTAIN KIDD: I don't understand this. How did you get here? How did you find us?

CAPTAIN RAMROD: It was easy. Our ship anchored on the other side of the island.

2ND SOLDIER: We stole around to this side and hid in the bushes till we got the signal.

CAPTAIN KIDD: What signal?

3RD SOLDIER (*Imitating parrot*): Pieces of eight! Pieces of eight! Come and get 'em before it's too late!

CAPTAIN KIDD: You mean that horrible bird gave us away?

CAPTAIN RAMROD: Of course. Bony is in his Majesty's service, too, and so is Captain Custard.
PIRATES (*Ad lib*): Captain Custard! That traitor! (*Etc.*)
CAPTAIN RAMROD: *Admiral* Custard will be his new title when we get back to England. (*Unties* CUSTARD) Sorry, sir. I hope you have not been uncomfortable.
CAPTAIN CUSTARD: Thank you, Captain Ramrod. I promised that every one of these men would get what's coming to him.
CAPTAIN RAMROD: The hangman will see that your promise is kept, sir. (*To* PIRATES) Off with you! March!
CAPTAIN CUTLASS: I always said he wasn't a real pirate!
CAPTAIN CUSTARD: And you were right. (*Patting bird*) But good old Bony is a real parrot, and he learned his lesson well. When I took him down to the beach, I knew Captain Ramrod and his men would come running when they heard him squawking: Pieces of eight! Pieces of eight! Come and get 'em, before it's too late!
CAPTAIN RAMROD (*As* SOLDIERS *march pirates offstage.*): And now, Captain Custard, we must get back to the ship.
CAPTAIN CUSTARD: If you will excuse me, I am not going.
CAPTAIN RAMROD: Not going? But you are the hero of the day. The King himself will want to give you a medal of honor.
CAPTAIN CUSTARD: Just the same, I want to stay here and enjoy my treasure.
CAPTAIN RAMROD: What treasure? What are you talking about?

CAPTAIN CUSTARD: Captain Kidd himself gave me this treasure chest.

CAPTAIN RAMROD: But there's nothing in it.

CAPTAIN CUSTARD (*Lifting lid*): Oh, yes, there is. The treasure chest has a false bottom. Watch! (*Lifts out a tray of books*) See! This is the *real* treasure.

CAPTAIN RAMROD: Books! Nothing but books!

CAPTAIN CUSTARD: That's right, Captain! Books! The greatest treasure in the whole world. Here are all my favorite books which I've never had time to read. Now all I ask of you is to leave me here in peace where I can enjoy them.

CAPTAIN RAMROD: What will the King say?

CAPTAIN CUSTARD: He will no doubt say he envies me this chance to catch up on my reading.

CAPTAIN RAMROD: But we can't leave you here for the rest of your life!

CAPTAIN CUSTARD: Oh, no! Come back and pick me up about this time next year. I'll need another supply of books by then.

CAPTAIN RAMROD: But your medal—the parades in your honor!

CAPTAIN CUSTARD: Tell them to give the medal to Bony! He deserves it! And he'll look pretty in the parade, perched on the King's shoulder. (*To parrot*) Goodbye, Bony. Don't let them forget to come back for me.

VOICE OF PARROT (*Offstage*):
Pieces of eight! Pieces of eight!
Come and get 'em before it's too late!

CAPTAIN CUSTARD: And now, Captain Ramrod, if you will excuse me, I am very busy. (*Settles himself with a book*)

CAPTAIN RAMROD: Goodbye, sir. I hope you won't be lonely!

CAPTAIN CUSTARD: Don't worry, Captain. I won't be. (CAPTAIN RAMROD *exits*.)

CAPTAIN CUSTARD: Poor Captain Ramrod! He doesn't know what he's missing. How could I be lonely? I have everything I need. (*Holds up one book at a time, as he recites the following*)
A book that answers "how" and "why,"
A book that makes you laugh or cry.
A book of facts, of things to do,
A book of folks like me and you.
A book of knights and golden deeds,
A book that fills a dozen needs.
A book of pictures and of rhymes,
A book of all the ancient times.
And all this treasure just for me,
Here on my island in the sea!

And that reminds me, you boys and girls out there! You'd better get busy and make out a list of the ten books you'd like to have for company on a desert island! You just never can tell when such an adventure might happen to you! And it's best to be prepared! (*Curtain*)

THE END

THE ABC'S THANKSGIVING

Characters

PILGRIM GIRL
PILGRIM BOY
MODERN GIRL
MODERN BOY
26 LETTERS OF THE ALPHABET
4 EXTRA LETTERS (I, G, O, N)
FLAG BEARER

SETTING: *Bare stage.*
AT RISE: *Each letter of the alphabet is represented by a child wearing a large placard with his letter printed on it. Those wearing the letters* T-H-A-N-K-S-G-I-V-I-N-G *are standing in the proper order on a low platform down center. The other letters are grouped on either side. A* PILGRIM BOY *and a* PILGRIM GIRL *stand on either side of the group which spells* THANKSGIVING. *All are singing "The Alphabet Song."*

ALL *(Singing)*:
A, B, C, D, E, F, G,
H, I, J, K,
L, M, N, O, P,
Q, R, S,
and T, U, V,
W and

X, Y, Z.
Look us over here and see
Every one from A to Z!

PILGRIM GIRL:
Long, long ago in Plymouth Town,
The children learned to spell.

PILGRIM BOY:
And now, today, we'd like to see
If we can do as well.

PILGRIM GIRL:
The ABC's decided
That they should have a meeting,

PILGRIM BOY:
To celebrate Thanksgiving Day
And help us send a greeting!

PILGRIM GIRL:
This word is *Thanksgiving*,
You know it so well.

PILGRIM BOY:
A big word, a great word,
But easy to spell.

PILGRIM GIRL: T.
LETTER T: T is for *Turkey*, the Thanksgiving meat.
PILGRIM BOY: H.
LETTER H: H is for *Happy Day*, *Holiday* treat.
PILGRIM GIRL: A.
LETTER A: A is *America*, all fifty states.
PILGRIM BOY: N.
LETTER N: N is the *Nation* each one celebrates.
PILGRIM GIRL: K.

THE A B C'S THANKSGIVING

LETTER K: K is for *Kinfolk*, the whole family flock,
PILGRIM BOY: S.
LETTER S: S is for *Settlers* on old Plymouth Rock.
PILGRIM GIRL: G.
LETTER G: G is for *Guests*, both the first and the last.
PILGRIM BOY: I.
LETTER I: I is for *Indians*, out of the past.
PILGRIM GIRL: V.
LETTER V: V is for *Visiting*, so much is done.
PILGRIM BOY: I.
LETTER I: I—*Invitation* to join in the fun.
PILGRIM GIRL: N.
LETTER N: N is *November* with this day of days.
PILGRIM BOY: G.
LETTER G: G is for *God* whom we honor and praise!
LETTERS T-H-A-N-K-S-G-I-V-I-N-G:
 Thanksgiving, Thanksgiving
 For great and for small.
 Thanksgiving, Thanksgiving,
 The best day of all!
OTHER LETTERS: What about us? What about us?
PILGRIM BOY AND GIRL:
 Quiet! Quiet!
 You're making too much fuss!
LETTERS (*At right*):
 You've spelled the word *Thanksgiving*,
 But we're important too.
LETTERS (*At left*):
 We want to join the party,
 So tell us what to do.

PILGRIM GIRL:
Thanksgiving is a big word,
It's long enough this way.

PILGRIM BOY:
The rest of you will have to wait.
Come back another day!

OTHER LETTERS: No! No! We want to take part in *Thanksgiving!* (*Some of them try to crowd into the* T-H-A-N-K-S-G-I-V-I-N-G *group.*)

LETTERS T-H-A-N-K-S-G-I-V-I-N-G: No room! No room! Go away! Go away! (MODERN BOY *and* GIRL *enter, each with a book.*)

MODERN BOY *and* GIRL: Wait a minute! Wait a minute! Perhaps we can help you.

MODERN GIRL:

It takes so many, many words
To tell the old-time story
About our own Thanksgiving Day
In all its proper glory.

MODERN BOY:

We have a special spelling book,
And by the time we're done,
We'll use up every letter,
Yes, every single one.

MODERN GIRL: The first word is *Turkey*. (*The T and K step out of the "Thanksgiving" word group, leaving space for U, R, E, and Y, who take their places as* MODERN GIRL *says next speech.*)
You cannot spell *Turkey*, you can't if you try,
Without using *U*, and *R* and *E Y*.

THE A B C'S THANKSGIVING

ALL: T-U-R-K-E-Y—*Turkey!*

LETTERS T-U-R-K-E-Y:
>*Turkey* is a dandy word,
>And turkey is a dandy bird!
>
>(LETTERS *return to their original places.*)

MODERN BOY: The next word is *Pilgrims.* (*Two I's, a G and an S step out of the word* T-H-A-N-K-S-G-I-V-I-N-G, *leaving space for the other letters as* MODERN BOY *completes his speech.*)
>You cannot spell PILGRIMS, you know about them,
>Without using P, and L, and an M.

ALL: P-I-L-G-R-I-M-S—Pilgrims!

LETTERS P-I-L-G-R-I-M-S:
>The PILGRIMS reached this land of plenty,
>Our history says in sixteen twenty!
>
>(LETTERS *return to original places.*)

MODERN GIRL: The next word is FOOD.

ALL (*Spell the word as letters step into place*): F-O-O-D—FOOD!

LETTERS F-O-O-D:
>We're thankful when our prayers are said
>For FOOD and drink, and daily bread.
>
>(LETTERS *remain in place*)

MODERN BOY:
>You can change the word,
>By changing one letter.
>I'd do it myself,
>But you can do better!

LETTER W:
>I know! I know!

That's where I go.
(F *and* W *change places*)
ALL (*Spelling aloud*): W-O-O-D. That's not a Thanksgiving word!
LETTERS W-O-O-D: Yes, it is! Yes, it is!
MODERN GIRL:
Decide if you are right or wrong,
As you sing this happy song.
ALL (*Singing to tune of* "*Over the River and Through the Wood*"):

"Over the river and through the wood,
To grandfather's house we go;
The horse knows the way to carry the sleigh,
Through the white and drifted snow.
Over the river and through the wood,
Oh, how the wind does blow!
It stings the toes and bites the nose,
As over the ground we go.
Over the river and through the wood,
To have a first-rate play;
Hear the bells ring, "Ting-a-ling-ding"!
Hurrah for Thanksgiving Day.
Over the river and through the wood,
Trot fast my dapple gray!
Spring over the ground like a hunting hound,
For this is Thanksgiving Day!"
LETTER W:
You need me for Thanksgiving,
It's very plain to see,
You couldn't sing this jolly song,

If it were not for me.

PILGRIM GIRL:
And there's a more important word
To every thankful heart,

PILGRIM BOY:
Another real Thanksgiving word
In which you play a part.

PILGRIM GIRL:
We left our homes across the seas
That we might *Worship* as we please.
(LETTERS *from the word* W-O-R-S-H-I-P *come forward.*)

ALL (*Spelling*): W-O-R-S-H-I-P—*Worship!*

MODERN GIRL:
And even now, we all rejoice
That we may have religious choice.

MODERN BOY:
Another song, as you will see,
Makes use of letters C and B.
(ALL *sing first verse of* "*America.*")

LETTER C:
America is spelled with C.
My *Country* makes good use of me.

LETTER B:
And *Liberty's* another word
In which my voice is plainly heard.
(*Enter* FLAG BEARER *with American flag.*)

MODERN GIRL *and* **BOY:**
May this flag ever wave above
The home of the free,

And the land that we love!
(ALL *give the pledge to the flag.*)
ALL: "I pledge allegiance to the flag of the United States of America, and to the Republic for which it stands; one nation, under God, indivisible, with liberty and justice for all."
LETTER J:
In *Justice*, there's the letter J,
Important on Thanksgiving Day.
LETTER Q:
Americans believe that all men are born free and *equal*,
With *equal* justice and opportunity for all.
PILGRIM BOY *and* GIRL:
Congratulations, Letter Q,
Our country makes good use of you.
LETTERS X *and* Z:
But we must weep,
And we must pout,
Because we two
Are both left out!
MODERN GIRL:
Poor X and Z! How bad you feel!
But we still have some *Extra Zeal*
To celebrate Thanksgiving Day,
So here are parts you both can play!
LETTER X:
I like that word *Extra*. It makes me feel *Extra* special.
And Thanksgiving is an *extra special day!*

LETTER Z:
   I like the word *Zeal*. It also means *Zest*
   And both of those words mean doing your best!
MODERN GIRL:
   You need every letter
   To spell every word,
MODERN BOY:
   To send out a greeting
   That's bound to be heard
PILGRIM GIRL:
   By all of the people
   Under the sun,
PILGRIM BOY:
   And wish Happy Thanksgiving
   To every last one!
ALL (*Singing to tune of "America"*):
   With thankful hearts we pray
   On this Thanksgiving Day
   To Thee above.
   Our grateful thanks to thee,
   For life and liberty,
   And ever keep it free
   This land we love.
            (*Curtain*)

THE END

BARTHOLOMEW'S JOYFUL NOISE

Characters

ISAAC ALLERTON
BARTHOLOMEW ALLERTON
MARY ALLERTON
REMEMBER ALLERTON
JOHNNY BILLINGTON
MARY CHILTON
ELIZABETH TILLEY
CAPTAIN MILES STANDISH

TIME: *A November morning in the 1620's.*
SETTING: *The* ALLERTON'S *cabin.*
AT RISE: BARTHOLOMEW *is sitting on top of a long wooden table, beating a crude homemade drum, and shouting commands to his sisters,* MARY *and* REMEMBER, *who are drilling with wooden sticks instead of guns.*

BARTHOLOMEW (*Beating a march rhythm*): Left, left, left, right, left! Left, left, left, right, left! Left, left, left, right, left! Watch it, Mary. You're out of step. Left, left, left, right, left! (*Throwing down drumsticks in disgust*) For mercy's sake! Don't you know your left foot from your right?
MARY: Of course, I do. (*Demonstrating*) *This* is my left foot and *this* is my right.
BARTHOLOMEW: Then try it again, and keep in time.
REMEMBER: I'm tired of this game. Besides, Father wouldn't like us to be playing soldier.

BARTHOLOMEW: Father never likes us to play anything. All he wants us to do is *work*.

MARY: You should not speak that way of Father, Bartholomew. He is the kindest man in Plymouth. Isn't he, Remember?

REMEMBER: I wouldn't want anyone else for my father.

BARTHOLOMEW: Well, neither would I. But I wish he would let us have more fun—like Mr. Billington.

MARY: You'd better not let him hear you speak of Mr. Billington, or Johnny Billington either.

BARTHOLOMEW: Johnny Billington is my friend.

REMEMBER: But Father has forbidden you to play with him. He's always getting into trouble.

BARTHOLOMEW: No talking in the ranks! 'Ten-shun! Mark time—mark. Left, left, left, right, left! Left, left, left, right, left! Forward, march! Left, left, left, right, left! Left, left, left, right, left! (*Marching continues until* MARY *and* REMEMBER *march straight into* ISAAC ALLERTON *as he enters.*)

ALLERTON: What is the meaning of this?

MARY: Excuse me, Father!

ALLERTON: Bartholomew Allerton! What are you doing on that table? And where did you get that drum?

BARTHOLOMEW (*Scrambling down from table*): We were just having our morning drill, Father. Captain Standish says we should all learn to defend ourselves.

ALLERTON: Captain Standish never said anything about young girls playing at soldiering. Mary, you should know better. Remember, I am surprised at you!

REMEMBER: I'm sorry, Father.

ALLERTON: As for you, Bartholomew, you have not answered my question. Where did you get that drum?

BARTHOLOMEW: I—er—I made it, sir.

ALLERTON: Let me see it. (*Looks at drum*) Umm! This looks very much like the instrument of Satan I saw in the hands of that young rascal, Johnny Billington.

BARTHOLOMEW: 'Tis very like it, sir.

ALLERTON: I think it is the very same.

BARTHOLOMEW: 'Tis possible, sir.

ALLERTON: I am asking you, Bartholomew, is it, or is it not, the same?

BARTHOLOMEW: It is the same, Father. Johnny showed me how to make it.

ALLERTON: How many times have I told you to stay away from John and Francis Billington?

BARTHOLOMEW: I—I don't know, sir.

ALLERTON: I can see I will have to refresh your memory with a switch.

BARTHOLOMEW: Please, Father, Johnny and I made the drum before you refreshed my memory the last time.

ALLERTON: Very well. I will not punish you twice for the same fault. But you will not see this drum again.

BARTHOLOMEW: But, Father, half of it belongs to Johnny.

ALLERTON: Then he may have his half, after I have chopped it in two!

MARY: Why is a drum so wicked, Father? Captain Standish has one.

ALLERTON: Captain Standish is a soldier, Mary. He uses the drum to call his company to order.

REMEMBER: But we march to meeting with a drum, Father.

ALLERTON: That is the Captain's order. He is in charge of our safety, and if he commands us to march to his drumbeat, I must obey with the others. But I will not have a musical instrument in my own house. We Allertons do not hold with such worldly inventions.

MARY: Are you going with Captain Standish and the other men to hunt game for the Thanksgiving feast, Father?

ALLERTON: Yes, child. We need all the deer and turkeys we can get.

BARTHOLOMEW: Oh, please, Father, please, let me go with you.

ALLERTON: Nay, Bartholomew, you are too young for a hunting party.

BARTHOLOMEW: Joseph Rogers is going. He told me so himself.

ALLERTON: Joseph Rogers is fifteen.

BARTHOLOMEW: But, Father . . .

ALLERTON: Stop pestering me, Bartholomew. You know I never change my mind.

REMEMBER: You might get lost in the woods like Johnny Billington.

ALLERTON: I will hear no more talk about Johnny Billington in this house.

BARTHOLOMEW: It wasn't his fault that he got lost. He didn't do it on purpose.

ALLERTON: Silence!

BARTHOLOMEW: I wish I could get lost forever and ever and ever! And never come back to this hateful place!

ALLERTON: Bartholomew Allerton! Never let me hear such wicked words from you again. Think of the many blessings we have received. We have much to be thankful for.

BARTHOLOMEW: I can't think of a single thing. I would be thankful to be back in England where we had a proper house and proper food. We never have any fun here.

ALLERTON: One more word out of you, Bartholomew, and I'll give you something to be thankful for! I am afraid I have spoiled you by sparing the rod, since your mother died. (*Gets Bible and opens it on table*) You shall, however, learn the lesson of Thanksgiving from the Holy Book. When I come home, I will expect you to recite the whole of the ninety-fifth Psalm from memory.

BARTHOLOMEW: But, Father, there are eleven verses! 'Twill take me an age to learn it. Couldn't I do just as well with the hundredth Psalm? That has only five verses.

ALLERTON: Be thankful I didn't make it Psalm number one hundred nineteen.

MARY: That has one hundred seventy-six verses.

ALLERTON: I'm glad you know your Bible so well, my child.

MARY: Thank you, Father.

ALLERTON: I trust you girls will find some useful tasks while I am gone.

REMEMBER: Mistress Brewster is going to let me help with the baking today.

MARY: I am going to help Mistress White take care of Baby Peregrine.

ALLERTON: 'Tis good to keep busy. Satan always finds mischief for idle hands. As for you, Bartholomew, you will not stir from this house until you have learned your verses.

BARTHOLOMEW: No, sir.

ALLERTON: For every mistake, you can expect a sharp reminder from my cane. Do you understand?

BARTHOLOMEW: I understand, Father.

ALLERTON: Now, I must join the hunting party. I trust you will all be faithful to your tasks.

ALL: Goodbye, Father.

ALLERTON (*Picking up drum*): And on my way, I will destroy this heathenish instrument. (*Exits*)

REMEMBER: I'm sorry, Bartholomew. I know how much you liked your drum.

MARY: 'Tis hard sometimes to be a Puritan.

BARTHOLOMEW: Johnny and Francis Billington are lucky. Their father is not a Separatist.

REMEMBER: But they have to go to meeting and obey all of our laws.

BARTHOLOMEW: I'll bet Johnny never had to learn eleven Bible verses. I know I'll never learn them—never!

MARY: Try reading them over and over, out loud.

REMEMBER: Learning Bible verses is not hard for me. Perhaps that is why Mother and Father named me Remember.

MARY: They didn't know that when you were a baby. They named you first, and you learned to remember later.

REMEMBER: Then perhaps it is my name that helps me remember. I'm glad they didn't call me Forgetful.

BARTHOLOMEW: They should name every girl baby Chatterbox. All of you girls talk too much.

MARY: If that's the way you feel about us, we'll leave you to your verses. Come along, Remember.

REMEMBER: Goodbye, Bartholomew. I'm truly sorry about your drum.

BARTHOLOMEW: Goodbye, little sisters. I like you both, even if you are chatterboxes. (MARY *and* REMEMBER *exit.* BARTHOLOMEW *props his head in his hands and reads aloud.*)

"Oh, come let us sing unto the Lord;
Let us make a joyful noise to the rock of our salvation.
Let us come before his presence with thanksgiving,
And make a joyful noise unto him with psalms."

(*He squeezes his eyes shut and repeats the first two lines.* JOHNNY BILLINGTON *tiptoes on stage.*)

JOHNNY (*Looking around cautiously*): Psst! Bartholomew! Is the coast clear?

BARTHOLOMEW: Johnny! Johnny Billington! Where did you come from?

JOHNNY: From the fort. And wait till you see what I have for you outside.

BARTHOLOMEW: You know my father has forbidden you to come here.

JOHNNY: But your father has gone hunting with the rest of the men. Where is our drum?

BARTHOLOMEW: Father took it. He says it is an instrument of Satan.

JOHNNY: Never mind. You can forget about the old drum. Come out and see what I have.

BARTHOLOMEW: I can't. I dare not leave the house till I have learned the ninety-fifth Psalm.

JOHNNY: Then I will bring it inside. (*Runs offstage*)

BARTHOLOMEW: I only hope Father doesn't come back unexpectedly.

JOHNNY (*Re-enters with real drum*): Look! Isn't it a dandy?

BARTHOLOMEW: Johnny Billington! This drum belongs at the fort!

JOHNNY: I know. I wanted you to try a real drum for once.

BARTHOLOMEW: But this is the drum Captain Standish uses to call out the men.

JOHNNY: He won't be needing it today. He's gone with the hunting party. Besides, his drummer is sick with a fever. There's no one to play it.

BARTHOLOMEW (*Beating drum louder and louder*): This is great, Johnny. How I wish I could be a real drummer like Peter Brown.

JOHNNY: My father says a man has to have a feeling for a drum. He says Peter Brown never has got the hang of it.
BARTHOLOMEW (*Throwing down sticks*): Oh, what's the use? Father would skin me alive.
JOHNNY: You can practice all day, if you like. The men won't be home for hours.
BARTHOLOMEW: Did your brother Francis go with the hunting party?
JOHNNY: No. He and Johnny Cook are burning leaves. They just started a big bonfire. Want to go and watch?
BARTHOLOMEW: I can't. I have eleven verses to learn, and I know only one.
JOHNNY: I'll bet we could see the fire from here, if we climbed up on the roof. (MARY *and* REMEMBER *run in, breathless and excited.*)
MARY: Bartholomew, come quickly! There's a fire at the end of the village!
REMEMBER: The boys were burning leaves, and the brush has caught fire.
JOHNNY: It's only a bonfire.
MARY: It started out as a bonfire, but it's out of control.
REMEMBER: Mistress White is crying. She says, with this wind, the whole village may go up in flames.
JOHNNY: It just might. Father says these thatched roofs would burn like tinder. (MARY CHILTON *and* ELIZABETH TILLEY *enter.*)
MARY CHILTON: Is your father at home?

ELIZABETH: Mistress Carver sent us to round up every man and boy in town. The fire is getting worse by the minute.

BARTHOLOMEW: Father went with the rest of the men.

MARY CHILTON: Do you know which way they went? They can't be far.

JOHNNY: I'll go search for them.

MARY CHILTON: There isn't time.

REMEMBER: If only there were some way to summon them.

BARTHOLOMEW: There *is* a way. (*Snatches drum from table and rushes out*)

MARY: Where is he going?

REMEMBER: What is he going to do?

JOHNNY: I think I know. Listen! (*Very loud offstage roll of drum*)

MARY CHILTON: What's that?

JOHNNY: It's Bartholomew.

ELIZABETH: But why is he beating a drum at a time like this?

JOHNNY: If the men hear the drum, they will turn back. The drum roll is the signal for every man to muster arms. (*Another drum roll is heard offstage.*)

MARY: I never knew Bartholomew could drum like that.

JOHNNY: He never had the chance to try.

REMEMBER: Father will be furious.

JOHNNY: Not if Bartholomew saves the village.

ELIZABETH: Let's not waste any more time. Let's see what we can do to help.

MARY CHILTON: I'll run from house to house and get the women to fill every jug and pitcher with water. (*Goes toward exit*)

ELIZABETH: You take the lower half of the village. I'll take the other half. (*Exits with* MARY CHILTON)

REMEMBER (*Collecting utensils*): I'll take this and this . . . (*Exits*)

MARY: Come on, Johnny. If you help me, we can carry the rain barrel from under the eaves. (MARY *exits with* JOHNNY. *There is another drum roll and* BARTHOLOMEW *enters, carrying drum.*)

BARTHOLOMEW: If the men are within earshot, the drum should bring them on the double. (*Opens blanket chest and pulls out quilt*) If I soak this in water, I can help beat out the flames. (*As he rises from floor,* CAPTAIN MILES STANDISH *and* ALLERTON *enter.*)

ALLERTON: Bartholomew! Thank heaven you are safe.

BARTHOLOMEW: Father! Captain Standish!

ALLERTON: Where are your sisters?

BARTHOLOMEW: They went to help with the fire. How did you get here so soon?

CAPTAIN: We were barely out of sight of the village when we heard the drum. The men will put out the blaze before it can do any real damage.

ALLERTON: We got here in the nick of time.

CAPTAIN: I can't understand it. Peter Brown is ill with a fever. Who could have sounded the alarm?

ALLERTON (*Picking up drum*): I think my son can answer your question, Captain.

CAPTAIN (*In surprise*): 'Tis the drum from the fort. But how did it get here, and who was the drummer?

BARTHOLOMEW: Johnny Billington brought it here, Captain Standish. He wanted me to try a real drum instead of the one we made.

CAPTAIN: You mean it was this lad who sounded that drum roll?

BARTHOLOMEW: I'm sorry, Father. It seemed the only thing to do.

CAPTAIN: Sorry! You have no call to be sorry, my boy. When Peter Brown was in the best of health, he could not roll a drum in that fashion. What would you say to being my drummer boy from this day on?

BARTHOLOMEW: Oh, Captain Standish, do you really mean it?

CAPTAIN: I certainly do. Is it a bargain? (*Extending hand to* BARTHOLOMEW)

BARTHOLOMEW (*Starts to shake hands, but suddenly drops his hand and turns aside*): I'm sorry, sir. My father would not allow it.

CAPTAIN: Not allow it! (*To* ALLERTON) Come, sir, you cannot be serious.

ALLERTON: I am a serious man, Captain Standish. I do not want my son to play an outlandish musical instrument.

CAPTAIN: This outlandish musical instrument has saved our settlement. You can be thankful your son knows how to wield a pair of drumsticks.

ALLERTON: I am also thankful that my son respects the

wishes of his father. Bartholomew, have you learned the verses I assigned you?

BARTHOLOMEW: Only the first one, Father. "Oh, come, let us sing unto the Lord; let us make a joyful noise to the rock of our salvation."

CAPTAIN: Do you hear that, Master Allerton? "A joyful noise . . ." Surely Bartholomew has made a joyful noise this day.

ALLERTON: The Scripture does not mention a drum, Captain Standish.

CAPTAIN: Not in so many words, Master Allerton.

BARTHOLOMEW: But there are other verses, Father . . . I have heard Elder Brewster read them in meeting. "Sing unto the Lord with the harp; with the harp and the voice of a psalm. With trumpets and sound of cornet, make a joyful noise before the Lord, the King."

ALLERTON: 'Tis the joyful heart that counts more than the loud noise, my son. And it is your heart that troubles me. You are not thankful for the many blessings we have received in Plymouth.

BARTHOLOMEW: I know what you mean, Father. But when I saw the fire about to destroy it, our new home was suddenly dear to me.

ALLERTON: Then you have learned the lesson I sought to teach you from the Holy Word.

CAPTAIN: I wager the lad would be even more thankful if you were to let him be my drummer boy.

ALLERTON (*Smiling*): You drive a sharp bargain, Captain. Between you and the Scriptures, what am I to say?

BARTHOLOMEW: Oh, Father, do you really mean it?

ALLERTON: I really mean it, son, on one condition.

BARTHOLOMEW: I'll learn a whole page of Bible verses, sir.

ALLERTON: Nay, lad, the condition is that your first act as the Captain's drummer boy shall be to summon our people to their feast of Thanksgiving.

CAPTAIN: You have your orders, Bartholomew.

BARTHOLOMEW: Thank you, Father, thank you. I will make such a joyful noise that everyone in Plymouth will hear and understand.

ALLERTON (*Folding his hands and lifting his head*): We will "enter into his gates with thanksgiving, and into his courts with praise."

CAPTAIN (*Bowing his head*): We will "be thankful unto Him, and bless His name." (*Curtain*)

THE END

THE RUNAWAY TOYS

Characters

TEDDY BEAR
TOY SOLDIER
DONALD DUCK
JUMPING JACK
SANTA CLAUS
TWINKLE ⎫
WINKLE   ⎬ *Santa's elves*
CRINKLE ⎭
FRENCH DOLL
RAG DOLL
DUTCH DOLL
JAPANESE DOLL
JIMSY MARSHALL
JANIE EVANS

TIME: *The present; Christmas Eve.*
SETTING: *The Marshall living room.*
AT RISE: TEDDY BEAR *and* TOY SOLDIER *are waiting by the fireplace.*

TEDDY BEAR (*Stretching and yawning*):
  Ho-hum!
  Why doesn't he come?
  I'm sleepy as I can be!
SOLDIER (*Standing stiff and straight*):
  As I often mention,
  Just stand at attention,
  And be a good soldier like me!
TEDDY BEAR: It's easy for you to talk. You're made of tin. But I am stuffed with sawdust.

SOLDIER: All right, old Button Eyes! Take a nap, if you like. I'll stand watch.
TEDDY BEAR: Did you tell anyone we were leaving?
SOLDIER: Only the toys in the next apartment. They want to join us.
TEDDY BEAR: If there are too many, Santa may not take us.
SOLDIER: Sh! I hear somebody coming.
DONALD DUCK (*Waddles in, quacking sadly*):
Quack quack! Quack quack!
I want to go back
'Cause nobody loves me, I fear.
Alas and alack!
My poor heart will crack,
If I have to remain around here.
SOLDIER: Halt! Who goes there?
DONALD DUCK: Quack! Quack! Quack! You scared the feathers right out of my back!
TEDDY BEAR: It's only Donald Duck.
SOLDIER: Where do you think you're going?
DONALD DUCK: Back to Toyland, if Santa Claus will take me. I can't stand it here any longer. No one will play with me.
TEDDY BEAR: I know how it is. Jimsy is too grown up to play with any of us.
SOLDIER: Better not let him hear you call him *Jimsy!* It must be *James* or *Jim!*
DONALD DUCK: It makes me quack real tears when I remember the good times we used to have. I had to go along every time he went for a walk in the park.

THE RUNAWAY TOYS

TEDDY BEAR: He took me to bed every night.
SOLDIER: And I stood guard on his bedside table.
DONALD DUCK: Now he keeps us shut up in that dark storeroom.
TEDDY BEAR: Lucky for us Mrs. Marshall forgot to close the storeroom door when she unpacked the Christmas trimmings. (JUMPING JACK *jumps in*)
JUMPING JACK: Oh me, oh my! I hope I'm not too late.
SOLDIER: Don't be so jumpy, Jack. You're in plenty of time.
DONALD DUCK: Are you going back to Toyland with the rest of us?
JUMPING JACK: I hope so. I can't make Jimsy laugh any more. He won't even look at me, and I can jump as well as ever. (*Does some of his best jumps and somersaults. The sound of sleigh bells is heard.*)
TEDDY BEAR: Listen! I hear sleigh bells. Santa is coming. (*There is a knock at the door.*)
DONALD DUCK: Someone's at the door. Quick! Let's hide!
SOLDIER: I'm ashamed of you, men. Stand your ground. Never retreat! (*Shouting*) Advance and give the password. (*Enter* RAG DOLL, FRENCH DOLL, DUTCH DOLL, *and* JAPANESE DOLL)
DOLLS: The password is *Merry Christmas!*
JUMPING JACK: Who are you? I never saw you before.
SOLDIER: These dolls belong to Janie Evans, the little girl in the next apartment. They want to go back to Toyland with us.

DOLLS: Janie doesn't love us any more. All she wants for Christmas is new clothes!

RAG DOLL:
Ruffles and ribbons, and sashes and laces,
Slippers for dancing to show off her graces.

DUTCH DOLL:
Bonnets and buttons, and earmuffs and mittens,
Made all of fur that is soft as a kitten's.

FRENCH DOLL:
A ring, and a wrist watch, a bracelet of charms,
To slip on her finger and wear on her arms.

JAPANESE DOLL:
She's finished with dolls, we've all heard her say,
And that is the reason we're running away!
(*Another jingle of sleigh bells.*)

SANTA CLAUS (*Offstage*): Whoa, Dancer! Whoa, Prancer! Easy there, Donner and Blitzen!

ALL: He's coming! He's coming!

TEDDY BEAR (*Running to fireplace and peering inside*): Let me look! Maybe I can see him!

DOLLS: Let us look! Ladies before gentlemen!

SOLDIER: Stand back! You'll get your dresses dirty.

TEDDY BEAR: I think I see one leg! Oh, my! I'm afraid he's stuck!

SOLDIER: Maybe we can pull him out. (*As the* TOYS *gather around the fireplace,* SANTA *enters left, followed by 3* ELVES *carrying packages.*)

SANTA (*Loudly*): Merry Christmas to all!

TOYS: Santa! Where did you come from?

SOLDIER: We thought you were stuck in the chimney.

SANTA: Nonsense! I took the elevator from the top floor.
FRENCH DOLL: But don't you always come down the chimney?
SANTA: Not in apartment houses, my dear. (*Putting his pack on the floor*) Aha! I see there are three stockings for us to fill. Put the boxes down and get busy, boys.
TWINKLE: You must stop calling us *boys*, Santa.
SANTA: Excuse me! I forgot you girls are working this season. Maybe we should have some introductions. These are my Christmas helpers, Twinkle, Winkle, and Crinkle.
ELVES: Merry Christmas.
SOLDIER: We are glad to meet you. I am Captain Tinby of the Toy Soldier Brigade, and these are my friends, Teddy Bear, Donald Duck, and Jack the Jumper. (*Each* TOY *acknowledges introduction with a bow.*)
FRENCH DOLL (*With a curtsy*): My name is Suzette. I come from Paree!
DUTCH DOLL: And my name is Gretchen from old Zuyder Zee!
RAG DOLL: And I'm just a plain old Raggedy Ann.
JAPANESE DOLL: My name is Kazuki. I come from Japan.
SANTA: But what are you toys doing here? You should be in the playroom where you belong.
SOLDIER: We have a favor to ask you, Santa.
SANTA CLAUS: Then be quick about it. I am very busy.
FRENCH DOLL: We want you to take us back to Toyland.

SANTA *and* ELVES: What?

DUTCH DOLL: Oh, please, Santa. We are so sad and lonely. Janie, the little girl who owns us, won't play with us any more. She says she is too old for dolls.

DONALD DUCK: And we have to stay in the storeroom all year long.

TEDDY BEAR: Jimsy says he has outgrown us.

SOLDIER: All he cares about is rockets and space ships and bicycles and baseballs.

TOYS: Please, Santa, please take us back to Toyland.
(*Singing to tune of "Jolly Old Saint Nicholas"*)
Jolly old Saint Nicholas,
Lean your ear this way.
Don't you say a single word,
Till we have had our say.
We are lonely as can be,
Lonely, sad, and blue,
Back to Toyland we would go.
Take us back with you!

Janie hates to play with dolls,
Wants a dress instead.
Jimsy has a lot of new
Notions in his head.
As for us, we're left alone,
Nothing here to do.
Have a heart, dear Santa Claus,
Take us back with you.

SANTA CLAUS: Bless my soul! I never heard of such a thing!

WINKLE: Nobody *ever* goes back to Toyland!
TOYS: Please, Santa, please!
SANTA CLAUS: Well, I'll think about it. But first, we must fill these stockings. Twinkle, do you have the letters from the Marshall family?
TWINKLE: I have the one from Mr. Marshall. (*Reading letter*)
Dear Santa, please bring me some books and a pipe,
And a pretty, new tie with a red and white stripe.
SANTA CLAUS: That order is easy to fill. Take the things out of my bag, Twinkle. Now for Mrs. Marshall.
CRINKLE (*Reading letter*):
Dear Santa, please bring me a new sewing kit,
Some stockings and gloves that will be sure to fit.
SANTA CLAUS: You'll find everything in my pack, Crinkle.
WINKLE: This letter is from James Marshall, Junior. (*Reading*)
Dear Santa, remember I play with *big* boys,
So don't bring me any of those *baby* toys!
I'd like to have rockets, a real two-wheel bike,
And anything else that you think I would like.
SANTA CLAUS: We have the bicycle on the freight elevator. The other things are in the boxes.
TWINKLE (*Picking up baby stocking from floor near fireplace*): Oh, look, Santa, here is a tiny, baby stocking. It was on the floor.
SANTA CLAUS: A baby stocking! Nobody told me there was a baby in this house.
SOLDIER: We didn't know.

JUMPING JACK: We never hear any news in that storeroom.
DONALD DUCK: A baby! A baby! Maybe it's a boy!
TEDDY BEAR: If Jimsy has a baby brother, I want to stay here. It will be like old times.
SANTA CLAUS: Is there a letter?
RAG DOLL: Babies can't write letters.
TWINKLE: But there *is* a letter. It must be from Mrs. Marshall.
Dear Santa, I'm writing for our Baby Sue.
She's not old enough to know about you.
Please make her first Christmas a day of pure joy,
And bring our new baby a well-chosen toy.
TOYS: The baby is a girl!
TEDDY BEAR: Of all the bad luck! Why couldn't it have been a boy!
FRENCH DOLL: A girl baby! A dear, little girl!
DUTCH DOLL: I hope she has curly hair and dimples.
SANTA CLAUS: Dear me! This is a problem. I didn't bring anything in my pack for new babies.
FRENCH DOLL: Oh, Santa, couldn't we stay here?
DUTCH DOLL: Every little girl loves a doll.
SANTA CLAUS: But she's just a tiny baby!
RAG DOLL: I could cuddle her at night.
FRENCH DOLL: I could sing her to sleep with a little French song. (FRENCH DOLL *sings* "*Allouette*")
DUTCH DOLL: I could make her laugh with my wooden shoes. (*If desirable, she does a wooden shoe dance*)
JAPANESE DOLL: I could keep her cool with my Japanese fan. (*If desirable, she does a short fan drill*)

SANTA CLAUS: But I can't give you away. You belong to Janie.
DOLLS: Janie wouldn't care. She doesn't love us any more.
JIMSY (*Offstage*): Janie, Janie, where are you?
JANIE (*Offstage*): Right here, Jimsy. Right beside you!
SOLDIER: That's Jimsy!
DOLLS: And Janie.
SANTA CLAUS: They must not find us here. Turn off the lights. (*There is a blackout during which* SANTA *and* ELVES *disappear.* TOYS *freeze into position.*)
JIMSY: Wait a minute, Janie. Wait till I turn on the lights. (*As lights come on,* JIMSY *and* JANIE *enter. They are surprised when they see the* TOYS.)
JANIE: Look! Look! There are all my dolls!
JIMSY: And my Teddy Bear and Toy Soldier! And look! There's Donald Duck and Jumping Jack!
JANIE: No wonder we couldn't find them in the storeroom.
JIMSY: But how did they get here?
JANIE: My mother must have brought my dolls over here.
JIMSY: And my mother must have had the same idea.
JANIE: Look, Jimsy. Aren't they beautiful? Here is Rag Doll. I think I love her best of all. But Suzette is the most beautiful, and Gretchen is the cutest, and as for Kazuki, well . . . there just never was a doll quite like Kazuki. I love them all.
JIMSY: That's just how I feel about my old toys, Janie. I'll never forget how Donald Duck used to waddle

after me in the park. And at night when I was scared, I'd hug the stuffing out of old Teddy Bear.

JANIE: Every time Mother wanted me to give my toys away, I just couldn't bear to part with them.

JIMSY: That's how I felt. I couldn't bear to think of giving my Toy Soldier away, and some other boy might have broken old Jumping Jack.

JANIE: But this year it's different. I know your baby sister will love my dolls as much as I did.

JIMSY: And I know your cousin Bob will take good care of my toys.

JANIE: Isn't it funny we found them right here in your living room?

JIMSY: I'll bet they're happy to be out of that storeroom. This will be a great Christmas for them.

JANIE: I'm glad we didn't stay in that storeroom any longer. It was dark and spooky up there. I was scared.

JIMSY: So was I—a little bit.

JANIE: We'd better get out of here before my mother misses me.

JIMSY: Or before Santa Claus comes.

JANIE: I almost feel like Santa Claus myself. It's almost as much fun to *give* your toys away as to get them.

JIMSY: I guess that's what Mother means by the Christmas Spirit.

JANIE (*Hugging each of her dolls*): Goodbye, Raggedy Ann. Goodbye, Suzette. So long, Gretchen. Be a good doll, Kazuki. And remember, I love you all. Goodnight, Jimsy. See you in the morning. (*Exit* JANIE)

JIMSY (*Yawning*): Goodnight, Janie. Ho-hum. I'm almost falling asleep. Goodnight, Teddy Bear. Goodnight, Captain. Goodnight, old Quack-Quack. Sleep tight, Jumping Jack. And if that Bobby Evans doesn't take proper care of you, just let me know. You're the best toys a fellow ever had. (*Exits*)
SOLDIER: Psst! You can come out now, Santa. The coast is clear. (SANTA *and* ELVES *re-enter.*)
SANTA CLAUS: Well, how about it? Do you still want to go back to Toyland?
TOYS: No, no! We want to stay here.
FRENCH DOLL: Janie loves us just as much as ever.
DUTCH DOLL: And we'll have so much fun with Baby Sue.
RAG DOLL: I will have someone to cuddle me again.
JAPANESE DOLL: This will be a merry Christmas after all.
SOLDIER: We'll have wonderful new adventures with Bobby Evans. I hope he knows how to build a fort.
TEDDY BEAR: I can hardly wait to see him.
JUMPING JACK: How surprised he'll be and how he'll laugh when I do my first somersault.
DONALD DUCK: Quack quack! Quack quack! A quackery-Quistmas to you! That's what I'll say to him.
SANTA CLAUS: Well, boys, I mean *girls*, I guess our job is done. We can't keep the reindeer waiting. (*All join in singing "We Wish You A Merry Christmas." Curtain.*)

THE END

SQUEAKNIBBLE'S CHRISTMAS

adapted from a story by Eugene Field

Characters

MR. GRANDFATHER CLOCK
MOLLY MOUSE
SQUEAKNIBBLE
MAMMA MOUSE
MASTER PUSS
FIVE LITTLE MICE

TIME: *Christmas Eve, ten o'clock.*
SETTING: *The Great Hall. In one corner stands* MR. GRANDFATHER CLOCK. *On the opposite side of the stage is a Christmas tree, on a low table. The center entrance bears a large sign, "Mousehole."*
AT RISE: MR. CLOCK *picks up a large hammer which is leaning against a chair, and slowly strikes ten on his gong.*

MR. CLOCK (*Replacing hammer*): Only ten o'clock! Dear me! At least eight more hours to go before the children come downstairs to see their tree and look at their presents! I get so lonely here, all by myself. I'd be glad to talk to anyone, even that little Molly Mouse. I wonder where she is tonight. Usually she's out here, scampering about in that patch of moonlight. Oh, ho! I think she's coming, and from the amount of noise she's making, she must be in a merry mood! (MOLLY MOUSE *enters from mousehole, skip-*

ping about and singing to the tune of "Jingle Bells.")
MOLLY MOUSE: Jingle bells, jingle bells,
Jingle all the way,
Oh, what fun it is to skip,
And scamper all the day!
Jingle bells, jingle bells,
Jingle all the way,
Oh, what fun it is to be
A mouse on Christmas Day!
MR. CLOCK: Well, well, well! You're unusually frisky this evening. Why all the dancing and singing?
MOLLY MOUSE: Because it's Christmas Eve, that's why. I always feel like dancing on Christmas Eve.
MR. CLOCK: Ah, me! How different you mice are today from the mice we used to have in the good old days! Now, there was your Grandmamma, Mistress Velvetpaw, and there was Grandfather, Mr. Sniffwhisker! How dignified they were! Many a night I've seen them dancing in this old hall, but always the stately minuet—such a dignified dance.
MOLLY MOUSE: Who wants to be dignified on Christmas Eve?
MR. CLOCK: Oh, come now! What does Christmas mean to you, little Miss Molly Mouse?
MOLLY MOUSE: It means a great deal to me. I've been good for such a long time! I haven't gnawed any holes, or stolen any canary seed, or worried my mother by running behind the flour barrel where that hateful old trap is set. In fact, I've been so good that

I'm sure Santa Claus will bring me something quite special.

MR. CLOCK (*Laughing*): Why, you silly mouse! You don't believe in Santa Claus, do you?

MOLLY MOUSE: I should say I do. Why shouldn't I believe in Santa Claus? Didn't he bring me a beautiful butter cracker last Christmas, and a lovely gingersnap, and a delicious rind of cheese? I should be very ungrateful if I didn't believe in him! Besides, I'd be *afraid* not to believe in Santa Claus.

MR. CLOCK: Afraid? Why would you be afraid?

MOLLY MOUSE: You see, I once had a sister named Squeaknibble who didn't believe in Santa Claus, and when I think of what happened to her, a shiver runs straight down my back from the tip of my whiskers to the tip of my tail. (*Singing to the tune of "Three Blind Mice"*)

One bad mouse, one bad mouse,
Lived in a house, lived in a house,
She had a terrible time because
She didn't believe in a Santa Claus,
And you know by now that our tale is about
That one bad mouse!

MR. CLOCK: Squeaknibble! Squeaknibble! That name sounds familiar.

MOLLY MOUSE: Surely you remember her.

MR. CLOCK: Let me see. Was she a fat, chunky little mouse with a very pink nose?

MOLLY MOUSE: No, that's not the one. Squeaknibble was always long and thin. Mother said she took after our New England ancestors. (*Scampers over to* MR. CLOCK *and curls up on the floor beside him*) The whole trouble with Squeaknibble was that she was such a disbelieving little mouse. I can remember when Mother first tried to tell her about the moon! It was right here in this very hall. (MOTHER MOUSE *pokes her head out of mousehole. She advances to center stage. If desired, a spot may be used to set off the parts of the play in which* SQUEAKNIBBLE *appears*.)

MAMMA MOUSE: Squeaknibble! Squeaknibble! Come here and look at the beautiful moon.

SQUEAKNIBBLE (*Entering from mousehole*): Where? Where? I don't see any moon.

MAMMA MOUSE (*Pointing*): You can see this patch of silvery moonlight on the floor. Way up there (*Pointing*), above the trees is the moon itself, sailing back and forth between the clouds.

SQUEAKNIBBLE: What is the moon, Mamma?

MAMMA MOUSE: As if I haven't told you a thousand times. The moon, my dear little mouse, is made of green cheese.

SQUEAKNIBBLE: Don't be silly, Mamma dear. The moon isn't made of green cheese at all! That's just a stupid notion for old mice and babies. A really clever mouse wouldn't be fooled for a second.

MAMMA MOUSE: Squeaknibble, you're much too smart for your whiskers. One of these days you'll be a sadder and wiser little mouse, if you don't start believing what we older mice tell you.

SQUEAKNIBBLE: I know, Mamma, but you always have

such tall stories! How can you expect me to believe them! It's the same way with Master Puss. You make up such terrible tales about him, I'd be scared out of my fur, if I believed half of them.

MAMMA MOUSE: You'd better believe me, if you expect to stay alive. That Master Puss is a monstrous creature. He has such sharp claws and such terrible teeth, you'd never stand a chance.

SQUEAKNIBBLE (*With a giggle*): Don't make me laugh, Mamma. Everybody knows a mouse is the fastest thing on four feet. That old Master Puss could never catch me! Do you know what I'd do? I'd go right up and stick my tongue out at him, and I'd say (*Singsong*): Ny'a, ny'a, ny'a, Mister Pussy Cat, ny'a, ny'a, you can't catch me! (*As she is singing and cavorting about the stage,* MASTER PUSS *enters stealthily behind her, claws outstretched.* SQUEAKNIBBLE *and* MAMMA MOUSE *see him just in time. Both run into the mousehole with many terrified squeaks.*)

MASTER PUSS (*Stamping his foot*): Aha! My little Squeaknibble! You've escaped me this time, but I'll get you yet! You just wait and see! What a nice, tasty morsel you would make for my Christmas dinner! Let me think. Tomorrow night is Christmas Eve. Maybe that's the very time I can catch you off guard. (*Stalking slowly offstage*) Indeed, I've been such a good Pussy Cat this year, I think I am entitled to Squeaknibble as my Christmas treat. (MASTER PUSS *makes his exit singing to the tune of "Pussy Cat, Pussy Cat, Where Have You Been?"*)

Pussy Cat, Pussy Cat,
What is your dream?
I'd like Squeaknibble all served up in cream!
Pussy Cat, Pussy Cat,
What will you do?
I'll catch Squeaknibble for my Christmas stew!
Meow! Meow! Meow! (MASTER PUSS *disappears under the table which holds the Christmas tree.*)

MR. CLOCK (*To* MOLLY MOUSE): It seems to me, Miss Molly, I am beginning to remember your sister, Squeaknibble. It was a long time ago! And I remember that particular Master Puss. He was a great, big black and white fellow, as smart as they come.

MOLLY MOUSE: That's right! Oh, dear! It still makes me shiver when I remember that Christmas Eve. Mamma brought us out here in the hall to show us the Christmas tree before she put us to bed. Squeaknibble had recovered from her fright of the day before, and was saucier than ever. None of us ever dreamed that Master Puss was under the table. (MAMMA MOUSE *sticks her head out of the mousehole, looks cautiously around, and then enters. She looks to see if all is well and then summons the* LITTLE MICE *to enter.*)

MAMMA MOUSE: The coast is clear. You may all come out. (FIVE LITTLE MICE *enter, followed by* SQUEAKNIBBLE.) There! (*Pointing to tree*) Isn't it a lovely tree?

ALL: Beautiful, just beautiful. (*From time to time during this scene,* MASTER PUSS *peers out from under the table.*)

MAMMA MOUSE: Now that you have all had a good look at the tree, you must scamper off to bed. Remember this is the night that Santa Claus will come.

FIRST MOUSE: How will Santa Claus get into our mousehole?

SECOND MOUSE: I hope he brings me a big piece of Roquefort cheese.

THIRD MOUSE: I'd rather have Edam cheese. It's milder.

FOURTH MOUSE: I'm hungry for good old English cheddar.

FIFTH MOUSE: I hope he brings me plenty of Muenster.

SQUEAKNIBBLE: You make me sick with all your silly talk about Santa Claus.

THIRD MOUSE: It's not silly talk. Santa's really coming tonight. Mamma said so.

SQUEAKNIBBLE: I don't believe it! So there!

SECOND MOUSE: If you'd hurry and come to bed, he'd be here in no time!

SQUEAKNIBBLE: I have news for you! I'm not going to bed at all!

SECOND MOUSE: Where are you going?

THIRD MOUSE: Santa Claus won't be able to find you when he comes.

SQUEAKNIBBLE: I don't care anything about old Santa Claus. I'm going to have a good romp here in the hall, all by myself.

MAMMA MOUSE: You're going to do nothing of the sort. You're going to bed with the others. Now, all of you get down that mousehole in a hurry. (*All exit.* SQUEAKNIBBLE *hangs back.*) Squeaknibble, you get along with the rest, if you know what's good for you. (*They all exit,* MAMMA MOUSE *giving* SQUEAKNIBBLE *a spank to speed her on her way.* MASTER PUSS *reappears from under the table.*)

MASTER PUSS: Meow! Meow! Meow! Bless my old white whiskers, but that naughty little Squeaknibble is going to get the surprise of her life. Something tells me she'll be back here as soon as her mother's back is turned! Now let me see! How can I fool her? She doesn't believe in Santa Claus, does she? That gives me an idea. I think I saw a fur coat and cap in the clothes closet. They would give me a perfect disguise. If only the door is open, I'll give that Squeaknibble the shock of her life. (MASTER PUSS *exits as* SQUEAKNIBBLE *enters from the mousehole.*)

SQUEAKNIBBLE: How good it is to get out of that mousehole and frolic here by myself. My stupid brothers and sisters have all gone to bed and are probably dreaming about Santa Claus this very minute. But not me! I'm out for a lark! And if I should see that old Master Puss again, I'd just say, Ny'a, ny'a, ny'a, Mister Pussy Cat, ny'a, ny'a, you can't catch me! (MASTER PUSS *suddenly appears wearing a fur coat and cap.*)

MASTER PUSS: Ho, ho, there, little mouse! What are you doing up so late on Christmas Eve?

SQUEAKNIBBLE (*Terrified*): Please, please, whoever you are, go away! Please, please, don't hurt me. I'm only a little mouse.

MASTER PUSS: Ho, ho, ho! I would never hurt a good

little mouse like you! Don't you know me? (*In a false, sweet voice*) I'm Santa Claus, and I've brought you a lovely piece of nice, fresh cheese.

SQUEAKNIBBLE (*Approaching* MASTER PUSS): How nice of you! I never believed there was a Santa Claus, but now—(MASTER PUSS *leaps at her with a terrible yowl. After a wild chase around the stage, he trips over his coat, and falls, just in time for* SQUEAKNIBBLE *to escape through the mousehole.*)

MASTER PUSS (*Shaking his paw as if it were a fist*): I'll get you yet, Squeaknibble! I'll get you yet!

MOLLY MOUSE: After that, my sister Squeaknibble was a reformed character. Later she went to live with my aunt, who was a country mouse, but when she came back on visits, she would tell us the story over and over again.

SQUEAKNIBBLE (*Entering with all the little mice*): Take it from me, children, it pays to believe in Santa Claus. I never heard of a child or a mouse who came to any good, who doubted him for a single minute. And remember, I know from experience. (*All sing to the tune of "Up on the House Top."*)

Squeaknibble taught us the Christmas laws,
We all believe in dear Santa Claus.
Into our mousehole we know he'll squeeze,
Just to deliver our Christmas cheese.
Ho, ho, ho, all of us know, ho, ho, ho, all of us know,
Santa will bring us something nice,
If we are good little Christmas mice! (*Curtain*)

THE END

GIFTS FOR THE NEW YEAR

Characters

KING OF THE CALENDAR
QUEEN OF THE CALENDAR
COURT JESTER
TICKETY-TOCK, *the Time Witch*
TRUMPETERS
ROYAL NURSEMAID
CHANCELLOR
MEMORY FAIRY
12 FAIRY GODMOTHERS, *representing the months of the year*

SETTING: *The throne room of the* KING *and* QUEEN OF THE CALENDAR. *Two thrones are upstage center, and in front of them stands a ruffled cradle. At one side stands a table covered with a white cloth; a sign reading* FOR BABY NEW YEAR *is tacked to table.*

AT RISE: *The* ROYAL NURSEMAID *is leaning over cradle, making cooing noises, as the* COURT JESTER *looks on.*

NURSEMAID: Gitchy, gitchy, gitchy, goo! I'm going to get you!
JESTER: Stop that silly talk. It's enough to make him sick to his stomach.
NURSEMAID: You're just jealous because I can make him laugh and you can't. Isn't he darling? (*Offstage sound of trumpets*)
JESTER: Quick! The guests have finished their banquet. They will be coming here at once.

NURSEMAID: I do hope they don't frighten this precious lamb.

JESTER: He will have to get used to strangers.

NURSEMAID: But he's never had so many visitors. All twelve of his Fairy Godmothers have been invited to the name-giving feast.

JESTER: Don't tell me Old-You-Know-Who is coming!

NURSEMAID (*Looking around nervously*): Sh-h-h! Be careful! Don't mention her name.

JESTER: I didn't mention any names. I just said Old-You-Know-Who!

NURSEMAID: That's the same thing. Don't even *think* about her! Of course, she's not invited.

JESTER:
Double, double,
Wreck and rubble!
I smell nothing
Here but *trouble!*

NURSEMAID (*Crossly*): Oh, be quiet! For a Court Jester, you're the gloomiest Gus I ever saw.

JESTER: Mark my words! Old-You-Know-Who will be on the warpath as sure as my name is Jester-de-Pester! (*Another offstage bugle is heard.*)

CHANCELLOR (*Entering with* TRUMPETERS *who stand at attention as court procession begins*): Make way! Make way! Their most royal Majesties—The King and Queen of the Calendar! (NURSEMAID *and* JESTER *bow as* KING *and* QUEEN OF THE CALENDAR *enter and take their places at thrones.*) Make way! Make way! The Twelve Fairy Godmothers of his Most Royal

Highness and Crown Prince of the Calendar—The Baby New Year. (*The* 12 FAIRY GODMOTHERS *enter and group themselves in a large semi-circle, six on either side of cradle.*)

KING:
Her Majesty, the Queen, and I,
Are glad to welcome you.
And in his crib, our son and heir,
Bids you a welcome, too!

QUEEN:
We're glad to have you see our boy,
To us he's very dear.
We know he'll bring us lots of joy.
Meet baby Prince New Year!

GODMOTHERS: All Hail to Baby New Year, Crown Prince of the Calendar.

JESTER:
Now tarry-a-diddle,
I'll give you a riddle,
And then you must answer me true.
I'll give you the start,
I'll give you the middle,
The rest will be up to you!

KING: Very well, Jester. You may tell us your riddle. But be sure it is a good one.

JESTER (*Holding up a battered silk hat which he picks up from behind the cradle*): Why is our King of the Calendar like this old hat? (FAIRY GODMOTHERS *consult among themselves and shake their heads.*)

KING: I'm not so sure I like riddles about myself.

JESTER: Oh, this is a good one, your Majesty. I promise you.
QUEEN: Is it because they have both seen many years of service?
JESTER: Not quite, your Majesty.
CHANCELLOR: I know! I know!
JESTER: The Royal Chancellor has the answer.
CHANCELLOR: Our King is like the hat, because he must always be at the *head*.
JESTER: Very clever! Very clever! But that is not the right answer.
ALL: We give up.
JESTER: The King is like this old hat, because each one has a *crown*. (*Applause and laughter*)
QUEEN: That is a very good riddle. I must remember it.
KING: And now that we have had our joke for today, the Chancellor will read the poem I have written for this great occasion.
CHANCELLOR (*Reads from scroll*):
Who is this baby, pretty and sweet,
Rings on his fingers, and bells on his feet?
Who is this baby, ever so dear?
Who could it be, but the Baby New Year?
(*Applause*)
KING: Our Baby New Year has twelve wonderful Fairy Godmothers who have been invited to his name-giving feast. The Court Jester may introduce them.
JESTER:
"January brings the snow,
Makes our feet and fingers glow."

She will be the first to say
What she brings the prince today.
JANUARY (*Holding up a baby blanket*):
Right from the tip of your dear little nose,
Down to the tips of your tiny, pink toes,
My gift will enfold you and keep you from harm,
A warm, woolly blanket with magical charm.
QUEEN: What a splendid present, Lady January! It is wonderful to know that no harm will ever befall our child. Thank you. (NURSEMAID *spreads blanket over cradle.*)
JESTER:
February, short and small,
Has more holidays than all.
FEBRUARY (*Leans over cradle and dangles a bunch of cherries*):
A bunch of red cherries, to dangle and shake,
And keep you enchanted, when you are awake.
The cherries will help you be honest and true,
And that is my present, dear baby, for you.
(*Puts bunch of cherries on cradle*)
KING: Thank you, Fairy February. Every father wants his son to be honest and true.
JESTER:
The Fairy March is next in line
With presents that are rich and fine.
MARCH (*Approaches crib; holds up first a toy lion, then a toy lamb*):
Hello, little New Year; I've brought you these toys:
A lamb and a lion—they're just right for boys.

Be brave as a lion, my dear little child.
But also be gentle and friendly and mild.
(NURSEMAID *places gifts on table.*)

QUEEN: Thank you, March. They are just what the Baby New Year needs.

JESTER:
April ushers in the spring—
Buds that bloom and birds that sing.
Lovely month, we bid you rise;
Give the baby your surprise.

APRIL (*Carrying a small umbrella, she approaches cradle*):
First there's March, then I come after
To bring the precious gift of laughter.
When storm clouds threaten you, young fella,
A smile will be your best umbrella.
(NURSEMAID *places gift on table.*)

KING: A merry heart is a great gift, Lady April. Our little New Year will make good use of it.

JESTER:
The April showers will bring May flowers,
And here is May to tell
About the gift she has in store
To serve our baby well.

MAY (*Approaches cradle with a big, golden ball*):
This golden ball I give you
Shines like the noonday sun.
May all your days be bright and fair
And happy, every one!
(NURSEMAID *places ball on table.*)

QUEEN: The gift of sunshine is a real treasure. Thank you, kind Fairy Godmother.

JESTER:
Here's June, the month of roses,
A charming lady fair;
She brings him fragrant treasures,
And days that are so rare.

JUNE (*Carrying a bouquet of red and white roses to cradle*):
Roses of red and roses of white,
To fill your years with sheer delight;
The gift of love these roses bring
To make your heart and spirit sing!

KING: Our thanks, Lady June. There is no greater gift than love.

JESTER:
A sparkling month is fair July
With flowers and fireworks, too.
Here, baby, open wide your eyes.
See what she has for you!

JULY (*Waving flag as she approaches cradle*):
Your country's flag, striped red and white,
With stars on field of blue:
It stands for freedom everywhere,
For hearts both staunch and true.

KING: Hurrah! Three cheers for the red, white and blue!

ALL: Hurrah! Hurrah! Hurrah! (NURSEMAID *places flag on table.*)

JESTER:
The August days are long and hot,

A time for rest and play.
So listen to Dame August.
Hear what she has to say.

AUGUST (*Carrying baseball, bat, glove, toy boat, car, and airplane, etc.*):
You're such a little baby, yes, such a tiny one,
I think you'll need my month of days for just plain having fun.
So here's a glove, a bat, a ball, just for your recreation.
A boat, a car, a bus, a plane! Do have a good vacation!

QUEEN: Remember that, Your Majesty. We must all go on a vacation in August. (NURSEMAID *places toys on table.*)

JESTER:
"The goldenrod is yellow,
The corn is turning brown."
And that's a sign September
Is coming back to town!

SEPTEMBER (*Carrying pad of paper, quill pen, and bottle of ink*):
When you grow up to be a man
You must be very wise;
And learn the secrets of the earth,
Of mountains, seas and skies.
You must not be a lazy boy
Or dare to play the fool,
So here's some paper, pen and ink,
For you to use in school.

QUEEN: Thank you, September. I hope the Baby New

GIFTS FOR THE NEW YEAR

Year will use your gifts wisely. (NURSEMAID *places gifts on table.*)

JESTER:
October's bright blue weather
Is always full of cheer.
And now she brings her present
For little Prince New Year.

OCTOBER (*Carrying basket filled with fruit and nuts, corn, gourds, etc.*):
The richest store of autumn's gold,
Young prince, I bring to thee:
The bounties of the harvest,
The fruits of field and tree.

KING: What a blessing! My son will never be hungry. (NURSEMAID *places basket on table.*)

JESTER:
They call her "Bleak November"
Because she's dressed in gray,
But Pilgrims chose this blessed month
To give their thanks and pray.

NOVEMBER (*Carrying songbook*):
For all your many blessings
Lift up your voice in praise.
To show your true thanksgiving
For healthy, happy days.
(*She hands songbook to* NURSEMAID, *who places it on table.*)

JESTER:
And now we greet December,
The last month of the year;

She brings a Christmas treasure,
Let's welcome her with cheer.

DECEMBER (*Carrying a silver star*):
This greatest gift I bring you,
A shining Christmas star;
May peace be with you always,
In lands both near and far.
(*There is a loud clamor offstage.*)

TICKETY-TOCK (*Harshly, from offstage*): Let me in! Let me in!

KING (*Rising*): Stop that noise! Let no one enter! Bar the door!

JESTER: It's Old-You-Know-Who!

TICKETY-TOCK (*Offstage*): You can't keep me out!

QUEEN (*Clutching* KING's *arm*): Oh, stop her! Stop her! Don't let her in!

TICKETY-TOCK (*Bursting in angrily*): Out of my way! Out of my way! (*She carries an alarm clock.*) Ha! Ha! Ha! Tried to keep me out, didn't you? You thought I wouldn't find this feast, eh?

ALL: The Time Witch! It's the Time Witch!

TICKETY-TOCK: Yes, it's the Time Witch, old Tickety-Tock herself, with a gift for our dear little Baby New Year.

QUEEN: Help! Help! Don't let her go near the baby!

TICKETY-TOCK (*Leaning over cradle and holding alarm clock close to the pillow*): Hear that, my little love? Hear that tick-tock, tick-tock. That's my present for you . . . a present from old Tickety-Tock.

KING: Take it away! Take it away!

GIFTS FOR THE NEW YEAR

TICKETY-TOCK (*As* CHANCELLOR *tries to take clock*): Keep your hands off that clock, you fat old Billy-kin! This is *my* gift to the new baby. It's the gift of time! May he use it well, for this time next year, on the very last stroke of twelve, this little baby will turn into a wrinkled old man and vanish from the face of the earth forever and ever!

ALL: Oh, no! Oh, no!

QUEEN: You can't do this to us!

TICKETY-TOCK: No one can stop Time, not even the King and Queen of the Calendar. In exactly twelve months, twelve hours, and twelve strokes of the clock, Baby New Year will be gone and forgotten. (MEMORY FAIRY *enters, carrying a big golden book and a golden wand*)

MEMORY FAIRY: Stop! Stop, you wicked old witch! I have a gift for the Baby New Year.

ALL: Who are you?

MEMORY FAIRY: My name is Memory. Alas, I cannot stop the Time Witch from making the Baby New Year disappear, but he will never be forgotten, thanks to this book of golden deeds.

KING: You are giving us hope, kind Fairy.

MEMORY FAIRY: Here in my golden book are listed all the years that will never be forgotten. Fourteen hundred ninety-two!

ALL: Columbus sailed the ocean blue!

MEMORY FAIRY: Sixteen hundred and twenty!

ALL: The Pilgrims found this land of plenty!

MEMORY FAIRY: Seventeen seventy-six, the year—

ALL: We won the freedom we hold dear!

MEMORY FAIRY: You see? You all remember those famous years and great events. And so it will be with our Baby New Year. Although he may be gone, he will never be forgotten, for he will live forever in the pages of history.

QUEEN: This is the greatest gift of all—the gift of being remembered.

(*Curtain*)

THE END

LINCOLN'S LIBRARY FINE

Characters

LINCOLN TAYLOR	TOM
MRS. TAYLOR, *his mother*	DICK
CAROL TAYLOR	BETTY HAYS
ANDY	GRACIE MOORE
PETE	MISS CRAWFORD

TIME: *A snowy February afternoon.*
SETTING: *The living room of* LINCOLN TAYLOR'S *home.*
AT RISE: LINC *is going through the contents of a toy box, scattering toys left and right as his friends,* ANDY, PETE, TOM *and* DICK, *wait impatiently on the sofa. All except* LINC *wear outdoor clothing.*

ANDY: Hurry up, Linc! We can't wait all day.
PETE: You've looked through that box three times!
TOM: If we don't go soon, the party will be over.
DICK: Why can't you look for that old book some other time?
LINC: Because Dad says I'm not to leave the house till I find it.
ANDY: Have you tried coaxing your mother? Maybe she'll let you go.
LINC: Not a chance!
TOM: Wow! I'm glad my parents don't make such a fuss about an old library book.

LINC: It isn't just an *old* library book, Tom. It's a brand-new one. Miss Crawford said I was first on the list.

DICK (*Moving to bookcase*): Maybe it's here some place. What's the name of it?

LINC: *Junior Jets*. And it's not there. I've had all those books off the shelves.

ANDY: Maybe you left it at school.

LINC: No such luck. I've searched high and low.

PETE: What about your bedroom?

LINC: I've already looked there, and Carol and Betty Hays are taking another look right now.

TOM (*Pulling off a chair cushion*): Sometimes things slide down under the chair cushions. (BOYS *pull cushions off sofa and chairs.*)

ANDY: Look what I found! A fountain pen!

LINC (*Putting it on desk*): That belongs to Dad. He was looking for it this morning.

DICK: And here's a set of car keys!

LINC: Mom was hunting all over the house for them last night.

PETE (*Holding up an object*): What's this?

LINC (*Looking at it*): A charm from Carol's bracelet. I'll bet she hasn't even missed it.

TOM (*Finding coin under a cushion*): Here's a penny. You can use it toward your library fine.

LINC: I'll need a lot more pennies. That book is weeks overdue now. The library sent a notice yesterday. That's how Mom and Dad found out I had lost it.

(CAROL TAYLOR *and* BETTY HAYS *enter.*)

CAROL (*Seeing toys and cushions scattered about*):

What goes on here? This room looks as if a cyclone struck it.

ANDY: We're hunting for Linc's library book.

CAROL: You'd better straighten things up before Mother gets back.

BETTY (*Replacing cushions*): I'll help.

PETE (*Holding out charm to* CAROL): Is this yours?

CAROL: Oh, it's a charm from my bracelet. Where did you find it?

PETE: Under one of the cushions.

LINC: Some people have all the luck.

BETTY: I'm sure we'll find your book, if we just keep looking.

DICK: But there isn't time. We'll be late for the party.

LINC: You'd better go without me. I'll never find it.

CAROL: Have you looked in the basement?

BETTY: Maybe it got mixed up with the newspapers and magazines.

LINC: That's an idea. I'll give it a try. (*He exits.*)

BETTY: What are we going to do? The whole party will be a flop without Linc. Carol, can't you coax your mother to let him go?

CAROL: I doubt it. When Mom says *no*, she means *no!* (MRS. TAYLOR *enters in coat and hat, carrying grocery bag.*)

MRS. TAYLOR: I think somebody's talking about me. What's the problem?

ANDY: Mrs. Taylor, please let Linc come to the party!

BETTY: It's a surprise party for him, Mrs. Taylor, a birthday surprise party!

MRS. TAYLOR (*Setting grocery bag on table*): Oh, dear! That's too bad. Carol, you didn't tell me the party was for Linc.

CAROL: It was a secret.

BETTY: We planned it at school. We thought it would be fun to celebrate Linc's birthday and Lincoln's birthday at the same time, since they were both born on February 12th, and they have the same name.

PETE: And now he says he can't go unless he finds that lost book.

MRS. TAYLOR: That's right, Pete. He's entirely too careless.

TOM: Then we might as well go without him. (CHILDREN *prepare to leave*.)

ANDY: It won't be much fun without Linc.

MRS. TAYLOR: I'm sorry, children, but that's how it is.

CAROL: Maybe I should stay home, too.

MRS. TAYLOR: Nonsense, Carol. (*Removes hat and coat*) Here, please hang up my things in the hall closet. And be sure to wear your boots.

CAROL: I thought the snow was melting.

MRS. TAYLOR: It can't melt too fast for me! I'll be glad to see the sidewalks again after these weeks of snow. Now run along and enjoy yourself.

BETTY: What about Gracie Moore? Aren't we going to wait for her?

CAROL: Oh, Gracie's always late. We'll probably meet her on the way.

MRS. TAYLOR: Goodbye, children. Have a good time.

ALL (*As they exit*): Good-bye, Mrs. Taylor.

LINC (*Entering from opposite side of stage*): It's not there. (*Sees* MRS. TAYLOR) Oh, hello, Mom. Where is everybody?

MRS. TAYLOR: They couldn't wait any longer, Linc.

LINC: Doggone that old book! It's spoiled all my fun!

MRS. TAYLOR: No use blaming the book. You spoiled your own fun, Linc. (*Picking up grocery bag*) I might as well put my groceries away. (*Finds car keys on table*) Oh, here are my car keys! How did they get there?

LINC: Dick found them under a chair cushion, and Andy found Dad's fountain pen, and Pete found a charm from Carol's bracelet! I'm not the only one in this house who loses things.

MRS. TAYLOR: It's bad enough to lose our own things, but your father and I are worried because you don't take care of other people's property. That library book isn't yours.

LINC: But suppose I *never* find it! Will I have to stay in the house forever?

MRS. TAYLOR: We'll talk about that later. (*Exits with bag*)

LINC (*Growling to himself*): I still don't see why I have to stay in the house. I've looked every place there is to look. (*Doorbell rings. Calling*) Come in. The door's open. (GRACIE MOORE *enters carrying the remains of a soaking-wet book, the cover of which is almost torn off.*)

GRACIE: Hello, Linc. Sorry I'm late. I'll bet the others have gone without me.

LINC: Oh, hello, Gracie. Yes, they've all left. (*Seeing book*) What's that? Gracie Moore, where did you get that book?

GRACIE: I just happened to see it on top of the stone gatepost at the bus stop. It has a library card in it with your name.

LINC (*Seizing it*): *Junior Jets*! Look at it! It's ruined!

GRACIE: It must have been lying there all through this deep snow.

LINC: What am I going to do? What am I going to do?

GRACIE: You'll have to return it to the library.

LINC: I can't take it back like this. Miss Crawford will be furious.

GRACIE: She sure will! One time my baby brother tore a page out of a library book and ate it. Miss Crawford almost had a fit! I'll bet she has two fits when she sees this.

LINC: She's not going to see it. (*Thrusts book into* GRACIE's *arms*) Here . . . take it.

GRACIE: But I don't want it. What will I do with it?

LINC: Hide it in another snowbank. I'd rather stay in this house until I'm in college than face Miss Crawford with that book.

GRACIE: But you'll have to face her some time.

LINC: I'll never set foot in that library again.

GRACIE: You could never stay away from books. You like to read almost as much as you like to eat.

LINC: I don't care. I just can't take that book back to Miss Crawford.

GRACIE: I thought you had more spunk!

LINC: Well, I haven't. Not when it comes to Miss Crawford.
GRACIE: After all, you can pay for the book.
LINC: You mean my dad can pay for it. Where would I ever get that much money?
GRACIE: What's wrong with working for it? You're no better than the other Lincoln, are you?
LINC: What are you talking about?
GRACIE: I'm talking about Abraham Lincoln, the President of the United States . . . the man you were named for.
LINC: And what does he have to do with my library book?
GRACIE: The same thing happened to him, you know.
LINC: How could it? There weren't any libraries in Lincoln's day.
GRACIE: And hardly any books either. Don't you remember the story Miss Martin read to us? Lincoln borrowed a book from a neighbor and stuck it in between the logs in the loft where he slept.
LINC: I still don't see what it has to do with me.
GRACIE: That night there was a terrible rain, and in the morning, when Lincoln woke up, the book was ruined.
LINC: So?
GRACIE: So Lincoln had to take the book back to this man—let me see—what was his name? Josiah something . . . Josiah Crawford.
LINC: Crawford! The same as Miss Crawford, the librarian. Gracie, you're making this up.

GRACIE: I am *not* making it up. You must have been absent when Miss Martin read us the story.

LINC: So what happened?

GRACIE: Well, he was very angry—even more than Miss Crawford will be, because books were very scarce in those days, and he knew Lincoln didn't have the money to pay for it.

LINC: What did Mr. Crawford do?

GRACIE: He made Lincoln work three days husking corn to pay for it.

LINC: You know very well Miss Crawford doesn't have any corn to be husked.

GRACIE: But you could do other things. There ought to be plenty of odd jobs around the library. At least you could try.

LINC: Maybe you have an idea, Gracie. Maybe I could try—if only I weren't so scared of Miss Crawford.

GRACIE: That other Lincoln was scared, too. But he took the book back all the same and did everything he could to make things right.

LINC: Is that a true story, Gracie?

GRACIE: Miss Martin read it to us just the way I told it to you.

LINC: Thanks, thanks a lot for telling me. Now you'd better hurry on to the party or you'll miss all the fun.

GRACIE: I hate to go without you, Linc.

LINC: I wouldn't have a good time anyhow with this on my mind. You'd better get going.

GRACIE (*Holding book*): Do you still want me to throw this in a snowbank?

LINC: No, not any more. Leave it here. And thanks a million for finding it. (*Takes book*)

GRACIE: You're welcome. And, Linc, if Miss Crawford makes a scene, just try to pretend you're really Abraham Lincoln, and maybe you won't be so scared.

LINC: I'll try, Gracie. So long. (GRACIE *exits*.)

MRS. TAYLOR (*Entering from opposite side*): I thought I heard someone at the door.

LINC: It was Gracie, Gracie Moore. She . . . she found my book!

MRS. TAYLOR: Oh, Linc, that's wonderful! I'm so glad! (*Suddenly she sees book. She points to it in horror.*) Lincoln Taylor! Don't tell me that thing is your library book!

LINC: It sure is, Mom. Gracie found it on top of the stone gatepost by the bus stop. It was buried in the snow.

MRS. TAYLOR: Oh, Linc, how could you have been so careless! Look at it! A brand-new book, utterly ruined. Wait till your father sees this!

LINC: He won't see it, Mom, because I'm going to take it back to the library right away.

MRS. TAYLOR: Do you have any idea how much a book like this will cost? Your father will have to pay for it.

LINC: No, he won't, Mom. I'm going to find a way to pay for it myself. (*Lays book on table*) Maybe you can find something to wrap this in while I get my coat. (*Exits.*)

MRS. TAYLOR (*As doorbell rings*): Now who could that

be? (*Goes to door*) Why, Miss Crawford! This *is* a surprise. Do come in.

MISS CRAWFORD (*Entering*): I just stopped by on my way to work to talk to you about Linc's library book, Mrs. Taylor. I suppose you got the overdue notice.

MRS. TAYLOR: Yes, we did, and we're very sorry about it.

MISS CRAWFORD: I was hoping that Linc could return the book today. We have so many calls for books about jets.

MRS. TAYLOR: Linc is getting ready to go to the library now.

MISS CRAWFORD: Good. I can save him a trip. (LINC *enters.*)

LINC: Hurry up, Mom. I want to get this over with as soon as possible. I know Miss Crawford will hit the ceiling. (*Sees* MISS CRAWFORD) Holy smoke! Miss Crawford!

MISS CRAWFORD: You seem shocked to see me, Linc. Maybe you'd better tell me why I'm going to hit the ceiling.

LINC: Well . . . er—you see—that is . . .

MRS. TAYLOR: Linc is trying to tell you that he has found his lost library book.

MISS CRAWFORD: Splendid! There are so many boys who can hardly wait to read it! If you'll give it to me, I'll put it on the shelf this afternoon.

LINC: Well—er—before I give it to you, I'd like to ask you a question.

MISS CRAWFORD: Go right ahead.

LINCOLN'S LIBRARY FINE

LINC: Are you any relation to Josiah Crawford?

MISS CRAWFORD: Josiah Crawford. I don't believe I ever heard of him.

LINC: He wasn't a librarian exactly, but he had a few books and he lent one to Abraham Lincoln.

MISS CRAWFORD: Oh, now I remember—a very touching story. Lincoln was careless with the book, and it was ruined by the rain coming through the chinks of the log cabin.

LINC: I'm glad you remembered the story, because almost the same thing happened to *Junior Jets*. Only it was snow, not rain. (*Hands her the book*)

MISS CRAWFORD: Good grief! My brand-new book! Ruined, utterly ruined! Young man, what are you going to do about this?

LINC: I'd like to pay for the book, Miss Crawford. I want to pay for it the same way Lincoln did—by working for you.

MISS CRAWFORD: Working! What could you do?

LINC: I could shovel snow, or help clean up, or run errands, or carry magazines. And I'd work every afternoon after school and all day Saturdays.

MISS CRAWFORD: I don't know. The library has very strict rules.

MRS. TAYLOR: Perhaps we could replace the book, Miss Crawford, and Linc could work for you until it is paid for.

LINC: Please let me, Miss Crawford.

MISS CRAWFORD: Very well, Linc. We'll give it a try.

LINC: Oh, good! Thanks, Miss Crawford. I guess I'm

not very much like Abe Lincoln, but I do love books, and I'll never be careless with another one!

MISS CRAWFORD: I'm sure Josiah Crawford was very proud of that other Lincoln. Maybe some day I'll be just as proud of you.

LINC: I hope so, Miss Crawford.

MRS. TAYLOR: And I'm proud of you right this minute, Linc. I'm sure you'll never forget this birthday, will you? (*Offstage singing of "Happy Birthday" is heard.* CHILDREN *enter carrying assorted packages, one of which is a birthday cake in a box.*)

PETE: Since you couldn't come to the party, Linc, we've brought the party to you.

BETTY (*Setting cake box on table and opening it*): And here's the best part, the birthday cake.

CAROL: Hurry up and light the candles, Linc.

LINC (*As* BETTY *hands him the matches*): Wow! What a surprise! (*Lights candles*)

MRS. TAYLOR: We didn't expect to be in on a birthday party, did we, Miss Crawford?

MISS CRAWFORD: Many happy returns of the day, young man!

CHILDREN: Make a birthday wish!

LINC: My birthday wish has already come true. I've found my library book, and I've found a way to pay the fine—thanks to Abraham Lincoln! (ALL *gather around* LINC *as he prepares to blow out the candles, and the curtain falls.*)

THE END

PRINCESS LONELY HEART

Characters

KING OF HEARTS
QUEEN OF HEARTS
PRINCESS LONELY HEART
6 KITCHEN MAIDS
3 LADIES-IN-WAITING
4 MESSENGERS OF KING
CUPID
FOOTMAN
PARTY GUESTS
2 PAGES

SCENE 1

TIME: *The day before Valentine's Day.*
SETTING: *The throne room of the King and Queen of Hearts. There are two thrones and a small table is beside each one. There is a crown on each table. In front of the Queen's throne is a larger table.*
AT RISE: *The* QUEEN *is sitting on her throne, cutting out cookies on the table, with a heart-shaped cutter. The* KING *is pacing up and down, his hands behind his back.* 6 KITCHEN MAIDS *stand beside the* QUEEN'S *throne.*

KING: I don't like it! I just don't like it!
QUEEN: What is it that you don't like, my love?
KING: I don't like to see you making cookies in the throne room. It isn't proper.

QUEEN: But where else can I make my cookies? It would not be proper for a queen to go into the kitchen.

KING: Why must you make cookies at all? We have hundreds of servants.

QUEEN: But only the Queen of Hearts knows the recipe for the royal Valentine cookies. (*Hands cookie tin to* 1ST MAID) Here is another panful. Please rush these to the royal oven and make sure they don't burn.

1ST MAID: Yes, your Majesty. (*She exits.*)

KING: I still don't like it! I just don't like it!

QUEEN (*Taking mixing bowl and spoon from* 2ND MAID): Never mind, my love. This is the last batch. (*To* 2ND MAID) A little more flour, please. (2ND MAID *shakes in some flour.* QUEEN *turns to* 3RD MAID) Another spoonful of sugar, please. (*To* 4TH MAID) A wee drop of vanilla, please. (*To* 5TH MAID) Just a pinch of salt. (*To* 6TH MAID) Now a handful of raisins. (*As* 6TH MAID *drops them in*) Whoops! One too many! Take out that last one. (1ST MAID *enters.* QUEEN *turns to her*) A dash of cinnamon and two shakes of nutmeg. (1ST MAID *obeys.*) Watch out, you careless girl! You gave three shakes instead of two.

1ST MAID: I'm sorry, your Majesty.

QUEEN: Never mind. Now help me count. I must beat the batter exactly twenty strokes.

ALL (*As* QUEEN *beats cookie batter*):
One, two, how do we do?
Three, four, beat some more.
Five, six, lots of licks,

Seven, eight, we can't wait.
Nine, ten, now again.
(*They repeat rhyme, ending with "Nine, ten, that's the end!"*)
QUEEN: Oh, dear! My arm is so tired.
KING: I don't like it! I just don't like it!
QUEEN: Stop saying that over and over again. I'm tired of hearing it.
KING: I don't see any sense to this cookie business.
QUEEN: But we must have the cookies ready for the children. Tomorrow is St. Valentine's Day.
KING: I don't like it! I don't like it at all!
QUEEN: This is one of your don't-like-it days, my love. You'll feel better after you eat some cookies.
KING: No, I won't. Your cookies always give me indigestion.
QUEEN: What a thing to say! (*To* 2ND MAID) Take this batter to the kitchen. Tell the cook to roll out the rest of the cookies and put them in the oven.
2ND MAID: Very well, your Majesty. (*She exits, holding bowl.*)
QUEEN (*Handing rolling pin covered with silver foil to* 3RD MAID): Make sure she uses the silver rolling pin.
3RD MAID: Yes, your Majesty. (*She exits.*)
KING: And take the rest of these things to the kitchen where they belong.
MAIDS: Yes, sire. (MAIDS *remove worktable, and exit.*)
KING (*Moving to throne*): Now, this is better. Put on your crown so you'll look like a queen.

QUEEN (*Putting on crown*): Why don't you put yours on?

KING: Because it gives me a headache.

QUEEN: It's not your crown that gives you a headache. It's your bad temper.

KING (*Putting on crown and seating himself on throne*): Maybe you're right.

QUEEN: Are you worried about something?

KING: Yes. I am worried about our daughter, Princess Merry Heart.

QUEEN (*With a sigh*): Ah, yes! So am I.

KING: She isn't merry any more.

QUEEN: I know. She does nothing but sit by herself all day long.

KING: Yesterday I heard the children calling her a name.

QUEEN: How dreadful! What did they call her?

KING: They were calling her Princess Lonely Heart, because she has no friends.

QUEEN: Maybe she is ill.

KING: In that case, we should see the royal doctor.

QUEEN (*Rising*): Let us go at once.

KING (*Rising*): I will order the royal coach.

QUEEN: And I will join you at the palace gate. (KING *and* QUEEN *exit right, as* PRINCESS *enters left with* 3 LADIES-IN-WAITING.)

1ST LADY (*Offering golden ball to* PRINCESS): Here is your golden ball, Princess. We can play a game in the palace garden.

PRINCESS: I don't want to play ball. Take it away.

2ND LADY: I have brought your favorite doll, Princess.

See how pretty she looks. (*Offers doll* to PRINCESS)
PRINCESS: I don't want my doll. Take it away.
3RD LADY (*With tea tray*): I have made some tea, Princess. We can have a tea party.
PRINCESS: I don't want any tea. Take it away.
1ST LADY: What would you like to play, Princess?
PRINCESS: I don't want to play anything. Please leave me alone.
2ND LADY: But we can't do that.
PRINCESS: Oh, yes, you can. All I want is to be alone.
LADIES: But, Princess . . .
PRINCESS: Please do as I command. Go!
LADIES (*Curtsying*): Very well, Princess. (*They exit. Then* PRINCESS *runs to* KING's *throne and pushes buzzer on arm of chair.* FOOTMAN *enters.*)
FOOTMAN (*Bowing*): You rang for me, Princess?
PRINCESS: Yes, I did. Has the mail come yet?
FOOTMAN: Yes, your Highness.
PRINCESS: Was there anything for me?
FOOTMAN: No, your Highness.
PRINCESS: Are you sure?
FOOTMAN: Quite sure, your Highness. Is there anything else?
PRINCESS: No, thank you. You may go.
FOOTMAN (*With a bow*): Very well, your Highness. (*Exits.*)
PRINCESS: Not a single valentine! Oh, dear! I'm afraid I'm going to cry. (*Sits on platform of throne and cries*)

MESSENGERS (*Calling softly offstage*): Princess Lonely Heart! Princess Lonely Heart!
PRINCESS: I hear someone calling.
MESSENGERS (*Offstage, calling louder*): Princess Lonely Heart! Princess Lonely Heart!
PRINCESS (*Rising*): Who's there? Who's there? (4 MESSENGERS *enter*.) Who are you? What do you want?
MESSENGERS: We want Princess Lonely Heart.
PRINCESS: There's no one here by that name.
1ST MESSENGER: Oh, yes, there is.
2ND MESSENGER: *You* are the Princess Lonely Heart.
PRINCESS: I am not! My name is Merry. I am Princess Merry Heart.
3RD MESSENGER: If you are merry, why are you crying?
PRINCESS: That is none of your business. Now get out of here at once.
1ST MESSENGER: You are all alone here.
4TH MESSENGER: So you *must* be Princess Lonely Heart.
PRINCESS: And what if I am? Who are you?
1ST MESSENGER: We are Cupid's messengers.
2ND MESSENGER: And we have a message for you.
PRINCESS: I don't want to hear it. Go away.
3RD MESSENGER: King Cupid knows that you are a lonely, unhappy little girl.
4TH MESSENGER: He knows that you were not invited to any parties.
1ST MESSENGER: He knows that you did not get any valentines.
PRINCESS: If King Cupid knows so much, maybe he knows what I can do about it.

4TH MESSENGER: That is our message.
PRINCESS: Maybe I will listen after all.
2ND MESSENGER: King Cupid wants you to be happy.
3RD MESSENGER: He wants you to have friends.
4TH MESSENGER: He wants you to live up to your name, Princess Merry Heart.
PRINCESS: But how? What can I do? I am the loneliest little girl in the world.
3RD MESSENGER: Oh, no, you're not.
1ST MESSENGER: You have a mother and father who love you.
2ND MESSENGER: You have loyal servants who love you.
3RD MESSENGER: And you could have hundreds of friends to love you.
PRINCESS: How? Tell me how.
1ST MESSENGER: If you would have your share of friends,
2ND MESSENGER: To love you all your days,
3RD MESSENGER: You first must learn to *be* a friend,
4TH MESSENGER: And practice friendship's ways!
PRINCESS: But no one needs me for a friend. All of the other children have friends of their own.
1ST MESSENGER: That is not true, Princess.
2ND MESSENGER: There are many boys and girls as lonely as you are.
3RD MESSENGER: Some are even lonelier.
4TH MESSENGER: They are waiting for a friend just like you.
PRINCESS: But who are they? Where can I find them?
1ST MESSENGER: They are not too far away, Princess.

2ND MESSENGER: When you really want to *be* a friend, you won't have far to search.

3RD MESSENGER: Just try looking around and asking questions.

4TH MESSENGER: And now we must go.

MESSENGERS (*Together*):
From Lonely Heart to Merry Heart
Is just a step away.
We hope St. Valentine's will be
A happy, happy day.
(MESSENGERS *exit.*)

PRINCESS:
If you would have your share of friends,
To love you all your days,
You first must learn to *be* a friend,
And practice friendship's ways.
If I want to learn to be a friend, maybe I could begin by having a party of my own! (KING *and* QUEEN *enter, each with large medicine bottle.* PRINCESS *runs to them.*) Mother! Father! I'm so glad you're here. I have a wonderful, wonderful plan.

QUEEN (*Feeling her forehead*): Do you have a fever?

PRINCESS: No, no! I'm just excited over the Valentine Party I'm having tomorrow.

KING *and* QUEEN: The what?

PRINCESS: The Valentine Party for my new friends. Oh, please say I may have a party.

KING: Nothing would please me more.

QUEEN: But who are your guests, my child? Who are your new friends?

PRINCESS: I don't know their names—not yet. But they are all little lonely hearts like me.

KING: You'll not be a lonely heart any longer, daughter, not after you take this medicine.

QUEEN: The doctor says this will cure your loneliness and make you as merry as ever.

PRINCESS: I don't need any medicine, Mother. Throw it away. (*Puts medicine bottles on table*) Now, please come and sit down. (*Leads* KING *and* QUEEN *to thrones*) I want you to help me with my guest list.

QUEEN: I don't know where to begin.

PRINCESS: Let's start with the lonely boys and girls in the village. Try to think of some.

KING: I guess the Blossom children are lonely. They just moved here from another city and haven't had time to make friends.

PRINCESS: Good. I will send each one of them a valentine and invite them to my party.

QUEEN: The Murphy children had to refuse all of their invitations because they have no party dresses.

PRINCESS: We'll send them two of my prettiest dresses at once, with an invitation to come to the palace party.

KING: Many of the children in the hospital are lonely.

PRINCESS: I will make a valentine for every child, and those who are well enough to travel can come to the party.

KING: I'll send the royal coach for them tomorrow afternoon.

PRINCESS: Thank you, Father.

QUEEN: There are some children in the village who have no mothers and fathers, no brothers and sisters.
PRINCESS: Oh, Mother, I do hope you baked enough cookies for all of them.
QUEEN: I baked hundreds of cookies. But what's come over you, child?
PRINCESS: Nothing, Mother, nothing . . . except that I am learning how to be a friend. I can hardly wait till tomorrow because I know I'm going to have the merriest heart in the whole kingdom. (*Curtain*)

* * * * *

SCENE 2

TIME: *The next day.*
SETTING: *Same as Scene 1.*
BEFORE RISE: 2 PAGES *enter before curtain from opposite sides, each holding half of an enormous cardboard heart. When they meet at center stage, they put the two halves together to read, "The Next Day." Then the curtain opens.*
AT RISE: *The room is crowded with* PARTY GUESTS. *Each* GUEST *wears a red cardboard heart hung around his neck by a string. The hearts are all shapes and sizes. The* KING *and* QUEEN *sit on their thrones.* PRINCESS MERRY HEART *stands on the platform slightly below them. The worktable is downstage left, and has four plates of cookies on it.*

ALL (*Singing to the tune of "Did You Ever See a Lassie?"*):
  Did you ever see a Princess, a Princess, a Princess,
  Did you ever see a Princess so merry and gay?
  For her friends are our friends,
  And our friends are her friends.
  Did you ever see a happier
  Valentine's Day?

KING (*Interrupting applause after song*): And now it is time for the main event of the afternoon—the prize awards for the Heart Contest. Her Majesty, the Queen, will award a plate of her Royal Cookies to the winner of each class. (*Applause*) And now . . . the winners! For the Biggest Heart, the prize goes to (*Announces name.* GUEST *with the biggest cardboard heart steps forward.*)

QUEEN (*Handing him plate of cookies*): Congratulations! (*More applause*)

KING: The winner of the Smallest Heart prize is (*Announces name*).

QUEEN (*Giving cookies to* GUEST): Congratulations! (*Applause*)

KING: The prize for the most beautiful heart goes to (*Announces name*).

QUEEN (*Giving cookies to* GUEST): Congratulations! (*Applause*)

KING: And here is (*Announces name*) to claim the award for the Funniest Heart.

QUEEN (*To* GUEST *with heart bearing a funny picture*): Congratulations!

KING: And now, my friends, that is the end of the contest. On with the games! (*Offstage bugle call is heard as* 4 MESSENGERS *enter*.)

1ST MESSENGER: We beg your pardon, King of Hearts,
The contest's not yet done.

2ND MESSENGER: We hate to interrupt you,
But there is more to come.

3RD MESSENGER: We have another prize to give
For the kindest heart and true.

4TH MESSENGER: We cannot name the winner.
(*To* GUESTS) The choice is up to you!

ALL: Princess Merry Heart! Princess Merry Heart!

1ST MESSENGER: For you, the Princess Merry Heart.
(*Hands her golden bow and arrow*)

2ND MESSENGER:
Little Cupid, king of love,
Sends you this valentine,
A bow and arrow like his own,
His little friendship sign.

3RD MESSENGER: He shoots his arrows everywhere,
Though you may never see one.

4TH MESSENGER: You've learned it's good to have a friend,
But better far to be one!

ALL: Long live Princess Merry Heart! Hurrah! Hurrah! Hurrah! (*Curtain falls as* GUESTS *repeat song* "Did You Ever See a Princess?")

THE END

WASHINGTON'S LUCKY STAR

Characters

COLONEL GEORGE ROSS	PRUDENCE WEST
MR. ROBERT MORRIS	BENJAMIN WEST
GENERAL GEORGE WASHINGTON	PATIENCE BLAKE
	EDWARD BLAKE
MISTRESS BETSY ROSS	MISTRESS BLAKE

TIME: *1777.*

SETTING: *The home of Betsy Ross, in Philadelphia.*

AT RISE: MISTRESS ROSS *is seated by a sewing table, on which there are some scraps of material, scissors, and several sheets of paper.* BENJAMIN *is seated on a large blanket chest.* PRUDENCE *and* PATIENCE *are on footstools.*

PRUDENCE: I'm sure I have it right this time. (*Unfolding paper she has just cut*) See my star! (*Looks in amazement at the lopsided result*) Oh, dear me! Something went wrong.

BENJAMIN: Ha! Ha! You call *that* a star!

PRUDENCE: I'm sure I did it just the way Mistress Ross showed us.

PATIENCE: You must have made a mistake. Look at mine. (*Unfolds her paper only to find one just as bad*) I don't see how you do it! (*Crumples paper and throws it on floor*) I give up!

MISTRESS ROSS: Fie, fie! And your name is Patience.
BENJAMIN: Girls are always clumsy. Now, watch me. (*Unfolds his star which is, if possible, worse than the other two.* ALL *laugh.*)
MISTRESS ROSS: You spoke too soon, Master Benjamin.
BENJAMIN: It looks so easy when you do it.
MISTRESS ROSS: I have had much practice.
PRUDENCE: Please show us again, Mistress Ross, from the very beginning.
MISTRESS ROSS: Very well, Prudence. And this time, we will all do it together—step by step. (*Note: Directions for cutting a five-pointed star may be found in many books on paper sculpture, as well as in standard reference books.* ALL *take another sheet of paper.*) You fold your paper, so. (*They follow her example.*) Then you fold it so . . . and so. . . . Now you are ready to cut. (*As* BENJAMIN *is about to cut his*) No, no, Master Benjamin! Place your scissors here, like this. Now, all together . . . cut! (*Unfolds her paper and reveals a five-pointed star*) See, a fine, big star with five points. Now let me see yours. (*As each child unfolds paper and shows star*) Good! Good! Excellent! I knew you could do it.
PATIENCE: We always have fun when we come here.
PRUDENCE: I'd come every morning and every afternoon, but Mother says we keep you from your work.
BENJAMIN: She says we're a nuisance.
MISTRESS ROSS: Oh, no, you're not. I love to have you. Since I have no children of my own, I have to borrow the neighbors' children to keep me company.

BENJAMIN: I'm glad I'm a neighbor's child. Are we ready to cut out our gold stars now, Mistress Ross?

MISTRESS ROSS: Yes, I think you have mastered the pattern. (*Taking scraps of gold cloth from workbasket*) Here are the gold patches I promised you.

PRUDENCE (*As she prepares to cut a cloth star*): I do hope I get it right.

PATIENCE: My brother Edward wears his gold star all the time. He says it brings him luck.

BENJAMIN: Just wait till the rest of the Arch Street boys see our gold stars. They'll all want to join the Sons of Liberty.

PATIENCE: "Wear a Star for Washington!" That's our motto, Mistress Ross.

MISTRESS ROSS: And a very good motto, Prudence. General Washington needs the loyalty of every man, woman and child.

PATIENCE: But some of the people right here on Arch Street don't like him. They call him names!

BENJAMIN: They'd better not call him names when I'm around.

PATIENCE: My brother was in three fights last week with Johnny Edwards because Johnny called General Washington a cowardly traitor!

PRUDENCE: A cowardly *trader?* How could Washington be a trader when he's a soldier? What does he have to trade?

BENJAMIN: Silly! Johnny was calling him a *traitor*—not a trader!

PRUDENCE: It sounds the same.

BENJAMIN: It isn't the same at all. A traitor, t-r-a-i-t-o-r, is a man who betrays his country.
PRUDENCE: But General Washington is fighting for his country.
BENJAMIN: You girls just don't understand what's going on. England used to be our country, and people like Johnny Edwards and his folks think it is wrong to fight against the king.
PATIENCE: But we don't have a king any more—not since last July.
PRUDENCE: Not since Mr. Jefferson wrote the Declaration of Independence. Even a girl knows that much. (EDWARD BLAKE *rushes in. His hair is badly mussed. He has a black eye, and his jacket, on which a gold star is pinned, is badly torn.*)
EDWARD: Oh, Mistress Ross, I am in terrible trouble. Please help me.
PATIENCE: Edward Blake! You've been fighting again! Wait till Mother sees you! You'll catch it!
EDWARD: I know. That's why I hope Mistress Ross can mend my jacket.
MISTRESS ROSS: 'Tis very wrong of you to fight, Master Edward.
EDWARD: I just couldn't help it. Johnny Edwards and Henry Willis were making fun of General Washington again.
BENJAMIN: I hope you gave it to them good and proper.
EDWARD (*Grinning*): I did my best. But I could never have won against both of them without my gold star! It brings me luck every time.

PATIENCE: I hope it brings you luck when Mother takes her switch to you!

EDWARD: Please, Mistress Ross, if you will mend my jacket, Mother may forget about the switch.

MISTRESS ROSS: Take it off, and I'll see what I can do.

EDWARD (*Removes first the star and then the jacket. He pins the star on his shirt front*): You're such a fine seamstress that you can fix anything. (*Hands her the jacket*)

MISTRESS ROSS: I'm afraid I can't mend your black eye.

EDWARD: Johnny Edwards has two of them!

BENJAMIN: Good for you!

MISTRESS ROSS: A fist fight is a poor way to settle an argument. You should have tried to reason with your friends. (*Works on jacket*)

EDWARD: They are not my friends, and they won't listen to reason. They want us to lose the war so they can hang General Washington and every man who signed the Declaration of Independence.

BENJAMIN: They'd better not try it!

PRUDENCE: What would our country do without General Washington?

EDWARD: Johnny Edwards and Henry Willis just laugh at our country. They say it's not a real country anyhow, because we don't even have a flag.

PATIENCE: But we do have a flag. We have lots of flags.

PRUDENCE: All of our ships have flags. Mistress Ross just made one last month for the Pennsylvania Navy.

BENJAMIN: And there's the Pine Tree Flag, and the Rattlesnake Flag, and . . .

EDWARD: That's just the trouble. We have too many flags. Every colony has one of its own. But instead, we should have one big, beautiful flag for the whole country.

PATIENCE: I'll bet Mistress Ross could make one.

PRUDENCE: Why don't you, Mistress Ross?

BENJAMIN: That's a great idea.

MISTRESS ROSS: Such a flag would have to be ordered by the government. (*There is a knock at the door.* MISTRESS ROSS *rises and hands jacket to* EDWARD.) Try this on, Edward. I may have to patch it after all. I'll answer the door. (*She exits left.*)

PATIENCE: I do hope she's not having company. (*Moves left and glances offstage*) Quick, Edward! It's Mother! She must have found out about your fight.

EDWARD: Zounds! Does she have her switch?

PATIENCE: I can't see, but, oh, my goodness! You'd better hide! She's coming in. (EDWARD *clambers into the big chest and closes the lid as* MISTRESS BLAKE *enters with* MISTRESS ROSS.)

MISTRESS BLAKE (*Out of breath*): I tell you, it's General Washington himself, Mistress Ross. He and another gentleman are in the coach with Colonel Ross. The minute I saw your husband's uncle I knew they were coming here!

MISTRESS ROSS: But you must be mistaken about General Washington.

MISTRESS BLAKE: No, indeed. I saw him plainly, and I knew you would not want the children here with such important visitors.

MISTRESS ROSS: But why would General Washington be coming here?

MISTRESS BLAKE: I have no idea, but the coach is almost at your door. Come along, children, and hurry!

PATIENCE: But, Mother . . .

MISTRESS BLAKE: There's no time for questions! Hurry! We must leave at once, and by the back door. (*She shoos the children ahead of her and they exit right. Knock on door is heard and* MISTRESS ROSS *exits left.* EDWARD *raises the lid of the chest, starts to climb out, but ducks back again as* MISTRESS ROSS *re-enters with* COLONEL GEORGE ROSS, ROBERT MORRIS *and* GENERAL WASHINGTON.)

MISTRESS ROSS: I am deeply honored, gentlemen.

COLONEL ROSS (*To* GENERAL WASHINGTON): General Washington, may I present my niece, Mistress Betsy Ross.

GENERAL WASHINGTON (*Bowing*): Colonel Ross has told me of your fine needlework, and of your courage in running your husband's business since his death. Our country has need of women such as you.

MISTRESS ROSS (*With a curtsy*): Thank you, your Excellency.

COLONEL ROSS: This gentleman is Mr. Robert Morris.

MISTRESS ROSS (*Curtsies again*): Every patriot is grateful for your contributions to the cause, Mr. Morris.

ROBERT MORRIS: Today we have come to ask *you* for help, Mistress Ross.

MISTRESS ROSS: I will give what I can, sir. You may be sure of that.

GENERAL WASHINGTON: We are asking for your skill, madam, not your money. Yesterday Congress adopted a design for our country's flag. Can you make it for us?

MISTRESS ROSS: I can try, sir.

ROBERT MORRIS: We have seen some fine examples of your flag-making.

MISTRESS ROSS: What is the design to be?

GENERAL WASHINGTON: Congress has decided the new flag must have thirteen stars on a field of blue. There must also be thirteen stripes of red and white.

MISTRESS ROSS: How are the stars to be arranged, sir?

GENERAL WASHINGTON (*Drawing a paper from his pocket*): I have a sketch of the design. (*They look at it together.*) What do you think of it?

MISTRESS ROSS: I like it very much. But since you ask my opinion, I think it would look better if the length were one-third more than the width.

GENERAL WASHINGTON: An excellent suggestion. Is there anything else?

MISTRESS ROSS: The stars are not arranged in any pattern, sir. Would it not be more pleasing if they formed a circle?

GENERAL WASHINGTON: What do you think, gentlemen?

ROBERT MORRIS: There is no end to a circle, and there can be no end to our new nation. It must go on and on.

COLONEL ROSS: A splendid thought, Mr. Morris.

GENERAL WASHINGTON: Have you any more ideas, Mistress Ross?

MISTRESS ROSS: The stars in this drawing have six points. I think that five-pointed stars would look much better.

GENERAL WASHINGTON: Isn't it difficult to cut a five-pointed star?

MISTRESS ROSS: Oh, no, sir. It is so simple that even a child can do it. Let me show you. (*Demonstrates with scissors and paper*) See!

GENERAL WASHINGTON: Excellent! We thank you, madam, for your fine ideas. We shall count on you to make our flag.

MISTRESS ROSS (*Curtsies*): I will do my best, your Excellency.

GENERAL WASHINGTON: I will have the artist make a new sketch and send it to you for a pattern.

MISTRESS ROSS: I will get to work as soon as I receive it. And before you go, gentlemen, I would like to show you a sample of red cloth I have on hand. You can tell me if it is the shade you want. (*Moves to chest where* EDWARD *is hiding*) I keep my supplies in this old chest. (*As she opens it,* EDWARD *stands up.* ALL *are amazed.*) Edward! Edward Blake! What are you doing in that chest?

GENERAL WASHINGTON (*As* EDWARD *steps out*): Is this a prisoner of war, madam?

ROBERT MORRIS: This young man must have been in a battle!

COLONEL ROSS: He looks as if he's had the worst of it.

EDWARD: Oh, no, sir. I won! You should see the other two boys!

GENERAL WASHINGTON: So you were outnumbered.

ROBERT MORRIS: It takes courage to fight, especially two against one.

COLONEL ROSS: You could have suffered a bad defeat, young man.

EDWARD: Oh, no, sir, not with my lucky star!

GENERAL WASHINGTON: What lucky star?

EDWARD (*Removing gold star from his shirt*): This one, sir. Mistress Ross is helping us make them. They are for the Sons of Liberty.

GENERAL WASHINGTON: The Sons of Liberty? And who are they, young man?

EDWARD: Well, sir, some of the boys on our street do not believe in our cause of liberty.

GENERAL WASHINGTON: Is that why you were fighting, Edward?

EDWARD: Yes, sir. They say we aren't a real nation, sir, because we don't even have a flag. But we'll show 'em, won't we, sir?

GENERAL WASHINGTON: I hope so, my boy, I hope so. At least, we'll show them that we have a real flag as soon as Mistress Ross can make one for us.

EDWARD: But most of us believe in our country even now, General Washington. That's why we made the gold stars, so everyone can see we're true patriots.

MISTRESS ROSS (*With her hand on* EDWARD'*s shoulder*): "Wear a Star for Washington"—that is their motto, sir.

GENERAL WASHINGTON: I am truly honored.

EDWARD: And the stars bring us luck, sir. They really do. Mine has helped me win four fights already.

GENERAL WASHINGTON: It is not good for small boys to fight, Edward. But I guess that is hard for you to believe when you see your fathers and brothers at war.

EDWARD: Yes, sir.

GENERAL WASHINGTON: Nevertheless, as one fighting man to another, I must honor you for your victories. I wish I had as many to my credit.

EDWARD: Oh, you will, sir. I know you will. Here, sir, please take my lucky star. (*Offers star*) If you wear it into battle, I know you will win.

GENERAL WASHINGTON (*Taking star*): Thank you, Edward. I need all the luck I can get against a powerful enemy.

EDWARD: I hope and pray it will bring you good fortune, sir.

GENERAL WASHINGTON: It has already brought me good fortune, Edward. Any general should thank his lucky stars for the love and loyalty of young Americans like yourself.

EDWARD: Thank you, sir.

GENERAL WASHINGTON: This flag which Mistress Ross is making will be like no other flag the world has ever seen. And it will be in your keeping. Promise me that you will always be ready to defend it with your life, your fortune, and your sacred honor.

EDWARD (*As he and* GENERAL WASHINGTON *shake hands*): I promise, sir. You can count on us. (*Curtain*)

THE END

THE WHITE HOUSE RABBIT

Characters

MR. RABBIT
PETER RABBIT
FLOPSY ⎤
MOPSY ⎥
THUMPER ⎬ *rabbits*
WHISKERS ⎥
COTTONTAIL ⎦
SCOTT HAYES
FANNY HAYES
PIERRE
MARIE
MRS. RUTHERFORD B. HAYES, *the First Lady*
CHARLES, *the White House gardener*

TIME: *1880.*

SETTING: *A corner of the White House lawn. Shrubbery at right conceals members of the cast. At left there is an outdoor garden bench, and mounted on a post pointing off left is a sign reading* TO THE WHITE HOUSE.

AT RISE: *A parade of* RABBITS *pulling toy wagons and wheelbarrows and carrying baskets, all filled with colored Easter eggs, is filing past* MR. RABBIT, *who stands center stage checking off each one in a notebook.*

MR. RABBIT (*To audience*): I suppose all of you have heard about the tradition of the Easter egg rolling on the lawn of the White House in Washington, D. C. . . . and I suppose some of you must have wondered how it all started.

Well, the history books say that Rutherford B. Hayes was the first President to welcome children to the White House lawn back in 1878—but what they don't say is *who* gave President Hayes the idea of the egg rolling. . . .

Today, we're going to tell you who really started it all. . . . (*To* RABBITS)
Hurry, hurry,
Scurry, scurry,
Rabbits on the run!

Hustle, bustle,
Bustle, hustle,
Get your day's work done!
PETER RABBIT (*Mopping his brow*):
With basket and barrow,
With wagon and cart,
Each Easter Bunny
Is doing his part!
THUMPER:

With yellow and purple,
And red, white, and blue,
We've dyed all the Easter eggs,
Just to please you!
MR. RABBIT: But we must have more! (*Louder*) More! More! *More!*
FLOPSY: Land sakes, Mr. Rabbit! We have more eggs now than we know what to do with!
MR. RABBIT: *I* know what to do with them.
THUMPER: What? What will you do with all these eggs?
MR. RABBIT: Never you mind! I have a plan!

COTTONTAIL: Tell us! Tell us!

MR. RABBIT: Not yet. It's a secret.

WHISKERS: We have a right to know.

COTTONTAIL: We won't haul any more eggs until you tell us.

MR. RABBIT: Come! Come! That's no way for Easter rabbits to act. You take this load of eggs behind those bushes and hide them in the grass. Then when you bring on your next load, I may have some news for you. Will you do that?

FLOPSY: It's a bargain! (RABBITS *continue across stage.* MR. RABBIT *stops* MOPSY, *the last in line.*)

MR. RABBIT: How many do you have in your basket, Mopsy?

MOPSY: Two dozen. And not a one of them cracked.

MR. RABBIT: Good!

THUMPER: Look at mine, Mr. Rabbit. I made them red, white, and blue, because they are White House Easter eggs.

MR. RABBIT: That was a fine idea, Thumper.

FLOPSY: And I made all of mine pink, because pink is the First Lady's favorite color.

MR. RABBIT: I am sure Mrs. Hayes will be pleased. Now hurry and hide these with the rest.

FLOPSY: Very well, Mr. Rabbit. But I don't understand why you want so many eggs this year. Little Scott and Fanny Hayes won't know what to do with all of these.

MR. RABBIT: Leave that to me, Flopsy. You just follow orders.

THE WHITE HOUSE RABBIT

FLOPSY: You're the boss, Mr. Rabbit. (*Exits*)

MR. RABBIT (*Figuring in notebook*): Thirty-two, forty-two, seventy-two, one hundred! Not enough!

SCOTT *and* FANNY (*Calling from offstage*): Mr. Rabbit! Mr. Rabbit! Where are you? (*They rush in.*)

MR. RABBIT: Here I am! Dear me, you look upset! What's the matter?

FANNY: We came to warn you.

SCOTT: It's Charles, the White House gardener. He hates rabbits.

FANNY: And he knows you're here.

MR. RABBIT: Don't worry. I know how to hide from gardeners.

FANNY: But you are in great danger.

SCOTT: You must leave at once.

MR. RABBIT: How can I leave before Easter? I have too much to do. Now tell me—have you asked your father about our surprise?

SCOTT: I meant to ask him last night, but he was so busy—

MR. RABBIT: This is a fine how-do-you-do! Here it is almost Easter, and you haven't yet asked your father about an Easter egg rolling on the White House lawn.

SCOTT: As President of the United States, he has more important things on his mind.

MR. RABBIT: How can you say such a thing? There's *nothing* more important. Don't you understand? We're making history.

FANNY: Please don't be angry, Mr. Rabbit. We'll ask him this afternoon. Honest!

MR. RABBIT: Well, you'd better hurry. Right now I have one hundred dozen eggs ready and waiting.

SCOTT: One hundred dozen!

MR. RABBIT: And we'll have twice that many by tomorrow—enough for all the children in Washington, D. C.

FANNY: Oh, Mr. Rabbit, it will be such fun. I can see all those boys and girls hunting Easter eggs on our lawn.

SCOTT: We never did anything like that when we lived in Ohio.

MR. RABBIT: And there's never been anything like it in Washington either. If you two do your part, we'll have a "famous first." Now run along.

SCOTT: We're on our way.

MR. RABBIT: And if you can't find your father, ask your mother.

FANNY: Not this morning, Mr. Rabbit. Mother is too upset about her Easter bonnet.

MR. RABBIT: What's the matter? Doesn't she like it?

SCOTT: She doesn't know. It hasn't come yet. And she's worried that it won't arrive in time.

FANNY: And besides, Charles, the gardener, wants to see her about you. He says you're ruining the garden.

MR. RABBIT: Nonsense! We Easter rabbits never hurt anybody's garden.

FANNY: Just the same, you'd better watch out for that gardener. He means business. Do promise you'll be careful.

MR. RABBIT: I'll be careful. Now, please hurry. (SCOTT

and FANNY *exit.*) Problems! Problems! Nothing but problems! (SCOTT *runs back onstage*)
SCOTT: Quick! Quick! Charles is coming this way. Run!
MR. RABBIT: Thanks. I'll go, but I shall return! (MR. RABBIT *hops off left as* SCOTT *exits right, and* CHARLES, *the gardener, enters.*)
CHARLES: If I could just get my hands on one of those pesky critters! I thought I saw one just a minute ago. He must be here somewhere. (*Pokes in shrubbery with rake, as* MARIE *and* PIERRE *enter.* PIERRE *carries a large, beribboned hatbox.*)
MARIE: Is it much further, Pierre?
PIERRE: I told you not to come. You always hate to walk in the sun.
MARIE: But I do want to see the White House and Mrs. Hayes. I've never seen a First Lady before.
PIERRE: And you might not see her now. Mamma said we may leave the hatbox with one of the servants.
MARIE: Let's sit down a minute, Pierre. It's so cool and shady here. And I want to look at the flowers.
PIERRE (*Placing hatbox on bench, and mopping his forehead*): All right. But we must not stay too long.
MARIE (*Stooping to pick flower*): Look at this pretty pink flower. I wonder what it is.
CHARLES: Here! Here! Here! Keep your fingers off those flowers, young lady!
MARIE: My goodness! You scared me! Who are you?
CHARLES: I am the White House gardener. And it's my business to take care of things here. We can't

have children running all over the grounds. Now off with you!

PIERRE: But we're *not* running all over the grounds. We're here on business.

MARIE: Important business. We are from La Belle Bonnet Shoppe, and we have come to deliver the First Lady's Easter bonnet.

CHARLES: Is that so?

PIERRE: Yes, sir. My mother designed it especially for Mrs. Hayes.

CHARLES: In that case, I suppose I cannot chase you out. But keep moving. (*Pointing*) The White House is that way. Now I must go tend to my lilies.

MARIE: Please, sir, may we go with you? We haven't seen any lilies since we left France.

PIERRE: We are homesick for the sight of lilies.

CHARLES: They are my favorite flower, too. Come along. I'll let you have a peek.

MARIE *and* PIERRE: Oh, thank you, thank you!

CHARLES: But mind you don't touch anything.

MARIE: We won't, we won't!

PIERRE: We'll be most careful. (*As* CHARLES, MARIE, *and* PIERRE *exit right, leaving hatbox on bench,* FLOPSY *and* MOPSY *enter left.*)

MOPSY: Did you find out why Mr. Rabbit wants so many eggs this year?

FLOPSY: Not a word. It must be a state secret.

MOPSY (*Pointing to hatbox*): Look! What is that?

FLOPSY: Maybe it has something to do with Mr. Rabbit's secret.

MOPSY: Let's look! (*They remove lid and lift out a fancy Easter bonnet covered with flowers.*)
FLOPSY: An Easter bonnet!
MOPSY: I'm going to try it on. (*Does so*)
FLOPSY: It's beautiful! Let me tie the ribbons under your chin. There!
MOPSY: How do I look?
FLOPSY: It's very becoming.
MOPSY: Let's go show Mr. Rabbit. Maybe he will let me wear it in our Bunny Parade. (FLOPSY *and* MOPSY *exit right with bonnet and hatbox, as* MRS. RUTHERFORD B. HAYES, *the First Lady, enters left with* SCOTT *and* FANNY.)
SCOTT: Please, Mother, we have something to ask you.
FANNY: It's very important.
MRS. HAYES: It will have to wait until I have spoken with the head gardener. He is bothered about the rabbits on the White House lawn.
FANNY: Oh, Mother, don't listen to him. He just doesn't like rabbits.
MRS. HAYES: They can be very harmful to plants and flowers.
SCOTT: Not *these* rabbits. They wouldn't hurt a thing.
MRS. HAYES: I must say, the garden looks lovely. I don't see any damage. (CHARLES *enters right with* MARIE *and* PIERRE.)
PIERRE: The lilies are beautiful, sir. Thank you for showing them to us.
CHARLES: I think they will be perfect by Easter morning. (*Sees* MRS. HAYES.) Ah, good morning, ma'am.

I'm sorry I was not here to greet you. I was just showing our lilies to these children from La Belle Bonnet Shoppe.

MRS. HAYES: La Belle Bonnet Shoppe? Then you must have brought my Easter bonnet.

PIERRE: Yes, ma'am. It's right here—(*Turns towards bench and finds box is gone*)

MARIE: Pierre! Pierre! The box is gone!

PIERRE: But I left it right there—right on that bench!

MARIE: It was all done up in a beautiful hatbox.

FANNY: You must be dreaming.

SCOTT: There was no hatbox there when we came.

PIERRE: But I put it there myself!

MRS. HAYES: My Easter bonnet! Where could it be?

CHARLES: There was no one else in the garden, ma'am. And we were gone only a few minutes.

PIERRE: Oh, Madame Hayes, please forgive us. I know we must seem very careless.

MARIE (*Starting to cry*): And it was so beautiful. Mamma went to such pains. Oh, dear, what shall we do?

MRS. HAYES: There, there! Don't cry, child. It must be here some place.

FANNY: Maybe it blew into the bushes.

SCOTT: Impossible. There's hardly any wind.

FANNY: Just the same, we can look, can't we? (*As* FANNY *and* SCOTT *start to search bushes,* MR. RABBIT *enters with hatbox.*)

MR. RABBIT: Excuse me. Is this what you are looking for?

ALL: The hatbox!

FANNY: Oh, Mr. Rabbit, where did you find it!

CHARLES (*Brandishing rake*): There he is! This time I'll get him! (*Grabs* MR. RABBIT *by coat collar*)

SCOTT (*Rushing to his rescue*): Let him go! Don't hurt him!

FANNY: He is our friend.

MR. RABBIT (*Freeing himself from* CHARLES, *he tips his hat to* MRS. HAYES *with a deep bow.*): With my compliments and best wishes for a happy Easter. (*Hands hatbox to* MRS. HAYES.)

MRS. HAYES: Thank you, thank you! (*Opening box and lifting out bonnet*) It is lovely. There will not be another one like it in all of Washington. (*To* PIERRE *and* MARIE) You may tell your mother I am well pleased.

MARIE (*With a curtsy*): Thank you, ma'am.

PIERRE: Thank you.

MRS. HAYES: As for you, Mr. Rabbit, how can I thank you for finding my beautiful Easter bonnet?

CHARLES: Please, ma'am, this is one of those pesky critters I was telling you about. He's good for nothing but a dish of rabbit stew.

SCOTT: Oh, please, Mother, don't let anyone hurt him.

FANNY: He's our friend, Mother.

CHARLES: The White House lawn will be ruined if it is overrun with rabbits.

SCOTT: Don't listen to him, Mother.

FANNY: These rabbits never hurt anything.

MR. RABBIT: If I may be allowed to say a word, ma'am. . . .
MRS. HAYES: You have my permission to speak.
MR. RABBIT: As you can see, I'm no ordinary rabbit. My card, ma'am. (*With a bow, he hands* MRS. HAYES *a card.*)
MRS. HAYES (*Reading*): "Mr. Easter Rabbit—Colored Eggs a Specialty."
CHARLES: Stuff and nonsense!
SCOTT: But he really is the Easter Rabbit, Mother.
FANNY: And he has one hundred dozen Easter eggs hidden on our lawn.
MRS. HAYES: One hundred dozen!
MR. RABBIT: With more to come, ma'am, as soon as my helpers finish dyeing them.
MRS. HAYES: But how can we possibly use all of those eggs at the White House?
SCOTT: That's what we wanted to ask you, Mother.
FANNY: Mr. Rabbit has the most wonderful idea.
MR. RABBIT: Perhaps I can explain, ma'am. There are many children in this city who believe in the Easter Rabbit, but they never have the pleasure of hunting for Easter eggs. Now, it is my idea, ma'am, that this big lawn would make an ideal place for an Easter egg rolling.
CHARLES: Never! Never! Not on the White House lawn. I won't stand for it.
MRS. HAYES: But the White House belongs to the people of the United States and to their children. Mr. Rabbit,

this is a fine idea. I am sure President Hayes will approve.

SCOTT *and* FANNY (*Hugging her*): Oh, Mother! Mother! Thank you! Thank you!

MR. RABBIT: Madam, you have won a place for yourself in history. You will always be remembered as the First Lady who started the custom of rolling eggs on the White House lawn!

MARIE: And may Pierre and I come too?

MRS. HAYES: Of course, my dears. The White House egg rolling must be for one and all. But are you sure, Mr. Rabbit, that you will have enough eggs?

MR. RABBIT: You may see for yourself, ma'am. (*Blows whistle and* RABBITS *enter again with baskets of Easter eggs.*)

RABBITS (*Singing to tune of "Skip to My Lou"*):
Rabbits at the White House,
What will they do?
Rabbits at the White House,
What will they do?
Rabbits at the White House,
What will they do?
What will they do for Easter?
They'll dye the Easter eggs
Red, white and blue,
They'll dye the Easter eggs,
Red, white and blue,
They'll dye the Easter eggs,
Red, white and blue,
That's what they'll do for Easter!

MR. RABBIT: Attention, fellow workers! I have an announcement from Mrs. Hayes, First Lady of the land!
MRS. HAYES: Tomorrow we will have an Easter egg rolling on the White House lawn.
SCOTT: For all the children of Washington, D. C.
MR. RABBIT: Well, what do you say? How do you like the idea?
RABBITS: Hooray! Hooray! Hooray!
CHARLES: I *still* don't like it!
MRS. HAYES, SCOTT *and* FANNY (*Singing to tune of "Skip to My Lou"*):
Rabbits at the White House,
CHARLES: Shoo! Shoo! Shoo!
MRS. HAYES, SCOTT *and* FANNY:
Rabbits at the White House,
CHARLES: Shoo! Shoo! Shoo!
MRS. HAYES, SCOTT *and* FANNY:
Rabbits at the White House,
CHARLES: Shoo! Shoo! Shoo!
MRS. HAYES, SCOTT *and* FANNY:
We'll have a jolly Easter!
ALL:
We'll roll the Easter eggs,
That's what we'll do.
Eggs of red and white and blue,
We'll roll them on the White House lawn,
That's what we'll do for Easter!
(*Curtain*)

THE END

BASKETS OR BONNETS

Characters

MOTHER NATURE
WEATHERMAN
MARY SUNSHINE
PANSY ⎫
JOHNNY-JUMP-UP ⎪
JACK-IN-THE-
   PULPIT ⎪
DAFFY ⎪
DILLY ⎬ *flowers*
IRIS ⎪
3 TULIP TRIPLETS ⎪
VIOLET ⎪
LILY ⎪
HYACINTH ⎭

PITTER ⎫ *raindrops*
PATTER ⎭
4 WINDS
MR. RABBIT
MRS. RABBIT
FLIPPITY ⎫
FLOPPITY ⎬ *little rabbits*
HIPPITY
HOPPITY ⎭
MARY
POLLY
RUTH
SUSIE

TIME: *The day before Easter.*
SETTING: *A park. Right stage is a counter stacked with small hatboxes. Left is a portable chalk board with a diagram labeled "Easter Weather." Up center is a large bush.*
AT RISE: MARY SUNSHINE *is behind the counter.* MOTHER NATURE *is trying to keep order in the line of flowers waiting for hats—*PANSY, JOHNNY-JUMP-UP, DAFFY, DILLY, IRIS, TULIP TRIPLETS, VIOLET, LILY, *and* HYACINTH.

The WEATHERMAN, *pointer in hand, is seated on a tall stool explaining the diagram in pantomime to the* WINDS *and the* RAINDROPS, *who are seated on the floor. Each of the* WINDS *has a long silver trumpet beside him.*

MOTHER NATURE: No pushing or shoving! Keep in line! (*As* JOHNNY-JUMP-UP *tries to push ahead*) Johnny-Jump-Up, you stay here where you belong—right behind Pansy.

PANSY: I'm so excited. I can hardly wait to see the color of my new bonnet.

MARY SUNSHINE: I have a purple one for you this year, Pansy.

PANSY (*Taking box*): Oh, thank you. Purple is my favorite color. (*Exits*)

JOHNNY-JUMP-UP (*Jumping up and down*): I'm next! I'm next!

MARY SUNSHINE: Yours is blue, Johnny. Same as last year.

JOHNNY-JUMP-UP: That suits me fine. I'll try it on right away. (*Starts to open box*)

MOTHER NATURE: You move along, Johnny. Daffy and Dilly are next.

JOHNNY-JUMP-UP: Oh, all right. (*Exits*)

MARY SUNSHINE (*With two boxes*): Two just alike for our daffodil twins.

DAFFY *and* DILLY: Thank you, Mary Sunshine. (*They exit.*)

MARY SUNSHINE (*With box*): This one is for Jack-in-the-Pulpit. Where is he? (JACK-IN-THE-PULPIT *runs in.*)

JACK-IN-THE-PULPIT: Here I am! Here I am!

MARY SUNSHINE: You're late this year.

JACK-IN-THE-PULPIT: Jack Frost held me up. (*Takes box*) Sorry I kept you waiting. (*Exits*)

MOTHER NATURE: And here is Iris, right on time.

IRIS: I do hope my new bonnet has a green ribbon.

MARY SUNSHINE (*Handing her box*): Mother Nature never makes a mistake. (IRIS *exits.*)

MOTHER NATURE: We have some bright colors for the Tulip Triplets.

MARY SUNSHINE (*Handing each one a box*): A red one, a yellow one, and a pink one.

TULIP TRIPLETS: We like bright colors—the brighter the better. (*Exit*)

MARY SUNSHINE: The next bonnet is for Violet. (*Leaning over counter*) Where is she?

VIOLET: Here I am.

MARY SUNSHINE: You are so tiny I could hardly see you.

MOTHER NATURE: But she's just as sweet and pretty as ever.

VIOLET: You shouldn't say such things, Mother Nature.

MOTHER NATURE: Don't be so modest, child. You know you are one of my sweetest spring flowers.

VIOLET: Thank you. (*Exits with box*)

MOTHER NATURE: And here is my lovely Lily. Goodness me! How you've grown!

LILY: All of us lilies are tall.

MARY SUNSHINE: Your new white bonnet will make you look even taller. (*Hands her a box.* LILY *exits.*)

MOTHER NATURE: I can tell the next one is Hyacinth. (*Sniffing*) Umm. She always smells so sweet.

HYACINTH: Thank you. I had a white bonnet last year, and a purple one the year before. I hope this one is pink.

MARY SUNSHINE (*Handing her box*): Just what you ordered.

HYACINTH: I can hardly wait to try it on. (*Exits*)

MARY SUNSHINE (*Holding up two boxes*): The Cardinals and Blue Jays have not stopped by for their topknots. Shall I deliver them?

MOTHER NATURE: Please do, and thank you for your help. (*As* MARY SUNSHINE *exits*) I am sure we will have a beautiful Easter day.

PITTER *and* PATTER (*Shouting and stamping their feet in front of the* WEATHERMAN): No fair! No fair! No fair!

PITTER: Boo hoo! Boo hoo! We want to come, too!

PATTER: Boo hoo! Boo hoo! I'm telling on you.

MOTHER NATURE (*Crossing to* WEATHERMAN): Dear me, Mr. Weatherman, what's the matter with Pitter and Patter?

WEATHERMAN: I was just giving them your orders, Mother Nature, but they won't listen to me.

PITTER: We want to see the Easter Parade.

PATTER: The Sunbeams saw it last year.

PITTER: This year it's our turn.

MOTHER NATURE: There won't be any Easter Parade at all unless you Raindrops stay at home.

PATTER: That's what you say every year!

PITTER *and* PATTER:
Rain, rain, go away,
Never come on Easter Day.

WEATHERMAN: The four Wind brothers are as bad as the Raindrops. They all want to blow at once. (*Four* WINDS *crowd around, each with his trumpet*)

EAST WIND: I blew last year and everybody liked me.

WEST WIND: If you blow in the morning, I want to blow in the afternoon.

NORTH WIND: I can blow all day and never get tired.

SOUTH WIND: I know how to blow the soft little breezes that are just right.

WEATHERMAN: Mother Nature must decide.

MOTHER NATURE: Now let me think. We'll start the day with East Wind for early morning.

EAST WIND: Goody! Goody! I'll see all the people going to church.

WEATHERMAN: Now you run along and practice. And take the Raindrops with you.

PITTER *and* PATTER: Boo hoo! Boo hoo! We're feeling blue!

MOTHER NATURE: Never mind. We'll have an April Shower party next week just for you. (*As they exit*) Now what about the rest of the day?

WEATHERMAN: I think we could trust South Wind. He is always gentle.

MOTHER NATURE: Good. He and West Wind work well together.

SOUTH WIND: I'll blow soft and warm all afternoon.

WEST WIND: And I'll cool things off around sunset.

WEATHERMAN: Excellent! Excellent! Now be on your way. (SOUTH WIND *and* WEST WIND *exit*)

NORTH WIND: What about me?

WEATHERMAN: Sorry, old boy. But you know what would happen. All of those pesky snowflakes would want to come along. When North Wind doth blow, we shall have snow.

NORTH WIND: Can't I blow for just a little while this afternoon? I need the exercise.

MOTHER NATURE: But you always blow up a storm.

NORTH WIND: I promise not to be rough or blustery.

WEATHERMAN: I did hear that some children are coming to the park today to fly their kites. Maybe they would like a good, strong wind.

MOTHER NATURE: But not too strong. That's the trouble with North Wind. He always blusters.

NORTH WIND: I'll be as gentle as a lamb.

MOTHER NATURE: Very well. If you promise to behave.

NORTH WIND (*Climbing up on stool with trumpet*): I promise.

WEATHERMAN: I'd like to speak to you about the temperature for tomorrow, Mother Nature. Perhaps you'd like to look at my thermometer.

MOTHER NATURE: Indeed I would. We don't want it too hot or too cold.

WEATHERMAN (*As they exit*): Now remember, North

Wind, none of your tricks! (*As* WEATHERMAN *and* MOTHER NATURE *exit left,* RABBITS *enter right.*)

MR. RABBIT: This is the place. I saw Mary Sunshine putting out the bonnets this morning.

FLIPPITY: A new bonnet! A new bonnet! I can hardly wait!

FLOPPITY: Will mine have a pink ribbon on it, Daddy?

HIPPITY: I want a blue hat with yellow flowers.

HOPPITY: I want a hat with a veil. Please, Mamma, may I have a veil?

MRS. RABBIT: Veils are not for children. Now be quiet.

MR. RABBIT: See, there is the bonnet counter.

MRS. RABBIT: But where are all the hats? And where is Mary Sunshine?

NORTH WIND: If you're looking for Mary Sunshine, she left long ago.

MRS. RABBIT: Did she take all the Easter bonnets with her?

NORTH WIND: She and Mother Nature gave them all out.

RABBITS: All of them?

MR. RABBIT: Didn't they leave any for us?

NORTH WIND: Who ever heard of bonnets for bunnies? Rabbits don't wear hats.

MRS. RABBIT: But this is Easter. Everybody gets a new bonnet for Easter.

NORTH WIND: You can see for yourself they are all gone.

MRS. RABBIT: Just like a man to get our hopes up for nothing!

LITTLE RABBITS: You promised! You promised!

MRS. RABBIT: No use crying about it! We've gone this

long without Easter bonnets. I guess we'll get through another year.

NORTH WIND: I could help you get some bonnets, if I hadn't promised to behave.

RABBITS: How? How?

MR. RABBIT: Oh, please, Mr. North Wind. Please help us.

NORTH WIND: I can't. I promised I wouldn't play any tricks.

MR. RABBIT: But this is so important. It means so much to Mother Rabbit and the children.

HIPPITY: What would you have to do?

NORTH WIND (*Pointing offstage*): See all those people over there?

RABBITS: Yes, yes.

NORTH WIND: All of them are wearing hats, aren't they?

RABBITS: Yes, yes, every single one.

NORTH WIND: All I'd need to do would be to blow one or two big blasts, and swoosh! Every one of those hats would sail right over here into the park and you could take your pick.

RABBITS: Oh, please, please, do it for us, Mr. North Wind.

NORTH WIND (*Climbing down from stool*): All right! I'll do it! Mother Nature will be angry, but it will be a lot of fun.

RABBITS: Thank you! Thank you!

NORTH WIND: Now be ready to catch them when they come your way. Here I go. (RABBITS *line up facing left stage as* NORTH WIND *exits.*)

MRS. RABBIT: Isn't he wonderful?

MR. RABBIT: He's a jolly good fellow all right. (*If possible, use offstage sound effect of wind. Offstage or behind screen, someone stands on a stool and tosses the hats onto the stage, one at a time.*)

HOPPITY: Look out! Here they come! (*As first hat sails on stage, there is a scramble.* FLOPPITY *catches it.*)

FLOPPITY: Look! Look! A pink ribbon! It's mine! It's mine!

HIPPITY (*Catching second hat*): A blue one! A blue one! That's for me!

FLIPPITY (*As third hat arrives*): This one is mine. See the pretty flowers!

HOPPITY: I hope this one has a veil.

MRS. RABBIT (*Catching fourth hat*): This one is mine. Veils are not for children. You may have the next one.

HOPPITY (*Catching a red hat*): Goody! Goody! A red one! A red one!

MR. RABBIT: I hope he's not forgetting me.

ALL: Here it comes! Catch it!

MR. RABBIT (*Catching a top hat*): Fine and dandy! Fine and dandy!

MRS. RABBIT: We'll be the finest family in the Easter Parade.

NORTH WIND (*Entering*): That was lots of fun. How do you like your hats?

ALL: Beautiful! Wonderful!

NORTH WIND: Let's see how they look. (RABBITS *try to*

put on hats, only to discover they can't wear them because of their long ears.)

MRS. RABBIT: Ouch! Ouch! It pinches my ears!

LITTLE RABBITS: Mamma, Mamma, they hurt! They hurt!

MR. RABBIT: Mine doesn't fit!

NORTH WIND (*Jamming* MR. RABBIT's *hat down*): Oh, for goodness' sake! Can't you jam it down over your ears?

MR. RABBIT: Ouch! Ouch! You're giving me an earache. Stop it! (MOTHER NATURE *and* WEATHERMAN *enter.*)

WEATHERMAN: What's going on here?

MOTHER NATURE: What is the meaning of this?

MR. RABBIT: It's our new hats.

LITTLE RABBITS: They hurt our ears.

MOTHER NATURE: Of course they hurt your ears. Rabbits were never meant to wear hats. Where did you get them?

MRS. RABBIT: Mr. North Wind brought them for us, but they don't fit.

WEATHERMAN: So that's what all the fuss was about.

MOTHER NATURE: North Wind, you've broken your promise. You've been up to your old tricks—blowing off hats. Shame on you!

NORTH WIND: I was only trying to help the Easter Rabbits.

MOTHER NATURE: But rabbits don't need hats.

MRS. RABBIT: All my life I've wanted an Easter bonnet more than anything else in the world.

LITTLE RABBITS: Everybody else dresses up for Easter.
MR. RABBIT: Maybe we could cut holes for our ears.
MOTHER NATURE: But they're not *your* hats. They belong to somebody else.
LITTLE RABBITS: Oh, please let us keep them. They are so pretty. (MARY SUNSHINE *enters with six Easter baskets.*)
MARY SUNSHINE: I just remembered the Easter baskets, Mother Nature. The Rabbits will be waiting for them. (*Puts them on counter*)
MOTHER NATURE: They are prettier than ever, Mary Sunshine. But the Rabbits won't be needing them this year.
MRS. RABBIT: But how will we deliver our Easter eggs?
MR. RABBIT: We *must* have baskets.
MOTHER NATURE: Baskets or bonnets? You can't have both.
MR. RABBIT: What good is an Easter Rabbit without a basket?
MOTHER NATURE: You should have thought of that before. Baskets or bonnets? Take your choice.
MRS. RABBIT: I can't give up this beautiful bonnet.
WEATHERMAN: Here come the children looking for their hats. Suppose we let them decide.
MOTHER NATURE (*To* RABBITS): Quick! Hide behind the bushes. The children must not see you. (RABBITS *hide behind bush, as* MARY, POLLY, RUTH, *and* SUSIE *enter.*)
GIRLS: Where are they?
MARY: I was sure we'd find them in the park.

SUSIE: Let's look behind the bushes.

MOTHER NATURE: Wait a minute, children. I'd like to ask you a question.

POLLY: Sorry. We must find our hats before the wind blows them any farther.

WEATHERMAN (*Looking sternly at* NORTH WIND): Don't worry about the wind. I can promise you it will be very quiet.

MOTHER NATURE: I want to ask you if you believe in the Easter Rabbit?

GIRLS: Of course.

RUTH: He always brings us such beautiful baskets.

POLLY: We love to hunt for eggs on Easter morning.

MARY: This year Mother says there will be a surprise.

SUSIE: It wouldn't be Easter without the Easter Bunny.

MOTHER NATURE: Thank you, girls. That's all I wanted to know.

GIRLS: But where are our hats?

MARY SUNSHINE: Come with me. I will help you look for them. (*Leads* GIRLS *off right*)

WEATHERMAN (*To* RABBITS): The coast is clear. You may come out.

MOTHER NATURE: Well, what have you decided?

WEATHERMAN: Which will it be? Baskets or bonnets?

RABBITS: Baskets!

MR. RABBIT: We couldn't disappoint the children.

MRS. RABBIT: They really believe in us.

LITTLE RABBITS (*Giving hats to* MOTHER NATURE *and* WEATHERMAN): Here are the bonnets. Now give us the baskets.

MOTHER NATURE: Help yourselves. (RABBITS *take baskets from counter.*)

MR. RABBIT (*As he takes basket*): Baskets are better than bonnets.

MRS. RABBIT (*With basket*): They're stylish for Rabbits this year.

LITTLE RABBITS: If our heads were tied up in bonnets, we wouldn't be able to hear!

NORTH WIND: That's right! You wouldn't be able to hear the children wishing you a happy Easter.

WEATHERMAN: Quiet! Not another word out of you! I'm going to lock you up so you won't play any more tricks.

NORTH WIND: Oh, no! Please! Please, let me return the children's hats. I can blow them over the hill before you can say "Happy Easter."

WEATHERMAN: I don't trust you!

MOTHER NATURE: But I do. I'm sure North Wind wants everyone to have a Happy Easter, so he may return the hats.

NORTH WIND (*Collecting hats*): Thank you, Mother Nature. I'll be as good as gold.

MOTHER NATURE: Before you go, you may blow one big blast on your wind trumpet to summon the Easter flowers. I want them to practice for the Easter Parade. (NORTH WIND *blows on trumpet and exits as* FLOWERS, *wearing their colorful flower hats, march in to music of "Easter Parade." All line up and sing.*)

FLOWERS:
Watch the Easter Rabbit

And get the Easter habit
Of making someone happy
In the real Easter way.
Be as bright and sunny
As any Easter Bunny
And you will find you're heading for
A big Easter Day!

ALL (*Shouting and waving*): Happy Easter! (*Curtain*)

THE END

MERRY-GO-ROUND FOR MOTHER

Characters

TERRY O'BRIEN
SHARON O'BRIEN
MRS. O'BRIEN
ELSIE HEATH
MRS. HEATH
JIM BLAKE
MRS. BLAKE
EMILY HAINES

MRS. HAINES
FRED FOSTER
MRS. FOSTER
CARLA CRANE
MRS. CRANE
GARY BAKER
MRS. BAKER

SCENE 1

TIME: *A day in May.*

BEFORE CURTAIN: TERRY *is seated on a tall stool, stage right. He wears a high silk hat marked "Tickets," and holds a roll of tickets in his hand. His sister,* SHARON, *stands just left of stage center. The sound of merry-go-round music is heard from behind the closed curtain.* MRS. HEATH *and* MRS. BLAKE *enter left and approach* TERRY.

TERRY (*In traditional "barker" style*): Right this way, folks, right this way for a ride on the merry-go-round! Hurry! Hurry! Hurry! Get your tickets here for the ride of your life! No admission charge! Tickets absolutely free. (*As* MRS. HEATH *and* MRS.

BLAKE *reach him*) Two tickets, ladies, for the greatest ride on earth. (*Tears off a ticket for each*)

MRS. HEATH: Why, Terry O'Brien, where in the world did you get that outfit? You look like a real barker at the county fair.

MRS. BLAKE: Listen, Mary! I think I hear merry-go-round music!

SHARON: That's right, Mrs. Blake. You *do* hear merry-go-round music, and I hope you enjoy your ride. You, too, Mrs. Heath. Won't you ladies step inside?

MRS. HEATH: My goodness! I don't know what to expect next.

MRS. BLAKE (*Pointing off right*): Oh, look! Here come Mrs. Haines and Mrs. Foster. (*To* SHARON) Is it all right if we wait for them?

SHARON: Certainly, ladies. The more the merrier!

TERRY: Right this way, ladies! Right this way for your free ride on the marvellous merry-go-round.

SHARON (*To* MRS. HAINES *and* MRS. FOSTER): Good afternoon, Mrs. Haines. Hello, Mrs. Foster. We're so glad you could come.

MRS. HAINES: We wouldn't have missed it!

MRS. FOSTER: Not for the world.

TERRY (*Tearing off tickets*): And here are your tickets, ladies. You're just in time for the first ride of the season.

MRS. HEATH: Do you ladies know what this is all about?

MRS. HAINES: It's a mystery to me.

MRS. BLAKE: Do you suppose there really *is* a merry-go-round in there?

MRS. FOSTER: It's impossible! But there *must* be a merry-go-round. Don't you hear the music?

MRS. HEATH: What's the mystery, Terry? Aren't you going to tell us?

TERRY: Take my word for it, ladies, it's the greatest show on earth! (*Calls*) Hurry! Hurry! Hurry! Just step inside for a wonderful ride—a ride on the merry-go-round.

MRS. BLAKE: Come on, girls, I can't wait another second. (*Ladies exit behind curtain, which* SHARON *pulls aside slightly.*)

TERRY: Tickets! Tickets! Get your tickets here for a free ride on the merry-go-round. Right this way, folks, right this way! No admission charges! Tickets absolutely free. (MRS. CRANE *enters and approaches* SHARON *and* TERRY.)

SHARON: Here comes Mrs. Crane, Terry. Keep it up, you're doing fine.

TERRY: Hurry! Hurry! Hurry! All aboard for a free ride on the merry-go-round.

MRS. CRANE: Terry O'Brien! Have you lost your senses? You'll have the whole neighborhood in an uproar!

TERRY: Here's your ticket, lady. Step right inside and have the most exciting ride of your life. No charge, lady, and keep the change!

MRS. CRANE: This is the oddest thing I've ever heard of! How could you children manage to get a merry-go-round inside your house?

SHARON: Won't you step inside, Mrs. Crane, and see for yourself?

MRS. CRANE: Indeed I will, Sharon. I just wonder if your mother knows about this. (SHARON *holds curtain aside briefly as* MRS. CRANE *goes behind it.*)

TERRY: Are they all here, Sharon? I'm just about out of breath.

SHARON: Mrs. Baker isn't here yet, but I think I see her coming. Whoop it up, Terry, you're doing great.

TERRY: Can't you get me a drink of water or something?

SHARON: You'll be finished in half a second. Here's Mrs. Baker now. Now go into your act! (MRS. BAKER *enters and approaches* TERRY.)

TERRY: Right this way, folks, right this way for the most exciting ride of your life. And it's all free, absolutely no charge. A free ride on the merry-go-round! Ah, good afternoon, Mrs. Baker. Here's your ticket for the merry-go-round.

MRS. BAKER: Thank you, Terry. I don't know what this is all about, but when I got that invitation I just *had* to come. Am I the first one here?

SHARON: No, indeed, Mrs. Baker. You'll find a lot of ladies you know.

MRS. BAKER (*Beaming*): Just as the invitation says! I declare, I've read it so many times I think I know it by heart.

"Come take a ride on the merry-go-round;
It's a Mother's Day surprise!
You'll meet your friends, and see some sights
That will make you blink your eyes.

"You're cordially invited
To come and take a ride.
Just ring the bell at half-past two,
And meet your friends inside!"
Now who could resist an invitation like that?

SHARON: We're so happy to have you, Mrs. Baker, and we're almost ready to begin.

MRS. BAKER: Then I'll go right in, because I don't want to miss a single bit of it! (MRS. BAKER *exits through curtain opening.*)

SHARON (*To* TERRY): That's the last one, Terry. Come on, let's get started.

TERRY: But where's Mom?

SHARON: Carla Crane asked Mom to help her select a present. She promised to keep Mom downtown until it was time to come. Jim Blake is standing down on the corner to give us the signal when he sees them coming.

TERRY: Then everything's set, because here comes Jim now. (JIM *runs on stage.*)

JIM: Your mother's on her way! Is everything under control here?

SHARON: All set and ready to go.

TERRY: Then what are we waiting for? Let 'er roll! (*Curtains open to reveal merry-go-round.* JIM, SHARON, *and* TERRY *take their places onstage.*)

* * * * *

SCENE 2

SETTING: *The living room of the O'Brien home, set up for the merry-go-round party. The merry-go-round consists of a circle of chairs, one for each guest, grouped around a central pole, such as a tall clothes tree or Maypole. Colored crepe-paper streamers run from the pole to the chair backs, which are decorated with paper-bag animal heads to represent the prancing steeds of a merry-go-round. The chairs are arranged so that each "rider" faces the back of her chair. Tall wands or dowel sticks wrapped with colored paper may be placed between the chairs to serve as side supports for the "riders."*

AT RISE: *All of the mothers are seated on the chairs, astride or sidesaddle, and each child stands at a pole beside his mother. A vacant chair has been left down center for* MRS. O'BRIEN. JIM *enters and takes his place beside* MRS. BLAKE. TERRY *perches himself on a stepladder, stage left, and* SHARON *stands beside the record player, which is playing merry-go-round music. She turns off record.*

TERRY: Welcome, ladies and gentlemen, welcome to the Mother's Day merry-go-round. I see you have all found your places. Is everybody comfortable? Is everybody happy? (*All applaud enthusiastically.*)

MRS. HEATH: This is a perfectly wonderful idea, Terry. I don't see how you ever thought of it!

MRS. BLAKE: And you really *do* have a perfect merry-go-round, with all these beautiful animals. (*Pats her horse's head*)

MRS. FOSTER: Just look at my magnificent giraffe!

MRS. CRANE: I adore my zebra!

MRS. BAKER: I don't see how you ever managed to do all this work!

SHARON: Oh, we had plenty of help, Mrs. Baker. The boys made the animals and we girls made most of the decorations.

MRS. FOSTER: Fred Foster! You knew all about this and never breathed a word!

FRED (*Laughing*): Oh, we know how to keep a secret.

ELSIE: And we wanted it to be a surprise!

EMILY: A surprise for every mother in the neighborhood!

MRS. HAINES: But where is *your* mother, Terry?

MRS. HEATH: Yes, where *is* Mrs. O'Brien?

MRS. CRANE: Is she in on the secret?

TERRY: Oh, no! Mom doesn't know a thing about it!

SHARON: Carla is our secret agent to keep Mom out of the way till the last minute. You see, this is a double surprise for her.

TERRY: Mom never had a surprise party in her life, and she never rode on a merry-go-round, so this will be a two-in-one surprise!

MRS. CRANE: She'll love it!

MRS. HEATH: I can't wait to see her face.

GARY: Be sure to yell *surprise* the minute she comes in the door.

JIM: And make it good and loud.
ELSIE: The louder the better!
SHARON: Oh, Terry, I can hardly wait!
TERRY: Sh! Here they come now. (MRS. O'BRIEN *enters with* CARLA, *who runs to her mother at merry-go-round.* MRS. O'BRIEN *stops in amazement.*)
ALL: Surprise! Surprise!
MRS. O'BRIEN: What is it? Terry! Sharon! What on earth's going on here?
TERRY (*Running to her*): It's a surprise party, Mom.
SHARON (*Joining them*): And it's all for you!
MRS. O'BRIEN: My goodness! It's the most exciting thing I ever saw! I was never so surprised in all my life!
SHARON: You always said you wanted a surprise party, and here it is!
MRS. O'BRIEN: But darling, it's not my birthday.
SHARON: It's Mother's Day.
ALL: Happy Mother's Day, Mrs. O'Brien.
MRS. O'BRIEN: Oh, thank you, thank you! And Happy Mother's Day to all of you ladies. (*Stopping and pointing*) But look! Look! It's a merry-go-round! A merry-go-round right in my own living room!
TERRY: It sure is, Mom, and that's for you, too.
MRS. O'BRIEN: How did you ever think of such a wonderful thing?
TERRY: You said you always wanted to ride on a merry-go-round, and here's your chance.
SHARON (*Leading her mother to empty chair*): We saved a good place for you, Mother. How do you like it?

MRS. O'BRIEN (*Admiring*): It's beautiful! Just beautiful! I've never seen anything like it. Look, my horse has a real mane and tail.
SHARON: And we have real merry-go-round music, too. Want to hear it?
TERRY: Just a minute, Sharon. It's time for my speech.
ALL (*Applauding*): Speech! Speech!
TERRY (*Making a formal bow and addressing everyone on the merry-go-round*):
This merry-go-round's for mothers,
To take you far away,
And ride you round and round and round,
And stop at yesterday!

You mothers are so good and kind,
And so unselfish, too,
That we, your loving children,
Have made a game for you.

When you were just about our age,
You longed for just One Thing,
And now, you're sure to get it—if
You catch the golden ring.
MRS. O'BRIEN: I don't understand.
MRS. BAKER: It sounds so mysterious.
ELSIE: It's all part of the surprise.
EMILY: We're tired of giving you the usual presents, like potholders and handkerchiefs.
GARY: We tried to think of something you've always wanted, but never had.

JIM: All of you mothers try to give us the things you never had when you were little.

TERRY: Mother never misses a chance to have a party for us, because she never had one when she was a little girl.

SHARON: And she was always disappointed because she never got a chance to ride on a merry-go-round, so now we're making her little-girl wish come true.

MRS. O'BRIEN: That's wonderful, darling! And it's a beautiful merry-go-round, even better than I dreamed of.

MRS. HEATH: But I still don't understand the part about the golden ring.

SHARON: You'll understand as soon as we start to play the game. Terry will explain it.

TERRY: When the music starts, we want all of you to march around the merry-go-round, and as you pass the stepladder, reach for the lucky ring. (*Indicates the box of paper rings on shelf of stepladder*) When the music stops, whoever has the golden ring will get a big surprise.

MOTHERS: This sounds like fun. (*Preparing to march*)

MRS. O'BRIEN: I've already had my surprise, so I'll watch the others. (*As* SHARON *starts the music,* TERRY *hands out the paper rings.* ELSIE'S *mother,* MRS. HEATH, *gets the first golden ring.*)

SHARON (*As music stops*): Congratulations, Mrs. Heath. You got the golden ring.

MRS. HEATH: What do I do now?

ELSIE: Just step over here, Mother, and I'll show you. (*Takes her mother to pile of gifts on table with record player*) Do you remember how badly you wanted a bright red dress or hair ribbon when you were a little girl?

MRS. HEATH: I certainly do, but I never got it. Mother said it didn't go with my red hair.

ELSIE (*Handing her mother a package*): Well, see how you like this. And Happy Mother's Day.

MRS. HEATH (*Opening package and holding up string of bright red beads*): Oh, Elsie! They're beautiful. Just what I've always wanted. But do you think I'd dare to wear them?

ELSIE: Read what the card says. Maybe that will help you make up your mind.

MRS. HEATH (*Reading from card*):
I know your favorite color
Has always been bright red.
You never dared to wear it,
But now go right ahead.
(*Putting on beads*) And that's just what I'll do. See how beautiful they look?

SHARON: They look lovely, Mrs. Heath. And now line up for the second game. Are you ready? (*Starts music*) Here we go. (*This time,* TERRY *gives the golden ring to* JIM's *mother,* MRS. BLAKE. JIM *escorts her to the present pile.*)

JIM: You've wanted this for a long time, Mom. Remember how disappointed you were when you found a clothesline instead of a birthday present?

MRS. BLAKE: Oh, I'll never forget it. I saw my father come home with a package from the hardware store. I was sure it was a red skipping rope for my birthday . . . but instead, it was a new clothesline for my mother. (*Opening package*) But this makes up for it a thousand times. (*Displays skipping rope*) I'll have a wonderful time skipping now, Jim. And listen to what the card says:
A jumping rope for Mother,
It comes with love from Jim.
It's better than a diet
For keeping slim and trim.
You rascal! (*Jumps a few turns with rope*) Look! Look! It's working! It's working! I feel myself getting thinner with every jump.

SHARON: Here we go with round three! Everybody ready? (*Starts music.* EMILY's *mother,* MRS. HAINES, *gets the golden ring.*)

EMILY (*Escorting* MRS. HAINES *to the gift table*): Hurry up, Mother. I can hardly wait for you to see your surprise.

MRS. HAINES (*Opening present, which is a mouth organ*): A mouth organ! (*Blows on it*) And it really plays! Oh, thank you, Emily! You did remember my ten-year-old birthday!

EMILY: How could I forget it? It's one of your best stories.

MRS. O'BRIEN: Let's hear it, Mrs. Haines.

MRS. HAINES: When I was ten years old almost every child in my classroom had a mouth organ. I wanted one more than anything else in the world and I was sure that was going to be my birthday present. The box was just the right size and shape. But when I opened it, what do you think was inside?

ALL: What?

MRS. HAINES: A toothbrush and a tube of toothpaste! (*Others moan in sympathy.*)

EMILY: Read your card, Mother. It's really part of your present.

MRS. HAINES (*Reading*):
Your teeth are really lovely,
And brushing helped, I know.
But here's a real mouth organ,
For you to blow and blow!

I'll bet I can play "America" without even practicing. (*Plays mouth organ as she returns to her place*)

SHARON: You go right ahead and play, Mrs. Haines, while the rest of the ladies get going on the next round. (FRED's *mother,* MRS. FOSTER, *gets the golden ring on this round.*)

FRED: Come along, Mom. You'll never guess what your surprise is.

MRS. FOSTER: I'm not even trying. I'll just wait and see.

FRED: Better read the card first and brace yourself for the shock.

MRS. FOSTER (*Reading card*):
You wanted pets, but Grandma said:
"No, no, my little Myrtle."
Well, here at last, a wish come true,

A real, live, tiny turtle!
(*Opening box*) Oh, isn't it cute! Wait till your father sees this! He'll say we can really open the Foster zoo. We already have pigeons, a dog, two cats, a parakeet, and now a turtle! Thank you, Fred! I'm just delighted.

MRS. O'BRIEN: I always imagined you lived in a household of pets when you were a child, Mrs. Foster, because you have so many animals now.

MRS. FOSTER: No, indeed. I never had a single pet when I was a child. I've often told Fred how I tried to smuggle a turtle into my room, and he remembered the story.

FRED: And now your story has a happy ending, Mom, even for the turtle! He'll have a good home with us.

SHARON: Everybody ready for the next game. Forward march! (*Starts music.* CARLA'S *mother,* MRS. CRANE, *receives the golden ring.*)

CARLA: Read the card, please, Mother. I hope you like it.

MRS. CRANE (*Reading*):
You longed for brush and paint set
When you were just a tot;
Now you can paint bright pictures
Of things the way they're not.
(*Holding up present*) See! A box of water colors.

CARLA: You'll have to tell your story, Mother, so everybody can appreciate your present.

MRS. CRANE: When I was a little girl, I dearly loved to paint with water colors. I was always allowed to have them, until the day I painted a sunset on my mother's best tablecloth. That ended my career as an artist . . . that is, until today.

MRS. O'BRIEN: I'm sure you won't make the same mistake now, Mrs. Crane.

TERRY: You might as well step forward and claim the lucky ring, Mrs. Baker. You're the last one. (*Hands gift to* MRS. BAKER)

GARY: And just wait till you open your package, Mom.

MRS. BAKER: I'd better read the card first. (*Reading card*)

You always were a tomboy
So take this ball and glove,
To prove you're not too grown up
To play the game you love!

This is a wonderful present for a baseball fan, Gary. Thank you so much.

MRS. O'BRIEN: I never knew you were such a baseball fan, Mrs. Baker.

MRS. BAKER: How could I help it? I grew up in a family with four boys, but they would never let me play ball with them. Now I have my very own ball and glove and I'm going to get this ball autographed by my favorite pitcher! Thanks again, Gary. This is what every mother needs.

MRS. O'BRIEN (*Center stage with* SHARON): And this party is what every mother needs, especially on Mother's Day.

TERRY (*Descending ladder*): Did you really like it, Mom?

MRS. O'BRIEN: Like it? I loved it. How about the rest of you mothers?

MOTHERS (*Ad lib*): Marvellous! Wonderful! I've never had such fun. (*Etc.*)

MRS. O'BRIEN: We mothers feel as if we are on a merry-go-round most of the time. We tear round and round and round looking after our families till we are almost too busy and dizzy to notice how much our children really love and appreciate us.

MRS. HEATH: It's wonderful to know that you took all this trouble just for us.

MRS. HAINES: And all the planning!

MRS. FOSTER: And all the imagination!

MRS. BLAKE: And all the work!

MRS. BAKER: And all the careful thought!

MRS. CRANE: And all the love!

MRS. O'BRIEN: Yes, love—and remember, children, that is the most priceless ingredient for any Mother's Day celebration.

MOTHERS:
If you want to get your mother
A gift for Mother's Day,
A gift that she'll remember
Forever and for aye,
It doesn't really matter
What the gift turns out to be,
So long as you remember
This simple recipe.
If you buy a penny candy,
A goblet or a glove,

Be sure to send it tenderly
With all your dearest love.
CHILDREN (*Applauding*): We'll remember that.
TERRY: And now . . . it's all aboard for the merry-go-round! (*Everyone takes his place as* SHARON *starts the merry-go-round music. All wave to the audience as curtains close.*)

THE END

THE MAGIC PENCILS

Characters

SUSIE	MISTRESS MARY
BILLY	MR. WIZARD
EDDIE	MR. SCALAWAG
TED	MISS CURRY
FRED	TONY
CARL	AMANDA
BOBBY	CATHY
JANE	BETTY

TIME: *The end of the school year.*

SETTING: *The Garden of Learning. The Fountain of Knowledge is center stage; to the right of it is the Paper Plant, and to the left the ABC Tree. The Magic Pencil Tree is right stage, and left stage are the Number Bush and a flower bed labeled* BOOKS IN BLOOM. *Each section of the garden is labeled with an appropriate placard, and there are three arrow signs attached to a post or tree pointing to* HOMEWORK HILL, EXAMINATION MOUNTAIN, *and* TO THE NEXT GRADE.

AT RISE: MISTRESS MARY *is watering the trees and plants.* MR. WIZARD *is on his knees, weeding the flower bed, Books in Bloom.*

THE MAGIC PENCILS

MISTRESS MARY: The garden is perfect, Mr. Wizard. I have never seen it look prettier.

MR. WIZARD: Thank you, Mistress Mary. I hope the school children will like it.

MISTRESS MARY: I'm sure they will. Who is coming today?

MR. WIZARD: Miss Curry always brings her boys and girls to the Garden of Knowledge for their closing-day picnic. (*Offstage motor horn is heard.*)

MISTRESS MARY: The buses must be arriving now. Let's take a last look to see that everything is just right.

MR. WIZARD (*Rising*): There's not a weed in sight. (*Suddenly seeing sign on Magic Pencil Tree*) Oh, dear! That Mr. Scalawag has been up to his old tricks again. Look! He has changed the sign on the Pencil Tree!

MISTRESS MARY: I wonder where he has hidden it this time. I'll run and look.

MR. WIZARD: It's too late. Here they come. (MISS CURRY *and children enter right.*) Good morning!

MISTRESS MARY: Good morning! Welcome to the Garden of Learning.

MISS CURRY: Good morning. (*To children*) Boys and girls, this is Mr. Wizard.

ALL: Good morning, Mr. Wizard.

MISS CURRY: And this is Mistress Mary.

ALL:
Good morning, Mistress Mary!
How does your garden grow?
With Pencil Trees and ABC's

And picture books all in a row?
MISTRESS MARY:
You're right on time.
The garden's fine.
Do enter, if you please.
Feel right at home,
And free to roam
Among the flowers and trees.
CATHY: What a beautiful garden!
BETTY: It's even prettier than I imagined.
SUSIE: May we pick the flowers?
BILLY: May we walk on the grass?
EDDIE: May we climb the trees?
MISS CURRY: You may do anything you like.
TED: I'm thirsty. I'd like to drink out of that fountain.
OTHERS (*Ad lib*): So would I. We'd like a drink. We're thirsty, too. (*Etc.*) (*At fountain,* TED, SUSIE *and* BETTY *pretend to take drink.*)
CATHY: Look at all the picture books! (*Sits down*) Here is my favorite story, *Heidi*.
BOBBY (*Also sitting by flower bed*): I want a book about rockets.
BILLY: Here is a picture book about space.
CARL (*At Number Bush*): Look at all these numbers! Enough to solve all the problems in the world.
FRED (*Picking numbers from bush*): Five times six, plus ten, minus eight, divided by four, multiplied by seven equals . . .
CARL: Here is the answer—see? (*Holds up No. 56*) The answer is 56.

MISS CURRY: Correct!

FRED: Let's try it again. (*Removing numbers as he talks*) Seven plus seven, times ten, divided by five, multiplied by nine!

CARL: I have it! I have it! (*Holding up numbers.*) The answer is 252.

MISS CURRY: Right again!

CARL: I wish we had this Number Bush in our room at school, Miss Curry.

MISS CURRY: Maybe we do. Perhaps you have never noticed.

BETTY: I'd like to play a game.

MISTRESS MARY: Many children who come here enjoy playing under the ABC Tree.

MR. WIZARD: They like to play a game called Spello.

SUSIE: How do you play it?

MISTRESS MARY: We'll show you. First of all, we need nine children. (*Nine children step forward.* MISTRESS MARY *takes letters from ABC Tree and hands them to* TONY, BILLY, *and* AMANDA.) To you three I will give these letters: C, U, E.

TONY, BILLY, *and* AMANDA (*Holding up letters*): C-U-E spells "cue."

MR. WIZARD: The next three children will get these letters: A, I, D. (*Hands letters to* CATHY, EDDIE *and* CARL.)

CATHY, EDDIE, *and* CARL (*Holding up letters*): A-I-D spells "aid."

MISTRESS MARY: And you last three get the letters T, O, N. (*She hands letters to* FRED, BOBBY *and* JANE.)

FRED, BOBBY, *and* JANE (*Holding up letters*): T-O-N spells "ton."

MR. WIZARD: Now you have three little words: CUE, AID, TON. When I blow this whistle (*Holds up whistle hanging on cord around his neck*), you must re-group yourselves to spell one long word with the nine letters. Ready, get set, go! (*Blows whistle. After much scrambling, the nine children move into a line and hold up their letters which now spell "EDUCATION."*)

CHILDREN (*Together*): Education!

MISTRESS MARY, MR. WIZARD *and* MISS CURRY (*Applauding*): Excellent! Splendid!

EDDIE: That was fun! Let's play it again.

MISS CURRY: I'm afraid we won't have time. Mr. Wizard and Mistress Mary are going to take us on a very important hike.

TED: Where are we going?

MISTRESS MARY: I am going to lead you up to Homework Hill.

MR. WIZARD: And I will take you up the trail to Examination Mountain. Who wants to go with me?

CHILDREN (*Ad lib*): I will. Let me go. I want to go with Mr. Wizard. (*Etc.*)

MISTRESS MARY: And who will come with me?

OTHER CHILDREN (*Ad lib*): I want to go with Mistress Mary, I do . . . (*Etc.*)

MISTRESS MARY: Everybody ready? Here we go! (*She leads her group around stage and then off in the di-*

rection of Homework Hill. As they walk around, they sing to the tune of "Here We Go Round the Mulberry Bush.")
This is the way up to Homework Hill,
Homework Hill, Homework Hill,
This is the way up to Homework Hill,
Along with Mistress Mary.

MR. WIZARD: Now right this way, boys and girls. Follow me and don't get lost. It's a long, hard climb to Examination Mountain. (*The other group of children follows* MR. WIZARD *around the stage and off, singing to the tune of "This Old Man."*)
One, two, three, one, two, three,
It's as easy as can be,
With a nick-nack, paddy whack,
Do the best you can,
You can pass any old exam!

MISS CURRY (*Starts to follow* MR. WIZARD, *but turns back as she sees that* AMANDA *and* TONY *are not coming*): Come along, Amanda. Hurry up, Tony. The others will get ahead of us.

AMANDA: I don't think I want to go with them, Miss Curry.

MISS CURRY: But why not?

TONY: I don't like the sound of those names—Homework Hill! Examination Mountain!

MISS CURRY: But when we come back, we will all be taking the path to The Next Grade. Don't you want to come along?

AMANDA: I'd rather stay here in the garden.
TONY: We could join you on the path to The Next Grade when you come back.
MISS CURRY: Don't be too sure of that, Tony.
AMANDA: You said we may do just as we like today.
MISS CURRY: So I did. Very well; you may stay here, but I warn you—you may be sorry.
AMANDA *and* TONY: Thank you, Miss Curry.
MISS CURRY: The children are almost out of sight. I must hurry. (*Exits*)
AMANDA: Thank goodness she's gone.
TONY: I can hardly wait to get one of those magic pencils.
AMANDA: I want the pink one with the rosebud on the end.
TONY: I'm going to take a blue one. Blue is my lucky color. (*As children approach tree,* MR. SCALAWAG *enters on tiptoe. He creeps up behind them and startles them with a loud "Boo!"*)
AMANDA: You scared the life out of me.
TONY: Who are you, and what are you doing here?
MR. SCALAWAG: I am Mr. Scalawag. I like to play tricks on people!
AMANDA: Are you a friend of Mr. Wizard and Mistress Mary?
MR. SCALAWAG: Not exactly. They chase me out of the garden every chance they get. But I have as much right to be here as they do. The Garden of Learning is for everyone. I see you are interested in the magic pencils.

AMANDA: I think they are beautiful.

TONY: We want to see how the magic works.

MR. SCALAWAG: You'll soon find out. Just help yourselves. (*He gives each one a large colored pencil.*)

AMANDA: They look like ordinary pencils, but they are much prettier.

TONY: But what is the magic?

MR. SCALAWAG (*Handing each one a sheet of paper from the Paper Plant*): Here. I'll show you. Sit down over there and write the answers to these questions. (TONY *and* AMANDA *sit on bench.*) What is the capital of the State of Maine? (*Children write.*) Who was the third President of the United States? (*Children write.*) Who was the first American to orbit the earth? (*Children write.*) How do you spell "receive?" (*Children write.*) Now for the answers. What is the capital of Maine?

TONY *and* AMANDA: Augusta.

MR. SCALAWAG: Right! Who was the third President?

TONY *and* AMANDA: Thomas Jefferson.

MR. SCALAWAG: Right! Who was the first American to orbit the earth?

TONY *and* AMANDA: Colonel John Glenn.

MR. SCALAWAG: Right! How do you spell "receive?"

TONY *and* AMANDA: R-E-C-E-I-V-E.

MR. SCALAWAG: One hundred percent correct! Now, do you understand what your magic pencils can do for you?

AMANDA: Do they always know the answers?

MR. SCALAWAG: Yes.

TONY: Oh, boy! With my magic pencil I'll never have to study again!

AMANDA: This is wonderful, Mr. Scalawag. Tony and I will get the highest marks in our class.

TONY: I had a lucky pencil once. Every time I used it I got an "A." But then I lost the pencil, and I haven't had an "A" since.

MR. SCALAWAG: Then you must take good care of this one.

AMANDA: I'm glad we didn't make that long, hard climb to Homework Hill or Examination Mountain.

TONY: Now we can take the path to The Next Grade as easy as pie. (MR. SCALAWAG *laughs loud and long.*)

AMANDA: What are you laughing at?

MR. SCALAWAG: Something tickled my funny bone!

TONY (*Laughing*): It tickles my funny bone, too, when I think how surprised Miss Curry will be.

AMANDA (*Laughing*): And what a good joke on the others who took the hard way to The Next Grade. (MISTRESS MARY *and* MR. WIZARD *enter, followed by children and* MISS CURRY.)

MR. WIZARD (*Advancing on* MR. SCALAWAG): So there you are! How many times have I told you to stay out of this garden? Get out of here and stay out!

MISTRESS MARY: You've been up to your tricks again! Where did you hide the sign for the pencil tree, you miserable creature?

MR. WIZARD (*Shaking him*): Tell us, or you'll be sorry.

MR. SCALAWAG: Let me go! Let me go!

MR. WIZARD: Tell us, or I'll tickle you to bits and pieces — (*Starts tickling*)

MR. SCALAWAG: Stop! Stop! You know how ticklish I am. Stop! Stop! Let me go! I'll tell! I'll tell! (*As* MR. WIZARD *releases him*) I hid the sign behind the tool shed.

MR. WIZARD: Run and look, Mistress Mary. He'd better be telling the truth. (MISTRESS MARY *exits*.)

MISS CURRY: And now, boys and girls, the time has come for us to leave the garden and take the path to The Next Grade. You have all done so well with Homework Hill and Examination Mountain that I'm sure you will find the way quite easy. (*Claps her hands*) Line up, everybody. (*As children form line to exit left,* TONY *and* AMANDA *fall in at the end*.) Just a minute, boys and girls. I have something to say to Tony and Amanda. I'm sorry, but I am afraid you will not be able to go along with us.

TONY *and* AMANDA: Why not?

MISS CURRY: Because you are not prepared.

TONY: But we have our magic pencils.

AMANDA: We will always have the right answers.

MR. WIZARD: My poor little friends! You have been sadly fooled.

MISS CURRY: There is no such thing as a magic pencil.

TONY: But they worked! Mr. Scalawag gave us a test, and every answer was right.

MISS CURRY: That was because you already knew the answers.

AMANDA: I even knew how to spell "receive." My magic pencil put the "e" before the "i."

MISS CURRY: Think how long we worked on that in school, Amanda. It was *you* who put the "e" before the "i"—not the magic pencil.

MISTRESS MARY (*Returning with sign,* PENCIL TREE. *She removes the* MAGIC PENCIL TREE *sign and replaces it with the right one.*): There! No more children will be fooled by Mr. Scalawag.

TONY: I still believe in my magic pencil.

MR. WIZARD: Mr. Scalawag, you must prove it was only a trick.

MR. SCALAWAG: Very well. Take your magic pencils and write the French word for "garden."

AMANDA: But we can't.

TONY: We haven't had French.

MISS CURRY: If your pencils were really magic, they would write the word all by themselves.

AMANDA: You are a bad, wicked fellow, Mr. Scalawag! (*Throwing down her pencil*) I hope I never see you again.

MR. SCALAWAG: I'm sorry. I meant no harm. It was only a joke.

TONY: Some joke! Now we can't go with the other boys and girls.

AMANDA: Oh, Miss Curry, please, please, please take us with you.

MISS CURRY: Are you willing to climb Homework Hill and go up Examination Mountain?

TONY *and* AMANDA: Oh, yes, yes, we'll do whatever you say!

MISTRESS MARY: Then come along. I will show you the way.

TONY (*About to leave*): Will you wait for us, Miss Curry? (*She hesitates.*)

AMANDA: *Please!*

MISS CURRY: What do you say, boys and girls? Shall we wait for Amanda and Tony?

ALL (*Ad lib*): Oh, yes. Let's wait for them. (*Etc.*)

MISS CURRY: Very well, children. We won't go without you.

AMANDA *and* TONY: Thank you! Thank you! (*They go off with* MISTRESS MARY.)

MR. WIZARD (*To* MR. SCALAWAG): As for you, you wicked fellow, you're going back to the tool shed, where you belong. Now, march! (*Escorts* MR. SCALAWAG *offstage*)

CATHY: Isn't it too bad the pencils are not really magic?

BETTY: They look so pretty. I'd like to have one.

ALL (*Ad lib*): So would I, so would I . . . (*Etc.*)

EDDIE: Maybe there's a teeny-weeny bit of magic in them after all.

MISS CURRY: There's a bit of magic in every pencil, boys and girls. But not the kind that Mr. Scalawag was talking about.

TED: What kind of magic is it, Miss Curry?

MISS CURRY: It's the magic you put into them through your own knowledge, Ted. A pencil can be a magic tool if you put it to good use.

SUSIE: I'd like to have one as a souvenir of the Garden of Learning.

CARL: I'd like to have one to use next year.

MISS CURRY: You may each have one. Step forward as I call your names. (*As she calls the roll, she gives each child a pencil from the tree.*) And now, before we go, let's practice our farewell song. (*Children sing to the tune of "School Days," as curtain falls.*)
School days, school days,
Dear old golden-rule days,
Reading and writing and numbers, too,
Solving the problems so hard to do!
There is so much a child must know,
We have a long, long way to go!
We're well on our way today—and so—
We bid you a friendly farewell!

THE END

PRODUCTION NOTES

THE LITTLE NUT TREE

Characters: 10 male; 7 female; extras for Sight-seers.
Playing Time: 15 minutes.
Costumes: Old-fashioned village costumes. Guide has sign on his hat and badge on his chest reading "Guide." Lord Mayor wears dignified black outfit. Princess Joanna, Heralds, Ladies-in-Waiting and Don Carlos wear regal, elaborate costumes. Princess wears a crimson dress.
Properties: Nut tree with silver nutmeg and golden pear (may be constructed from cardboard), stool or stepladder, bottles of polish, cloths, sprinkling cans, axe, trumpets, handkerchief.
Setting: The garden of the Poole family, in which the nut tree occupies a prominent place slightly right of center stage. Shrubbery, plants, etc., may be added to give the illusion of a garden. An exit at right leads to the house, at left to the street.
Sound: Trumpets.
Lighting: No special effects.

BANDIT BEN RIDES AGAIN

Characters: 12 male; 8 female.
Playing Time: 20 minutes.
Costumes: Sheriff, Miranda, Cowboys and Indians wear traditional cowboy and Indian costumes. Bandit Ben wears a dark-colored cowboy outfit with a black kerchief as a mask. Tilly, Milly and Willy wear city clothes.
Properties: Sheriff's badge, hand bell, fishing rod, bait can, workbasket with knitting, rolled up wigwams and tepees, bows and arrows, paint cans, peanut butter sandwich, broomstick horses, bag of loot, toy pistol, rope, card.
Setting: The Sheriff's office near the Bar-B.Q. Ranch. A crudely lettered sign at left reads "Sheriff's Office," and another sign reads "Bar-B.Q. Ranch." There is a rail fence at left, and at right a desk with hand bell on it and swivel chair nearby.
Lighting: No special effects.

SOURDOUGH SALLY

Characters: 7 male; 6 female.
Playing Time: 20 minutes.
Costumes: Modern everyday dress. The boys all wear jeans, and the prospectors wear beards of different colors. Sally wears a coat at the end. Miss Collins wears a dark dress.
Properties: Five spades, pie pan, phone, letter in envelope.

Setting: The Crane living room in Alaska. One door leads outside, another leads to the rest of the house. A large easel is located at center with a painting of the Alaskan flag.
Lighting: No special effects.
Sound: Doorbell.

ALOHA, MOTHER

Characters: 5 male; 7 female. Speaker may be male or female. 13 Visiting Mothers may be the mothers of children in the play, or may be played by members of the class.
Playing Time: 15 minutes.
Costumes: Modern everyday dress in Scene 1. Hawaiian costumes and leis for children in Scene 2. Speaker wears Hawaiian costume for speech between scenes.
Properties: Suitcase, ukelele, leis, flowers named in Scene 2.
Setting: A classroom. In Scene 1 a table with chairs around it occupies center stage; in Scene 2 the center is cleared and a row of chairs is at rear.
Sound: Ukelele or autoharp accompaniment for music and dances if possible.
Lighting: No special effects.

SO LONG AT THE FAIR

Characters: 9 male, 5 female; male and female extras.
Playing Time: 20 minutes.
Costumes: Children and Mrs. Webster may wear everyday clothes. Policeman wears blue uniform; Carousel Attendant wears dark suit and visored cap, and has badge on jacket; Gypsy wears brightly colored skirt, peasant blouse, and a kerchief on her head. Barkers wear colorful fair clothes. Johnny wears blue jeans and a red sweater.
Properties: Balloons; pocket notebook; pencil; tickets; small girl's straw hat; bunch of blue ribbons; coin for Johnny; silver chain with charm attached to it; stuffed animals; paper novelties.
Setting: Fairgrounds. Four tables representing booths are decorated gaily with crepe-paper streamers and colored pennants.
Lighting: No special effects.
Special Note: For the children's carousel, the players form a double circle. Children in the outer circle place their hands on the shoulders of their partners who stand in front of them forming the inner circle. Players in the inner circle join hands. Players in both circles step to the left as the music plays. The music may be sung by the children as they go around in the circle, or may be played on a record. The tempo of the music increases so that the children keep the "merry-go-round" moving as rapidly as possible without dropping their hands.

PRODUCTION NOTES

THE GLASS SLIPPERS

Characters: 7 male; 5 female; 8 male or female.
Playing Time: 20 minutes.
Costumes: Traditional fairy-tale costumes. Cobblers wear peasant shirts and trousers, with colorful sashes. Mother and Daughters wear elegant dresses. Cinderella wears ragged skirt and blouse. Old Woman wears dark dress, shawl, and scarf. Prince and Heralds wear court costumes; Prince wears crown. Customers wear dresses or shirts and trousers.
Properties: Shoes of all kinds, including gold slippers, silver slippers, bedroom slippers, and one pair of glass or plastic slippers; cobblers' tools, needle and thread, hammers, etc.; shoe boxes and bags; long table cover; bowl of soapsuds and long-stemmed pipe for blowing soap bubbles; cane.
Setting: The workshop of the Carefree Cobblers. At right is a long workbench with chairs behind it. At left is a small table with a chair at it. Downstage center is a display counter.
Lighting: No special effects.

THE MOUSE THAT SOARED

Characters: 5 male; 1 female; 12 male or female for other mice.
Playing Time: 20 minutes.
Costumes: Mice wear gray or brown outfits, with tights, sweaters, and mouse hats. Mamma Mouse and the girls who play parts of mice may wear skirts over their tights. Bill and Jake wear everyday clothes. Thomas Cat wears a black cat outfit with a bell on a cord around his neck. Orvie re-enters later wearing a space suit, which may be composed of dark tights, a heavy jacket and a helmet with strange-looking metal paraphernalia protruding all around.
Properties: Blindfolds, cardboard carving knife, torn scrap of newspaper, transistor radio, pencil and sheets of paper, rhythm band instruments, including fiddle for Thomas Cat.
Setting: Merry Mouse Meadow. There is a tree upstage, and there may be a backdrop depicting a green landscape.
Lighting: No special effects.
Sound: Loud rumble like rocket taking off; static from radio.

SMOKEY WINS HIS STAR

Characters: 14 male; 4 female. Mr. Bates should be played by an adult, if possible.
Playing Time: 15 minutes.
Costumes: Children wear modern school clothes. The 7 Safeties wear school safety baldrics over their clothes, and large gold stars. Smokey wears bear costume—brown shirt and hat, and dungarees.

Properties: Large can labeled "Trash," lunch baskets, thermos jug, ball, bicycle, sign reading "Pine Grove," hot dogs, metal forks, three boxes of wooden matches, large gold star for Smokey.
Setting: Scene 1 is set in a street. The stage is bare except for a large can labeled "Trash," at left. Scene 2 is set in a pine grove. There is a picnic table; a sign reading "Picnic Area" is displayed prominently, and sticks, logs, and dry leaves are scattered about.
Lighting: No special effects.

MEET MR. MUFFIN

Characters: 10 male; 9 female. (The cast is flexible, and more or fewer children may take part.)
Playing Time: 15 minutes.
Costumes: Children wear everyday clothes. Mr. Muffin wears an old English costume of the traditional smock and tall Welsh hat. Mrs. Muffin wears a full-skirted dress with an apron, toy spectacles and a ruffled cap. Little Muffins wear chef's aprons and hats over everyday clothes. Baker wears a high white baker's cap.
Properties: Wooden tray with muffins, flour sifter, muffin pan, hot pan mitt, bowl, spoon, wrench, basket, pail, notebook, large wooden spoon, baker's basket, and eight placards on sticks.
Setting: A playground. The stage may be bare or may be gaily decorated.
Lighting: No special effects.

THE ADMIRAL'S NIGHTMARE

Characters: 9 male; 3 female; extras for Sailors and Sea Monster.
Playing Time: 20 minutes.
Costumes: Columbus and Alfredo wear dark flowing costumes, hats, and swords. Alfredo wears a cloak. The children wear brightly colored old-fashioned clothes. Queen Isabella and Francesca wear elaborate court costumes; Isabella has a crown. The 4 Winds wear dark tights and wide capes of different colors. The Sea Monster, made up of a line of children, should have a green covering, a grotesque head, and tail. Sailors wear traditional tattered sea costumes—dungarees, torn shirts, bandannas, etc.
Properties: Necklace, crystal ball, three model ships (may be made of cardboard), one of which is tied to a string, small flags reading *Nina, Pinta, Santa Maria,* toy swords and daggers.
Setting: At right stage is a large sturdy platform representing the highest deck of the *Santa Maria,* where Columbus and Alfredo stand. On the platform are a canvas chair and a

sheet fashioned into a sail. The main stage is empty except for a long table near left entrance. Tacked on the outside edge of the table and extending above it is a long sheet of cardboard painted to represent the sea, with a scalloped top edge to resemble waves.

Lighting: A spotlight focuses on platform, and stage lights go up and down as indicated.

Sound: Crunching wood. Offstage noises may simulate thunder and wind during the storm.

Which Way to Halloween?

Characters: 15 male; 16 female.

Playing Time: 20 minutes.

Costumes: Halloween, Thanksgiving and Christmas characters wear traditional holiday costumes. Father Time wears old, worn clothes and may have a beard; Little New Year wears baby's diaper or infant clothes. Cupid should wear red tights, pointed hat and carry bow and arrow: March Wind wears flowing costume; April Fool wears light, elfin clothing. Pat and Mike are dressed in green; Bride wears bridal gown, Policeman wears uniform, and Parade Girls wear red, white and blue marching costumes with three-cornered hats. Miss Warner, Mother, Trudy, Lois and Eleanor wear modern everyday dress. All wear Halloween masks and costumes or sheets at end.

Properties: Pumpkin, turkey platter, ear of corn, peace pipe, broomsticks, pack of toys, baby coach, rattle, bow and arrow, big red heart, shamrock, palm leaf fans, purse on a string, sign reading "April Fool," bridal bouquet, flags, schoolbooks, Halloween masks.

Setting: A bare stage with one bench.

Lighting: No special effects.

Sound: Jingle Bells and march music—bugles and drums—offstage; clock striking twelve.

The Runaway Unicorn

Characters: 18 male; 5 female. (If desired, however, the parts of the Seven Dwarfs may be played by girls.)

Playing Time: 20 minutes.

Costumes: Traditional storybook costumes. Linda and Lewis wear school clothes. The Unicorn Keeper wears a uniform. The Unicorn wears a Unicorn costume, with a white body, a red head, and a single horn, which is black in the middle and red at the tip.

Properties: Horn for Robin Hood, and crown.

Setting: Storybook Lane. On stage are nine cardboard replicas of books, each large enough to conceal a child.

(*Hansel and Gretel* should be large enough for two children and *Robin Hood* large enough for three.)
Lighting: No special effects.

THE PARROT AND THE PIRATES

Characters: 7 male; as many male extras for Soldiers as desired.
Playing Time: 20 minutes.
Costumes: Pirates are dressed in usual pirate attire with colored bandannas. Soldiers wear uniforms.
Properties: A large, brightly feathered artificial parrot; shovels for pirates; map; chest with tray in it; books; 4 coconut shells; 2 bags of "gold"; muskets; sword for Captain Kidd.
Setting: A tropical island. There are palm trees at right and left, and a perch for the parrot hangs on a low branch of one of the trees. At the center of the stage there is a mound of earth and rocks (may be made of cardboard or painted construction paper) large enough to conceal treasure chest.
Lighting: No special effects.
Note: The Voice of the Parrot may come from offstage, or an actor concealed behind a tree may speak for the parrot. An excellent effect may be achieved through the use of an offstage microphone.

THE A B C's THANKSGIVING

Characters: 3 male; 2 female; 30 male or female.
Playing Time: 15 minutes.
Costumes: Pilgrim boy and girl wear traditional Pilgrim clothes. All others wear modern dress. Letters of the alphabet wear large placards, each with his letter printed on it.
Properties: American flag.
Setting: Stage may be bare, or may be decorated with a Thanksgiving theme. There may be a low platform down center, large enough to hold twelve children in a line.
Lighting: No special effects.

BARTHOLOMEW'S JOYFUL NOISE

Characters: 4 male; 4 female.
Playing Time: 20 minutes.
Costumes: Typical Pilgrim costumes, with aprons and caps for the girls, breeches and knee stockings for the boys. Captain Standish should have a more military or rough costume.
Properties: Wooden sticks, homemade drum, drumsticks, Bible, large drum, pails and pitchers, quilt.
Setting: A small Plymouth cabin. There are a large table and blanket chest against the walls. One door leads outside.
Lighting: No special effects.
Sound: Drum roll offstage as indicated.

The Runaway Toys

Characters: 6 male; 8 female.
Playing Time: 15 minutes.
Costumes: Janie and Jimsy wear everyday clothes. Santa Claus wears traditional Santa costume, and elves wear elf suits. Donald Duck and Teddy Bear may wear duck and bear costumes or may wear elf suits with duck and bear caps. Toy Soldier wears bright uniform. Jumping Jack wears clown costume. Rag Doll wears ragged dress and French, Dutch, and Japanese Dolls wear typical national costumes.
Properties: Four stockings, including one baby stocking; pack for Santa Claus; packages; four letters.
Setting: Living room with sofa, chairs, etc. There is a fireplace with a mantel. Door right leads to the storeroom and door left to the rest of the apartment.
Lighting: Blackout of stage as indicated in text.
Sound: Sleigh bells.

Squeaknibble's Christmas

Characters: 2 male; 3 female; 5 male or female.
Playing Time: 10 minutes.
Costumes: Mr. Grandfather Clock wears a large clock face and a long white beard. The mice wear gray or brown Brownie costumes with perky round ears and long, thin tails. Master Puss wears a furry costume with a long tail, pointed ears, and long whiskers. He has sharp claws on his paws.
Properties: Gong and hammer, for Mr. Grandfather Clock.
Setting: The Great Hall. Mr. Grandfather Clock is in one corner. On the opposite side of the stage is a Christmas tree, on a low table. There is an entrance on one side to the rest of the house, and a small entrance upstage center, bearing a large sign reading "Mousehole."
Lighting: No special effects necessary. If desired, a spot may be used to set off the parts of the play in which Squeaknibble appears.

Gifts for the New Year

Characters: 16 female; 3 male; extra courtiers if desired.
Playing Time: 20 minutes.
Costumes: Nursemaid may be dressed like traditional British nanny. Jester wears harlequin suit, belled cap, and slippers with bells at toes. King and Queen wear long robes of rich-looking fabric, and wear gold crowns. The Fairy Godmothers are dressed in long, flowing robes of various colors: January, frosty white and silver; February, red; March, green; April, pale blue; May, lavender; June,

pink; July, red, white, and blue; August, bright yellow; September, bright orange; October, brown and gold; November, gray; December, silver. Tickety-Tock wears a long black cloak and carries a big alarm clock. Chancellor wears long gray traditional court attire. The Memory Fairy is dressed in gold and carries a golden book and golden wand.

Properties: Man's silk hat; scroll; baby blanket; bunch of wax red cherries; stuffed toy lion and toy lamb; small umbrella; golden ball; bunch of red and white roses (may be artificial); small American flag; toy boat; baseball, bat, and glove; pad of paper; quill pen; bottle of ink; basket filled with fruit, nuts, Indian corn, gourds; songbook; large silver star; alarm clock.

Setting: The throne room of the King and Queen of the Calendar. Upstage center on an elevated platform there are two gold or elaborately decorated chairs representing the thrones for the King and the Queen. In front of platform stands a ruffled cradle. At one side there is a table covered with a white cloth; tacked to the table is a sign reading "For Baby New Year."

Lighting: No special effects.

Sound: Trumpets and bugles.

LINCOLN'S LIBRARY FINE

Characters: 5 male; 5 female.

Playing Time: 20 minutes.

Costumes: Modern everyday dress. All children except Linc wear outdoor clothing at opening.

Properties: Toy box, toys, car keys, charm from bracelet, penny, fountain pen, filled grocery bag, wet book, wrapped birthday gifts, birthday cake, candles, matches.

Setting: The living room of Lincoln Taylor's home. The room is comfortably furnished, with sofa, chairs and table.

Lighting: No special effects.

Sound: Doorbell.

PRINCESS LONELY HEART

Characters: 8 male; 11 female; 8 or more male or female extras for party guests.

Playing Time: 15 minutes.

Costumes: King, Queen, and Princess wear traditional court costumes of red and white, with heart motifs. King and Queen have crowns; Princess has a coronet decorated with hearts. Ladies-in-Waiting wear attractive long dresses. Kitchen maids wear white dresses, with tiny red aprons. Messengers, footman, and pages wear page costumes. Guests wear party clothes. Each party guest wears a red heart tied on a string hung around his neck.

Properties: Cookie batter, heart-shaped cookie cutter, cookie tin, bowl, spoon, flour sifter and flour, sugar bowl and sugar, vanilla bottle, salt shaker, raisin box, cinnamon and nutmeg shakers, rolling pin wrapped in foil, golden ball, doll, tea tray, 2 medicine bottles, heart (cut in halves) reading "The Next Day," four plates of cookies, golden bow and arrow.
Setting: The throne room. Two thrones are on a raised platform center stage. Beside each throne is a small table. There is also a larger worktable.
Lighting: No special effects.
Sound: Buzzer.

Washington's Lucky Star

Characters: 5 male; 5 female.
Playing Time: 15 minutes.
Costumes: Costumes of the Revolutionary period. Edward wears a torn jacket with a gold star on it. Colonel Ross and General Washington wear uniforms.
Properties: Sewing equipment, scraps of material (gold and other colors), scissors, several sheets of paper.
Setting: The living room of Betsy Ross. There are a sewing table near center and a large blanket chest upstage left. There are two footstools and several chairs. The rest of the room may be furnished as desired, in colonial style,
and there may be a fireplace.
Lighting: No special effects.

The White House Rabbit

Characters: 8 male; 5 female.
Playing Time: 20 minutes.
Costumes: Mr. Rabbit wears a red, white, and blue waistcoat, white tights or trousers, a silk hat, a large watch and chain across a red vest, and a whistle on a cord around his neck. Thumper, Whiskers, and Cottontail may be dressed similarly, but with different color combinations. Flopsy and Mopsy may wear white tights and skirts, and flowered bonnets. All the rabbits have large "cottontails," and long ears sticking up through their hats. Fanny and Scott Hayes and Mrs. Hayes are dressed in the clothes of the period. Charles wears overalls, a dark work shirt, and an old straw hat. Pierre and Marie may wear slightly more "dressy" clothes than Fanny and Scott, and both of them wear hats and coats.
Properties: Notebook and pencil; toy wagons, wheelbarrows, and baskets filled with colored Easter eggs; (there are plastic "eggs" available, or eggs may be made of colored paper); rake; hatbox; flowers for flower beds; flowered woman's hat; card.
Setting: A corner of the White House lawn. There is high

shrubbery (high enough to conceal members of the cast) along the back and side; an outdoor bench at right and a sign with an arrow pointing left which reads, To THE WHITE HOUSE. There are several flower beds visible, with flowers growing in them. These may be made from heavy cardboard and filled with enough soil to stick artificial flowers in; or flowerpots set in low boxes may be used.
Lighting: No special effects.

BASKETS OR BONNETS

Characters: 8 male; 17 female; 6 male or female.
Playing Time: 15 minutes.
Costumes: Flowers wear crêpe-paper flower costumes; at the end of the play they also wear flower hats. Rabbits wear white elf suits with powder-puff tails and caps with long ears. Pitter and Patter wear blue elf suits and Winds may wear elf suits of different colors. Girls wear spring dresses. Weatherman wears a suit and a top hat. Mary Sunshine wears a gay spring dress and a sunbonnet. Mother Nature wears a long dress and cap. Six other hats are required: one with a pink ribbon, a blue one, a flowered one, a veiled one, a red one, and a top hat.
Properties: Pointer, 4 long silver-colored trumpets, 13 small hatboxes, and 6 Easter baskets.
Setting: A park. A backdrop of trees and bushes may be used, if desired. There is a large bush up center. Right is a counter; left is a portable chalk board with a diagram labeled "Easter Weather."
Lighting: No special effects.
Sound: Sound of wind, if desired.

MERRY-GO-ROUND FOR MOTHER

Characters: 4 male; 11 female.
Playing Time: 25 minutes.
Costumes: Everyday dress for all. Children are dressed in school clothes, and mothers are dressed to look like grown-ups. Terry wears a high silk hat marked "Tickets." Mrs. Heath wears a red wig.
Properties: Roll of tickets, large rings made of colored foil, record player, and record of merry-go-round music. There are six packages, wrapped as gifts, each one containing a card, as described in the text, and one of the following gifts: a necklace of bright red beads, a jump rope, a mouth organ, a tiny turtle, a paintbox, and a baseball and glove.
Setting: Scene 1, before the curtain, requires only a tall stool. Scene 2, in the living room of the O'Brien home, is set up for the merry-go-round

party. A stepladder is at stage left, and a table for the gifts and record player at stage right. The merry-go-round is a circle of decorated chairs grouped around a central pole. Full details are given in the beginning of Scene 2, in the text.
Lighting: No special effects.

THE MAGIC PENCILS

Characters: 9 male; 7 female. (The parts of the children may be taken by all male or all female characters, or any combination the director wishes.)
Playing Time: 20 minutes.
Costumes: Children are dressed in everyday school clothes. Mistress Mary wears a long dress, a flowered bonnet, and carries a watering can. Mr. Wizard may wear overalls and a straw hat, or something distinctive. He could have a beard. Mr. Scalawag wears a fanciful costume, similar to a clown suit, and a half mask. Miss Curry wears a simple dress.
Properties: Books, letters, numbers, colored pencils.
Setting: The Garden of Learning. At center stage there is the Fountain of Knowledge, which may be constructed from a small garden bird bath, with a central wire and silver "icicles" representing the water spray. Right stage is the Magic Pencil Tree, made from an artificial table Christmas tree, trimmed with large colored pencils, the tops of which may be decorated with flowers. To the right of the fountain there is the Paper Plant, made of brightly colored paper, and to the left, the ABC Tree, also made from a small table Christmas tree trimmed with large, colored cutout letters, including E, D, U, C, A, T, I, O, N. There is a large flower bed at the right, labeled BOOKS IN BLOOM, and nearby is the Number Bush, on which large colored numbers are hanging. There are also three signs with arrows pointing to HOMEWORK HILL, EXAMINATION MOUNTAIN, and TO THE NEXT GRADE. Each section of the garden should be labeled with a large placard. At the beginning, the Pencil Tree is labeled MAGIC PENCIL TREE. Later, this sign is replaced with one reading, PENCIL TREE.
Lighting: No special effects.
Sound: Motor horn.